SPENSER'S
ANATOMY OF HEROISM

SPENSER'S
ANATOMY OF HEROISM

A COMMENTARY ON
THE FAERIE QUEENE

BY

MAURICE EVANS

Professor of English
University of Exeter

CAMBRIDGE
AT THE UNIVERSITY PRESS
1970

Published by the Syndics of the Cambridge University Press
Bentley House, 200 Euston Road, London N.W.1
American Branch: 32 East 57th Street, New York, N.Y. 10022

© Cambridge University Press 1970

Library of Congress Catalogue Card Number: 74-96087
Standard Book Number: 521 07662 5

Printed in Great Britain by
Alden & Mowbray Ltd
at the Alden Press, Oxford

CONTENTS

PREFACE

So many books have been written on *The Faerie Queene* during the last decade that the production of yet another might seem to call for an apology. Recent Spenserean criticism, although doing ample justice to the myths, the verbal techniques and the rhetoric of the poem, has tended to play down what once seemed the element of most importance, namely its didacticism. The object of this book is to place the emphasis once more upon Spenser's didactic intention, to analyse the rhetorical techniques by means of which he manipulates the reactions of the reader, and to redefine the logic which underlies the sequence of his six virtues. The famous phrase 'to fashion a gentleman' will be at the centre of the discussion, although it is in fact a misleading phrase; for Spenser's explicit concern is to fashion heroes, and he uses the heroic poem both as a means of anatomising the nature of heroism in his own sense of the term and of influencing the reader to embrace its values. For this reason, I have begun by reiterating some of the common Renaissance conceptions of the heroic poem before moving on to Spenser's personal and unique treatment of the genre. For Spenser wears his didacticism with a difference. His moral theme is more subtle than is generally recognised, and his language has much of the paradox and complexity normally associated with the Metaphysical poets but usually denied to *The Faerie Queene*. A surprising number of Spenser's lines, as we shall see, have a controlled ambiguity which lends itself to simultaneous and diametrically opposed interpretations: the description of Lucifera, for example, 'Looking to heaven; for earth she did disdayne' [I. iv. 10], would fit either pride or virtuous idealism, just as that of Archimago, 'And to the ground his eyes were lowly bent' [I. i. 29], could describe either humility or ignoble earthiness. In both cases, of course, Spenser is making the contrast between what people seem to be and what they are; and the double meanings implicit in 'disdayne' and 'lowly' mark the distinction between the erroneous vision of the truth, which is all that Red Cross is capable of at this early stage of his moral education, and the full truth which Spenser wishes to communicate to the reader. Not all of Spenser's ambiguities, however, are explicable in this way. The description of Acrasia bound by the Palmer in chains of Adamant, 'For nothing else might keep her safe and sound', leaves us genuinely uncertain whether she is kept safely locked up or safely preserved in her fetters of reason; and the frequency with which statements of this kind occur throughout the poem suggests that for Spenser both interpretations are valid, and that the moral vision which prompts them is an ambivalent one. I shall argue that *The Faerie Queene* embodies a double perspective throughout which replaces the simple distinction between virtue and vice by something altogether more complex.

Spenser makes no wholly explicit statement of his intention within the poem, and the nature of his moral vision emerges only gradually through the accumulation of innumerable instances. In exploring the theme, therefore, I have tried to follow the method of the poem by plunging into the current of its detail through the successive books and emerging with my general conclusions only in the final chapter. No book which deals with the whole of *The Faerie Queene* can hope to be completely original, and such originality as this one claims lies more in the attempt to reassemble what are often familiar materials into a new pattern than to produce fresh interpretations of individual details. My debt to previous critics—in particular, to Miss Williams, Alastair Fowler, Professor Berger, Professor Alpers and, of course, C. S. Lewis—is obvious and far greater than can be acknowledged in footnotes. Some of the ideas of this book have been raised tentatively and briefly in my book on sixteenth-century poetry, and I have used with modification material previously published by me in the *Review of English Studies, ELH, English Studies* and *Studies in Philology*.

PART I

Introduction to the poem

1

The Heroic Poem

[1]

Spenser's letter to Raleigh, published with the first three books of *The Faerie Queene* in 1590, is a humanist manifesto designed to place the poem in the great heroic tradition, just as E.K's Preface to *The Shepheardes Calender* a decade before advertised the fact that here was the genuine English Pastoral. As an ardent humanist Spenser worked his way through the traditional poetic genres, acclimatising them to the English language and usually drawing attention to the fact. In his desire to be recognised as the champion of the new literary movement, he perhaps laid claim to a purer humanism in his prefatory letter than is manifested in the poem itself, and his account of the author's intention stresses the epic qualities of the work but does less than justice to those which are mediaeval and native. We are reminded, for example, of the tradition of writing the poem in twelve books, the central hero, and the initial plunge *in medias res* which distinguishes the epic poet from the more orderly historiographer; but nothing is said about the romance techniques of the poem by which story melts into story and many actions are kept simultaneously afoot. Spenser makes no mention of the great Renaissance controversy over unity of action in the long poem, although his intention to unite the twelve separate stories under a common hero, Arthur, shows that he was well aware of the issue. Instead, he insists on the heroism which is the feature of both epic and romance, and presents himself as the latest practitioner in the great heroic line which embraces both genres: 'In which I have followed all the antique Poets historicall; first Homere...then Virgil...after him Ariosto...and lately Tasso...'

His identification of himself with the line of 'Poets historicall' reflects normal Renaissance literary theory: Puttenham, too,

3

defines heroic poetry in similar terms:[1]

Such therefore as gave them selves to write long histories of the noble gests of kings and great Princes entermedling the dealings of the gods, halfe gods or Heroes of the gentiles, and the great and waighty consequences of peace and warre, they called Poets *Heroick*, whereof *Homer* was chief and most auncient among the Greeks, *Virgill* among the Latines. (I. xi)

Spenser describes his poem as 'coloured with an historicall fiction', and the phrase offered less of a paradox to the Elizabethan reader than to us with our stricter ideas of what constitutes history. Puttenham, for example, divides histories into three kinds: wholly true, wholly false, and a third which he calls 'mixt', exemplified in Homer's 'fabulous or mixt report of the seige of Troy' (I. xix). The term 'historicall' is the label of the type of poetic subject rather than a guarantee of veracity, and the historical poet is free 'to devise many historicall matters of no veritie at all, but with purpose to do good and no hurt...' [ibid.]. In this respect the heroic poem is the direct ancestor of the historical novel and insists as strongly as the latter on its fictional quality. This follows inevitably from the usual Renaissance interpretation of Aristotle's term *mimesis* as 'feigning'; for Sidney,[2] the essence of poetry lies in fiction— 'it is not riming and versing that maketh a Poet,...But it is that fayning notable images of vertues, vices, or what els, with that delightfull teaching, which must be the right describing note to know a Poet by...' (p. 160). The distinctive quality of poetry lies in its ability to exceed the 'narrow warrant' of nature, and it is this which gives the poet his special status as a 'maker' and is the source of the specific delight which poetry affords.

The main object of the heroic poem, however, is not to please but to instruct through pleasing, and for this, fiction alone is not enough. A poem must create belief if it is to achieve its proper moral or cathartic effect; it must have the 'verisimilitude'

---

1 George Puttenham, *The Arte of English Poesie*, ed. Gladys Doidge Willcock and Alice Walker (Cambridge, 1936).
2 *An Apologie for Poetry*, in *Elizabethan Critical Essays*, ed. Gregory Smith (Oxford, 1964), vol. I.

upon which neo-classic criticism insisted so strongly, especially if it belongs to a literary 'kind' such as the heroic which has so much of the marvellous in its constitution. The solution was to attach the fiction to historical settings and characters since, as Aristotle had pointed out when discussing this problem of belief, what is thought to have happened is clearly possible and hence credible.[1] Modern or familiar history will not do because the truth is too well known to be tampered with, and the poet's task, therefore, is to find a historical figure sufficiently venerated to carry belief and authority but sufficiently remote and imprecise in detail to allow the poet free play; in the words of Tasso:[2]

In some ways the history of an age or a nation very distant from us appears a subject well-suited for a heroic poem, because, since those things are so buried in antiquity that there scarcely remains a weak and obscure memory of them, the poet is able to change them and change them again and tell of them as he pleases.

(*Discourses on the Heroic Poem*, II. 15)

The highest aim of poetry is to make men virtuous, and the heroic is the highest 'kind' of poetry because its blend of history and fiction performs this function best. The history gives it the authority of a great and credible example, while the fiction emancipates the poet from the limitations of a foolish world and enables him to improve on even the best of history. It is this combination which, in Sidney's judgement, made Xenophon a heroic poet: 'For Xenophon, who did imitate so excellently as to give us...the portraiture of a just Empire under the name of *Cyrus* (as *Cicero* saith to him), made therein an absolute heroicall Poem' (p. 160). By means of this idealised portrait of a historical figure Xenophon was able 'not onely to make a *Cyrus*, which had been but a particuler excellencie, as Nature might have done, but to bestow a *Cyrus* upon the worlde to make many *Cyrus's*' (p. 157). The feigned Cyrus of Xenophon, the feigned Aeneas of Virgil, are more 'doctrinable', to use Sidney's word, than their historical

---

1 For a fuller treatment, see Graham Hough, *A Preface to The Faerie Queene* (London, 1962).
2 In *Literary Criticism, Plato to Dryden*, ed. Alan H. Gilbert (Wayne Books), p. 482.

originals in Justin or Dares Phrygius. This exalted conception of
the moral impact of literature must stem, in part, from the
effect of the new medium of the printed book; and it only
differs from our own conception of the influence of the newest
medium, television, in that it springs from a deeper idealism.
Renaissance theory stressed the benign influence of the heroic
figure in literature, whereas we are more conscious of the
dangerous effects of the film or television gunman.

For the Renaissance reader and writer alike the most important thing about the heroic poem was, as its name implies, the
hero and Spenser seems to have been conscious of this quality
of the heroic genre to a quite unusual degree. *The Faerie Queene*
is very specifically a heroic poem and peculiarly rich in allusions to 'the olde heroes' who provide the touchstone for virtue
throughout. The word 'Heroick' is Spenser's highest term of
praise and one which he uses with precise and literal meaning:
Merlin, showing Britomart her descendants in his magic glass,
holds up Malgo for her admiration:

> 'How like a Gyaunt in each manly part
> Beares he himselfe with portly maiestee,
> That one of th'old *Heroes* seemes to bee:' [III. iii. 32]

Belphoebe is praised for her 'Heroick mind' [III. v. 55],
Britomart for her 'huge heroicke magnanimity' [III. xi. 19]; and
Calidore, seeing the virtue of the young Tristram, at once
assumes that he must be 'surely borne of some Heroicke sead'
[VI. ii. 25]. There are many descriptions of this kind throughout
the poem, as well as innumerable casual references to the 'old
Heroes' which keep the concept of heroism to the fore and play
an important part in the total meaning of the poem:

> *Phorcys*, the father of that fatall brood
> By whom those old Heroes wonne such fame;
>
> [IV. xi. 13]

The old heroes to whom Spenser so constantly alludes form a
very curious collection: there are British kings such as Brutus
and Malgo; 'famous founders' of 'puissant nations', of whom
Inachus and Albion are examples; literary and mythical heroes
like Orpheus, Odysseus, Hercules, Aeneas; and finally what

Puttenham calls the gods of the gentiles, a category which includes Bacchus, Isis and Osiris. This mixture of the semi-historic and the purely mythical resulted from the traditional euhemeristic explanation of pagan mythology as something based ultimately on historical fact:[1] the pagan gods and heroes of mythology were in their origin historical heroes, law-givers, civilisers who for their benefactions to mankind were first adored and eventually worshipped by posterity. Spenser's collection of 'old heroes' ranked as a historical list, and it is this fact which allows him to invoke Clio so frequently in *The Faerie Queene*. There was plenty of disagreement about the precise date and nature of the historical figures around whom the myths were woven, and Miss Rathbone[2] has shown that there were several candidates for the original Hercules and the original Jove—a fact to which Mutability alludes when she taunts Jove in the *Mutability Cantos*:

> Then, let me aske you this withouten blame,
> Where were ye borne? Some say in *Crete* by name,
> Others in *Thebes*, and others other-where;
> But, wheresoever they comment the same,
> They all consent that ye begotten were
> And borne here in this world, ne other can appeare.
>
> [VII. vii. 53]

The precise origin of Jove does not matter to Mutability since in any case he is 'mortall borne, and thrall to me'. The historicity of such figures was not in doubt, and Professor Seznec has drawn attention to the vast body of mediaeval and Renaissance literature concerned with tracing the genealogies of Saturn, Jove, Hercules or the Trojan line back to their fountain-head in Noah, or forward to their descendants among the reigning dynasties of the Renaissance. It was no uncommon thing in Renaissance courts to claim Hercules or Aeneas among one's great ancestors.

Spenser's familiarity with this time-honoured conception of myth is obvious throughout *The Faerie Queene*. His description

---

1 Jean Seznec, *The Survival of the Pagan Gods* (Harper Torchbooks), book I, part I, section I, 'The Historical tradition'.
2 Isabel Rathbone, *The Meaning of Spenser's Fairyland* (New York, 1937).

of the heroes of justice, for example, implies their eventual ascent to the level of mythology:

> Whilome those great Heroes got thereby
> Their greatest glory for their rightfull deedes,
> And place deserved with the Gods on hy. [v. ii. 1]

His account of Isis and Osyris, deified for their exercise of justice and equity while they reigned on earth, is an explicitly euhemeristic one:

> Well therefore did the antique world invent
> That Justice was a God of soveraine grace,
> And altars unto him and temples lent,
> And heavenly honours in the highest place;
> Calling him great *Osyris*, of the race
> Of th'old Aegyptian Kings, that whylome were;
> With fayned colours shading a true case:
> For that *Osyris*, whilest he lived here,
> The justest man alive, and truest did appeare.

> His wife was *Isis*, whom they likewise made
> A Goddesse of great powre and soveranity,
> And in her person cunningly did shade
> That part of Justice, which is Equity, . . . [v. vii. 2–3]

Their predominant virtues on earth caused them to be identified with the absolute virtues as they exist in heaven, and Spenser's terminology—'With fayned colours shading a true case'— suggests how this elevation came about. It is the poets who turn heroes into gods and 'feign' the myths by which men attempt to govern their lives; and it is of special relevance to *The Faerie Queene* that poetry, particularly heroic poetry, was credited with this power and this responsibility of myth-making. Puttenham once more makes the point in his chapter on the form of Poesie by which 'the great Princes and dominators of the world were honored'. The Poets, he begins,

being in deede the trumpetters of all praise . . . were in conscience and credit bound next after the divine praises of the immortall gods, to yeeld a like ratable honour to all such amongst men, as most resembled the gods by excellencie of function, and had a certaine affinitie with them, by more than humane and ordinarie vertues shewed in their actions here upon earth.   (Book I, chap. XVI)

The whole pantheon of Greek mythology thus arose out of the ministrations of Homer, Hesiod and the Greek poets:

Such personages among the Gentiles were *Bacchus, Ceres, Perseus, Hercules, Theseus* and many other, who thereby came to be accompted gods and halfe gods or goddesses [Heroes] and had their comedations given by Hymne accordingly or by such other poems as their memorie was therby made famous to the posteritie for ever after, . . .

It is this power which gave poetry its almost divine status in the Renaissance and enabled Puttenham or Sidney alike to claim that the poets were 'the first priests, the first prophets, the first Legislators and polititians in the world'. Orpheus could tame the savage beasts with his lyre because he was the son of the Muse, Calliope.

Nor is this simply the critic's view of poetry; the poets themselves make this claim for their own art. Ben Jonson, for example, makes the point in his *Epistle to Elizabeth Countesse of Rutland*,[1] though not without some touch of irony, perhaps to excuse the arrogance of a belief which his plays suggest that he took very seriously:

> It is the Muse, alone, can raise to heaven,
> And, at her strong armes end, hold up, and even,
> The soules, shee loves . . . There were brave men, before
> Ajax, or Idomen, or all the store,
> That Homer brought to Troy; yet none so live:
> Because they lack'd the sacred pen, could give
> Like life unto 'hem. Who heav'd Hercules
> Unto the starres? or the Tyndarides?
> Who placed Jasons Argo in the skie?
> Or set bright Ariadnes crowne so high?
> Who made a lampe of Berenices hayre?
> Or lifted Cassiopea in her chayre?
> But only Poets, rapt with rage divine?   (41–63)

Spenser seems to have accepted this high responsibility of

---

[1] Poems of Ben Jonson, ed. George Burke Johnston (London, 1954).

9

poetry without self-consciousness or hesitation, and his early poems make repeated profession of this poetic faith. In *The Ruines of Time*, for example, the personification of the ruined city Verulam asserts that poetry alone can give immortality, and whoever wishes to mount to heaven by his virtuous deeds 'on *Pegasus* must ride,/And with sweete Poets verse be glorifide' (426–). In *The Teares of the Muses*, Calliope, the Muse of Epic, boasts of the powers which she once exercised but which she now abrogates since men are no longer worthy of them:

> Therefore the nurse of vertue I am hight.
> And golden Trompet of eternitie,
> That lowly thoughts lift up to heavens hight,
> And mortall men have powre to deifie:
> *Bacchus* and *Hercules* I raisd to heaven,
> And *Charlemaine* amongst the Starris seaven.
>
> But now I will my golden Clarion rend,
> And will henceforth immortalize no more;   (457–65)

The Faerie Queene is Spenser's attempt to wipe away her tears and restore her broken trumpet.

[2]

These common aspects of Renaissance heroic theory form the background to *The Faerie Queene* and influenced Spenser's attempt at the heroic genre in a very fundamental manner. Following the best authorities, he chose a hero and a period at once very remote yet carrying historical authenticity for his own times: he chose Arthur, we are told in the letter to Raleigh, as being 'most plausible'. He set the historical period very precisely—Britomart starts out on her quest just after King Uther has beaten the pagans, Octa and Oza [III. iii. 52]—yet in showing Arthur as a prince before he came to the throne, he found a period of his hero's life not so documented by the chroniclers as to inhibit fiction. That Arthur was a historical figure was scarcely questioned in Spenser's day; and the large body of modern research into the Tudor myth has brought to light the good political reasons for which the Tudors were anxious to trace their descent from the original British kings of whom Arthur was the most illustrious. The British line, of course, goes back beyond Arthur through Brute to Aeneas, and so by way of his mother, Venus, to Jove himself, with Hercules, Helen and a host of others all in the family. Spenser outlines the genealogy from Aeneas downwards, starting in the middle as a poet should, instead of at the beginning in the manner of a historian. Book II, canto x, gives us the chronicle of Briton kings to the accession of Uther Pendragon, where it stops abruptly since that, for Arthur, was the present, and to go further would be to leave the chamber of memory for that of prophecy. This is what happens in III. iii, when Britomart goes to Merlin's cave and is shown in his magic glass the 'famous progenie' which shall spring from herself and Artegall and culminate in the Tudor dynasty. The first comes last of all, in III. ix, when Paridel traces the line from the birth of Aeneas through the fall of Troy to the founding of Rome, and so on to the conquest of Albion by the Trojan Brute, which is the point where Arthur's chronicle of Briton kings begins.

As a celebrated figure and the most famous of Elizabeth's ancestors, Arthur was obviously a very suitable epic hero and one who enabled Spenser to pay the compliment to his great patron which Virgil and Ariosto had paid to theirs: but there were pressing literary as well as political reasons for his choice. In his role of a prince of the Trojan line, Arthur was descended from heroes already celebrated in poetic myth and identified with the great tradition of heroic poetry: Homer had begun the epic tale, Virgil had carried it on as far as Rome, and now it was the time for the British heroic poet to deal with the British sequence. The epic of the third Troy follows those of the other two; and in continuing the heroic account of the same illustrious line, Spenser was very conscious that he was treading in the footsteps of Homer and Virgil and that his argument was very literally 'worthy of Maeonian quill' [II. x. 3]. A heroic poem about British Arthur is as much a piece of humanist myth-making as any Renaissance epic on a classical subject; and it is entirely natural that the actions of Arthur and the separate heroes should be modelled on those of Hercules and Aeneas, and that Elizabeth should play the successive roles of Diana, Venus and Astraea in the poem.

In writing *The Faerie Queene* Spenser was composing as the ancients were thought to have composed their epics and extending to Britain the heroic mythology which Homer and Virgil had already provided for their respective nations. He was bestowing immortality on those worthy of it and, in so doing, he was demonstrating that the poets were not merely the first civilisers of mankind among the ancients but still carried on the task. The dedicatory sonnets to the poem harp on this theme and throw light on Spenser's poetic intention: that to Essex promises to 'make more famous memory/Of thine Heroicke parts'; that to Howard identifies him with the old heroes whom the poem is celebrating:

> And ye, brave Lord, whose goodly personage
> And noble deeds, each other garnishing,
> Make you ensample to the present age
> Of th'old Heroes, whose famous ofspring
> The antique Poets wont so much to sing;
> In this same Pageaunt have a worthy place,...

those to Northumberland and Norris offer the everlasting fame which only virtue can deserve and the Muse can give. In dispensing immortality to those who deserve it, Spenser is playing the part of his own good poet, Bon font, before he lost that name by stooping to slander [v. ix. 26].

The Faerie Queene, therefore, is built around the idealised portrait of a great hero. The central position of Arthur has been challenged in view of the relatively small part which he plays in the story, and no one would claim that he is the most memorable figure of the poem. Nevertheless, such an attitude takes into account only the element of literal narrative in the poem and ignores the moral allegory; for though Arthur does relatively little in comparison with the total action, it is all of the highest significance and follows a consistent pattern. Rosemond Tuve[1] has shown that his virtue of Magnificence, which Spenser describes as 'the perfection of all the rest', is

---

1 Rosemond Tuve, *Allegorical Imagery* (Princeton, 1966), pp. 57–8.

not to be confused with Aristotle's Magnanimity but is identical with Christian 'perseverance'. It is this quality which enables Arthur to demonstrate the nature of each virtue with a completeness beyond the wavering powers of the separate knights. His demonstrations of holiness, temperance, justice and courtesy are obvious and will be discussed more fully later; but even in book III, where he scarcely appears at all, his very absence is an aspect of his perfection. Britomart's initial task is to discover her own physical nature and emancipate it from both the traditional fears and the false romanticism which surround sex. Arthur, however, is already past this stage of adolescence, as his account of his night with the Queen of the Faeries and the 'pressed grass' makes clear [I. ix. 15]: it is a flesh-and-blood mistress not an image in a glass or in a book which he follows from the start; and when, by book IV, Britomart has grown up to this stage, Arthur has already mastered the lusts of the flesh and learnt to control the discords which accompany the awakened sexual instinct. Throughout the poem he is drawn as the archetypal hero, the saviour, the law-giver, the civiliser in whose presence the Savage Man of book VI grows tame. It is a measure of his role as a hero that Spenser models so many of Arthur's adventures on the Labours of Hercules, his great forbear and the greatest of all the traditional heroes: the conquest of the mares of Diomedes, the slaying of Antaeus, of Geryon, of the Lernean Hydra, provide the patterns for his victories. All heroism in *The Faerie Queene* aspires to the quality of Hercules, but Arthur's most of all. More will be said about this at a later point: at the moment it is sufficient to say that Spenser identifies his chief hero with the generic hero of classic mythology and in so doing 'humanises' his British material and establishes the poem firmly in the great heroic tradition.

The Faerie Queene is explicitly designed to persuade the reader to virtue, and the presentation of the great hero is only one of the weapons in the battery of its rhetoric. It will be argued later that Spenser disagreed with Sidney's assertion in the *Apologie* that the image of the all-perfect hero was the best means of making men know and follow virtue; he seems to have recognised that to see an Odysseus does not necessarily help the average man in his own struggle to avoid the Sirens. Arthur provides the touchstone of virtue throughout the poem, but the heroes of the separate books start in imperfection and, in discovering the true nature of virtue as they proceed on their quests, educate both themselves and their readers. Such a method makes possible a much fuller anatomy of all the aspects of virtue than would be possible with a single hero, and Spenser makes the fullest use of the variety which the romance form offers him to explore virtue in all its ramifications.

The heroes themselves comprise a variety of types. There are historical figures such as St George and Artegall, the one a Saxon, the other a Briton, whose joint participation in the same quest and the same service is symbolic of the unity which the Tudors were credited with bringing to England. A second group, which includes Guyon and Britomart, consists of fictional figures whose actions nevertheless identify them with historical characters who have passed into mythology—in this case, Odysseus and Minerva. Yet a third group, notably Belphoebe, Timias and perhaps Calidore, involves fictional figures who are the projections of Spenser's own contemporaries—though it should be stressed that Belphoebe is not simply Elizabeth, nor Timias Raleigh, nor Colin Clout Spenser himself. Poetry does not immortalise the person but the virtues for which the person is notable just as Shakespeare's sonnets promise immortality not to the young man but to his beauty and truth. It is Elizabeth's 'rare chastitee' and Raleigh's invariable if very vulnerable chivalry which Spenser is celebrating, just as he prefigures his own generic skill as a poet under the guise of Colin. The historical level of allegory is a very real and constant dimension of *The Faerie Queene* as Professor Kermode has rightly insisted,[1] but there is never a simple one-to-one ratio between the living person and the fictional character. The heroic poet does not reproduce real people but selects those qualities worthy of chronicling and projects them in the form of a heroic fiction.

By means of his separate heroes Spenser carries out an extensive anatomy of heroism, examining its manifestations in terms of each individual virtue. Red Cross is the hero of faith,

---

[1] F. Kermode, *Spenser and the Allegorists*, Warton Lecture on English Poetry (British Academy, 1962).

and his actions demonstrate its nature and the factors which help or hinder its achievement. It is a Christian virtue and its archetypal hero, therefore, is Christ; but this does not preclude reference to the classical heroes who form the normal epic line. Red Cross's dragon of the *Revelation of St John* is also the dragon guarding the apples of the Hesperides just as Red Cross himself, in his fall, is at once an Adam and a Hercules wearing the shirt of Nessus. Although Spenser surrounds Red Cross with so much of the traditional panoply of the heroic, however, he explicitly denies him the highest heroic treatment:

> O gently come into my feeble brest,
> Come gently, but not with that mighty rage,
> Wherewith the martiall troupes thou doest infest,
> And harts of great Heroes doest enrage. . .
>
> Faire Goddesse lay that furious fit aside,
> Till I of warres and bloudy Mars do sing
> And Briton fields with Sarazin bloud bedyde, . . .
>
> [I. xi. 6–7]

He is addressing his Muse before he begins to describe Red Cross's fight with the dragon and, in the spirit of his invocation, lets down his 'hautie string' to a lower pitch by means of colloquial similes which have no place in the highest flights of heroic style. The dragon's blood pours out so profusely that 'The streame thereof would drive a water-mill' [22]: the waters of the Well of Life exceed not only those of Silo and Jordan but of 'th'English *Bath*, and eke the german *Spau*'. The reason for this is, presumably, that Red Cross's quest is not in the strictest sense of the term a 'heroic' one: the lesson he has to learn is not how to conquer in battle but how to be rescued by Grace when fallen, and faith itself is a virtue beyond and outside the sort of heroic virtue by which Artegall rescues Irena or Britomart kills Radegund. The fame which is the normal heroic aim is neither the beginning nor the end of human action, and Spenser is measuring the temporal against the scale of the eternal.

Once there is faith, however, virtuous action can flow from it and Guyon can proceed on his way as an orthodox hero, following in the footsteps of Odysseus. Books III and IV deal with types of heroism arising specifically from love:

> Well did Antiquitie a God thee deeme,
>   That over mortall minds hast so great might...
>   And stirredst up th'Heroes high intents,   [III. iii. 2]

but because Spenser's conception of love in this context involves procreation, he turns from mythical heroes to heroines to make his point:

> Where is the Antique glory now become,
>   That whilome wont in women to appeare?
>   Where be the brave atchievements doen by some?
>   Where be the battels, where the shield and speare,
>   And all the conquests, which them high did reare,
>   That matter made for famous Poets verse,...
>
>   [III. iv. 1]

The Trojan line is still his touchstone, but instead of Aeneas he quotes Penthesilea, the heroic Amazon who fought on the side of Troy and 'made a lake/Of *Greekish* bloud so oft in *Troian* plaine' [III. iv. 2]. In book III, Britomart's heroic task is to subdue another rebellion against Jove, that of Cupid in his triumphs, and she is drawn, therefore, in the role of a Minerva, helmeted and golden-haired, emulating her mortal half-brother Hercules in her conquest of another Busyrane.[1] The emphasis of book IV, in contrast, falls upon love as a source of peace:

> Which who so list looke backe to former ages,
>   And call to count the things that then were donne,
>   Shall find, that all the workes of those wise sages,
>   And brave exploits which great Heroes wonne,
>   In love were either ended or begunne: [IV. proem 3]

Spenser is now more concerned with the results than with the beginnings of love and the mythical heroes he quotes are the great peace-makers, the heroes of friendship such as 'great Hercules and Hyllus deare/Trew Jonathan and David trustie

---

1 Alastair Fowler, *Spenser and the Numbers of Time* (London, 1964), chap. X, p. 124.

tryde' who have their place in the garden of Venus along with
the rest. Cambina's magic potion which transforms Cambel and
Triamond into the very emblem of peace is compared to the
Nepenthe given to

> Such famous men, such worthies of the earth,
> As Jove will have advanced to the skie,
> And there made gods, though borne of mortall berth,
> For their high merits and great dignitie,...
>
> [IV. iii. 44]

Of all the virtues, however, justice is the most strictly heroic,
since its conquests are more public than the inner victories with
which the previous virtues are mainly concerned and its way
leads more obviously to fame. As the progenitor of the Tudor
monarchs, Artegall is inevitably the knight of justice rather
than of any other virtue and receives special treatment as the
most explicitly heroic of all the heroes. When we first hear of
him in book III, he is already performing all the deeds of the
archetypal hero:

> For he ne wonneth in one certaine stead,
> But restlesse walketh all the world around,
> Ay doing things, that to his fame redound,
> Defending Ladies cause, and Orphans right,
>
> [III. ii. 14]

and at the beginning of his own book he is introduced in the
line of the great heroes of justice:

> Such first was *Bacchus*, that with furious might
> All th'East before untam'd did over ronne,
> And wrong repressed, and establisht right,
> Which lawlesse men had formerly fordonne.
> There Justice first her princely rule begonne.
> Next *Hercules* his like ensample shewed,
> Who all the West with equall conquest wonne,
> And monstrous tyrants with his club subdewed;
> The club of Justice dread, with kingly powre endewed.
>
> And such was he, of whom I have to tell,
> The Champion of true Justice, *Artegall*:   [V. i. 2–3]

There is more extensive and direct reference to Hercules' Labours in book v than in any other book of the poem, and Artegall's own failure is described in terms of Hercules with Omphale just as Britomart's victory is in terms of Hercules and Hippolyta.

The last of the virtues, courtesy, would seem to follow the same pattern, when Calidore leads the Blatant Beast in chains as Hercules had led Cerberus before. Courtesy, however, is a more complex virtue than any except perhaps holiness, and one of very personal significance to Spenser as a poet. In one sense the true hero of book VI is Colin Clout, the generic poet who can see the vision denied even to the technical hero; and in the proem, the poet visualises himself as setting out upon a poetic quest comparable to the quests which face the other heroes:

> Guyde ye my footing, and conduct me well
> In these strange waies, where never foote did use,
> Ne none can find, but who was taught them by the Muse.
> [VI. proem 2]

The Proem is a prayer that he may achieve his proper virtue as a poet and not be tempted by the pleasures of the way to betray his high task, and we shall see later in the discussion of book VI the nature of these temptations which lie in the poet's way. Colin is not, however, the technical hero of the book, because his virtue, like holiness, is the source of heroism in others rather than heroic itself. Like Red Cross's vision of the Holy City, Colin's vision of the Graces provides the values by which men can become heroic, and Spenser links the two: the mountain which Red Cross ascends is compared first to that upon which Moses received the tablets of the Law, then to the Mount of Olives, and finally to the Muses' hill:

> Or like that pleasaunt Mount, that is for ay
> Through famous Poets verse each where renownd,
> On which the thrise three learned Ladies play
> Their heavenly notes, and make full many a lovely lay.
> [I. x. 54]

Colin sees both visions, and book VI brings us back to where we started in book I. *The Faerie Queene* turns upon an axis of which faith and poetry are the two poles, the vision which God sends to man and the vision which man attains of God: these define the code through which the man may grow into the hero.

[3]

I have traced Spenser's preoccupation with heroism in what may seem obvious and unnecessary detail, because it is a thread which runs through the whole poem and draws it together. Although Spenser is a long way from Carlyle, he could have titled his poem *Of heroes and hero worship* without impropriety and have called his separate books The Hero as Christian, as Lover, as Lawgiver, as Poet. There is more in this than the mere observance of the literary decorum appropriate to a heroic poem: Spenser dealt with heroes and wrote a heroic poem because he believed, like Carlyle, that the hero played a significant part in human history since the Fall. The image of history which he presents in *The Faerie Queene* comprises a bloody and dismal catalogue of human behaviour: the chronicle of Briton kings is an appalling picture of greed, ambition, treachery and lust—Locrine who 'fell to vaine voluptuous disease' [II. x. 17]; Madan, 'unworthie of his race:/For with all shame that sacred throne he fild' [21]; Ferrex and Porrex stirred up with 'the greedy thirst of royall crowne,/That knowes no kinred, nor regardes no right' [35], until the accumulated evil justly brings about the destruction of the sacred line of Brutus. When Merlin shows Britomart the future, it is a vision of overwhelming tragedy and horror:

> Then woe, and woe, and everlasting woe,
>   Be to the Briton babe, that shalbe borne,
>   To live in thraldome of his fathers foe;...
>   O who shall helpe me to lament, and mourne
>   The royall seed, the antique *Troian* blood,
>
> [III. iii. 42]

until Merlin himself can prophesy no more,

> As overcomen of the spirites powre,
>   Or other ghastly spectacle dismayd, [III. iii. 50]

Yet in spite of this, Britomart and Glauce go away rejoycing, full of 'hope of comfort glad With lighter hearts. . .' [51]. Their comfort derives from the fact that throughout the fallen line of history there springs up from time to time the hero, the saint, the law-giver, the giant-killer, the poet, who restores the lost ground and sets things to rights again:

> But evermore some of the vertuous race
> Rose up, inspired with heroicke heat,
> That cropt the branches of the sient base,
> And with strong hand their fruitfull rancknes did deface.
> [v. i. 1]

Such a man was Brutus himself who 'many Giants left on groning flore' [II. x. 10], or Bladud who

> in arts
> Exceld at *Athens* all the learned preace,
> From whence he brought them to these salvage parts,
> And with sweet science mollifide their stubborne harts.
> [II. x. 25]

or Rhodoricke 'whose surname shalbe Great' [III. iii. 45]. Figures such as these, immortalised in mythology, form Spenser's line of Elfin Emperors; and the purpose of his poem is to anatomise their quality for the benefit of mankind and to add to their numbers any British heroes yet unsung.

For the sake of emphasis, and also to give expression to the whole range of impulses within the heart of man, Spenser creates a parallel line of anti-heroes stemming from Paris and Helen, the destroyers of Troy, and opposed to the line of Aeneas which restored it. Paridel describes this line to Britomart in III. ix, himself the embodiment of those lusts of the flesh which destroyed Troy and would destroy the descendants of Aeneas if they could. Human nature and human history embody for Spenser the perpetual struggle between the good and the evil Trojan lines; and the aim of each quest in the poem is to make the line of history and that of myth one and the same, to make London identical with Cleopolis and everyman a hero. Spenser has no belief that such a happy state can ever be achieved in the fallen world of man: Gloriana's court is in

Faerie not on earth, and human heroism is at its best a fragile and uncertain thing. Artegall is built up to a great and heroic stature:

> Portly his person was, and much increast
> Through his Heroicke grace, and honorable gest.
>
> [III. ii. 24]

The crest which he bears in Merlin's mirror has for its device, 'Achilles armes, which Arthegall did win' [III. ii. 25]; and the implications are that as Paris's arrow slew Achilles, so Artegall may avenge him and perhaps, too, in his marriage to Britomart, achieve the final union of the warring lines of Greek and Trojan. Yet Artegall himself is slain like Achilles: in the next canto, before he even appears on the scene, we are told of his early death 'by practise criminall' [III. iii. 28]. Clearly Spenser's conception of the hero is not a simple romantic one, and the next chapter will explore more fully the beliefs upon which his conception is based.

2

Meaning and Myth

There is no 'spilt religion' in *The Faerie Queene*: the poem assumes an absolute distinction between earth and heaven and a separate scale of values for each. The world is irreparably fallen and true goodness and virtue, therefore, exist only in heaven: earthly virtue and fame have a relative goodness in that they are the best the world can achieve, but in the eternal scale they are less than nothing. As Chaucer makes his Troilus laugh from heaven at the passions which are so inescapably a real and valuable part of life on earth, so Spenser demands of his reader the same mediaeval capacity to care deeply about human virtue while simultaneously recognising its worthlessness in absolute terms. The first two of Spenser's *Fowre Hymnes* celebrate without reservation the joy and the virtue of earthly passions which, in the second two, are reviled in terms of the heavenly scale:

> And that faire lampe, which useth to enflame
> The hearts of men with selfe-consuming fyre
> Thenceforth seemes fowle, and full of sinfull blame;
> And all that pompe, to which proud minds aspyre
> By name of honor, and so much desyre,
> Seemes to them basenesse, and all riches drosse,
> And all mirth sadnesse, and all lucre losse.
>
> (*An Hymne of Heavenly Beautie*, 275–82)

Both sets of values are correct in their own places and the one does not invalidate the other. When Red Cross reaches the Hill of Contemplation, he sees afar off the heavenly city whose brightness dims even that of Cleopolis: it is not for him now, but when his quest is completed and he is raised among the Saints, he will look down upon the earth as Troilus did and despise the values which at present it is his whole object to defend:

> But when thou famous victorie hast wonne,
> And high emongst all knights hast hong thy shield,
> Thenceforth the suit of earthly conquest shonne,
> And wash thy hands from guilt of bloudy field:
> For bloud can nought but sin, and wars but sorrowes
> yield. [I. x. 60]

Until then, however, he may not hang up his shield as Verdant does in the Bower of Blisse but must carry on the fight, knowing that the corruption lies in the nature of the medium itself and not in the moral intention. The human quest is evil in that it is the product of the corrupt will working through fallen materials: it is good in so far as it is an attempt, at no matter how many removes, to reproduce on its own level the vision of the saint in book I and of the poet in book VI. These two achievements of the 'erected wit' placed at the beginning and the end of the poem enclose the action and justify what comes in between.

Spenser's view of the creation is in the main an Aristotelean one. The great pageants in which he embodies his conceptions of the world present a picture of life as composed of chaotic stuff which form is struggling with only partial success to subdue to its own likeness, and in which the constituent atoms war with each other in a very Aristotelean state of 'becoming'. This symbolism is most explicit in book IV, but it is the underlying assumption of the whole poem: life itself has good and evil inextricably mixed into its own raw materials and involves, therefore, a perpetual conflict, an inescapable choice. This is apparent in the great chronicle of Briton kings with its seemingly random mixture of villains and heroes, and human history only reflects the nature of the substance which composes it. Human love, from which life springs, is Janus-faced, offering a possible good and a possible evil:

> Fresh shadowes, fit to shroud from sunny ray;
> Faire lawnds, to take the sunne in season dew;
> Sweet springs, in which a thousand Nymphs did play;
> Soft rombling brookes, that gentle slomber drew;

23

High reared mounts, the lands about to vew;
Low looking dales, disloignd from common gaze;
Delightfull bowres, to solace lovers trew;
False Labyrinthes, fond runners eyes to daze;
All which by nature made did nature selfe amaze.

[IV. X. 24]

The ambivalence of love is embodied in this moral geography of the Garden of Venus with its carefully organised pairs of opposites: the shadows ironically preceding the sun and reinforced by the sinister word 'shroud'; the active nymphs and the slothful slumbers; the lofty vision and the low looking; the delightful bowers for true lovers and the false mazes for false ones. Even the serpent 'whose head and tail were fast combyned' around the legs of the statue of Venus suggests in this context not only the serpent of eternity, but the serpent of Eden which destroyed human immortality and so made necessary the eternity by succession which Venus makes possible [IV. X. 40].

If this is the essential nature of love, such too will be the nature of the fruits which follow. The great pageant of the rivers at the wedding of the Thames and the Medway in the next canto is Spenser's symbol of life in all its fertility; and the same ambivalence is implied by the procession of 'the seas abundant progeny'—the fifty daughters of Nereus, the six brethren slain by Humber, the three sons of Blomius and all the ramifications of parenthood which form the basic metaphor of the sequence. The sea-gods lead the way, their allegorical force stemming in part from their traditional roles in popular mythology but even more from the casual epithets which Spenser borrows from his source in Natalis Comes. It is not necessary to dig deeply into the iconography of the figures whom Spenser introduces for they normally speak for themselves and define their own significance in the context. On the one side there are the incestuous Astraeus, the sinister Orion 'that doth tempests still portend', and Phorcys, father of 'that fatall brood/By whom those old Heroes wonne such fame' [13]—the heroes being, of course, Perseus and Odysseus, and the brood including the Gorgons and Polyphemus. On the credit side are Brontes who helped forge Aeneas's armour; Neleus and Pelias, 'lovely brethren both'; Eurypulus who, like the Palmer, 'calmes the waters wroth', and 'faire *Euphoemus*, that upon them goth/As on the ground' [14], a veritable figure of Christ himself. The sequence is loaded with symbolism of good and evil, sin and redemption, which is carried on into the founders of 'puissant nations' who follow after them. Among these, for example, are Inachus, founder of Argos, and Agenor whose son, Cadmus, founded Thebes; but on the other side, Albion, 'father of the bold/And warlike people, which the *Britaine* Islands hold', who was slain by Hercules [15].

These are the symbols of the human will in its varied and opposed manifestations; and the rivers which follow suggest the materials upon which it works, the conflicting passions out of which the pattern of action is derived. Nereus who heads the procession is himself a figure of conflicting associations: he is 'th'eldest, and the best,/...then which none more upright,/ Ne more sincere in word and deed profest;/Most voide of guile,...' [18]; yet Spenser tells us at some length, perhaps as an initial warning of the bitter nature of life, that he foretold the fall of Troy [19]. The Nile inevitably comes first of the rivers as the indifferent source of all life, good and evil alike [III. vi. 8]; but those which follow drop for the most part into one or the other camp and carry specific moral associations. There is divine Scamander, for example, 'purpled yet with blood/Of Greekes and Trojans' [20], bringing to mind the fulfilment of Nereus's prophecy and perhaps, also, the figure of Lust with his great nose 'Full dreadfully empurpled all with bloud' [IV. vii. 6] who, whether in the persons of Paris and Helen or Paridel and Hellenore, is causer of the tragedy. There are Pactolus 'glistring with his golden flood', and 'Tygris fierce, whose streames of none may be withstood' [20], a pair resembling Mammon and Maleger on his tiger; and these in turn are balanced by 'immortall Euphrates', 'Alpheus still immaculate', and 'Tybris, renowmed for the Romaines fame' [21]. The story of Aeneas runs constantly below the surface, and the Tiber makes good the slaughter of Pactolus as the second Troy rises from the ashes of the first. Spenser concludes his list of world rivers with 'that huge River, which doth beare his name/Of warlike Amazons,...' [21], anticipating Radegund, the wicked Amazon of book V. 'And shame on you, O men', he declares in the next stanza, denouncing both Artegall for not asserting his proper virtue over her, and the British nation for its similar lack of imperialist ambition towards 'that land of gold' [22].

The British rivers which come last of all carry a smaller body of native mythology for Spenser to work on than their more famous brothers, but the overtones of allegory are still present. There is 'The wanton Lee, that oft doth loose his way' [29], for example—a symbolism to which he is presumably referring again in V. ii. 19, when Artegall kills Pollente in its waters; or again there is the Stour, a Hydra-like figure with its 'sixe deformed heads on hye' [32]. More commonly, however, Spenser links the British rivers with the tragedies or heroic triumphs which have taken place upon their banks or in their waters, so that the account reads at times like the chronicle of Briton kings:

> Then came those sixe sad brethren, like forlorne,
>   That whilome were (as antique fathers tell)
>   Sixe valiant Knights of one faire Nymphe yborne,
>   Which did in noble deedes of armes excell,
>   And wonned there, where now Yorke people dwell;
>   Still Ure, swift Werfe, and Oze the most of might,
>   High Swale, unquiet Nide, and troublous Skell;
>   All whom a Scythian king, that Humber hight,
> Slew cruelly, and in the river drowned quight.
>
> But past not long ere *Brutus* warlicke sonne
>   Locrinus them aveng'd, . . .   [IV. xi. 37–8]

The primary symbolism of this great procession is of fertility, the richness, the endless variety of creation; but underlying it all is the consistent pattern of good and evil in conflict and yet, at times, mysteriously leading into each other as the tragedy of Ino leads to the divinity of Palemon, the 'saylers frend' [13]. Life has an ambiguous and fluctuating texture which belongs to Mutability and will do so until literally the end of time when at last all things will be 'firmely stayd/Upon the pillours of Eternity' [VII. viii. 2].

[2]

The hero is born into this fallen state which presents by its very nature a perpetual choice between good and evil, and the 'Quest' in *The Faerie Queene* is the allegory of this challenge. Sloth, first of the deadly sins in the Palace of Pride, is the refusal or the inability to recognise that the choice must be made:

> Scarse could he once uphold his heavie hed
> To looken, whether it were night or day:
> May seeme the wayne was very evill led,
> When such an one had guiding of the way,
> That knew not, whether right he went, or else astray.
>
> [I. iv. 19]

The Faerie Queene takes its whole being from Spenser's profound sense of the Fall, and the most insidious temptation with which he faces anyone throughout the poem is that of forgetting its reality. The prime object of the poem, indeed, is to educate and train the hero and through him, the reader, to recognise all the infinitely subtle ramifications of Original Sin and to circumvent or to survive their challenge. The Fall brought sin and death into the world and *The Faerie Queene*, even more than *Paradise Lost*, is concerned to remind us how the spiritual death of sin may be escaped and the physical death of mortality made less significant. The books of the poem present a chain of virtues directed towards these two ends, so that by the conclusion of the poem Aaron may be as completely dressed as imperfect human nature will allow.

The underlying scheme of the poem then is the traditional Christian one. The Fall is answered by the Grace of God, manifesting itself through the Incarnation and the Passion which, paying the penalty of death incurred by the first Adam, allow the man of faith to rise again and stand once more 'On even ground against his mortal foe'. The Grace of God is the basis of everything—without it there could be neither redemption nor virtue, and Spenser never ceases to reiterate that 'all the good is Gods, both power and eke will'. Whatever virtue man is capable of is made possible by Grace and faith alone, and Spenser never suggests that such virtue has any merit in the theological sense of the word: it is the result, not the cause, of justification. Yet Christian virtue is necessary as a sign of faith and as pleasing to God; and since Spenser's main concern is with the practice of virtue itself rather than with its ultimate sanctions, he lays as much stress upon the effects of the Incarnation *per se* as upon the Passion which gave it fulfilment. He takes the Incarnation very literally and sees in Christ the pattern of the perfect and absolute hero whose humanity he adores as Hopkins adored that of his 'Chevalier':

> Mark Christ our King. He knows war, served this soldiering through;
> He of all can handle a rope best.   (*The Soldier*)

The Incarnation represents to Spenser an infusion of new virtue into corrupted human nature, there in every man, like the statue within the block of stone, waiting to be liberated by the act of faith and restoring in man the image of God. For Spenser as for Hopkins this Christ-like quality in the human heart is the true Aristotelean 'form' of man, the Inscape which deals out its being in the Christian life, 'Crying What I do is me: for that I came'. Once acknowledged it works like a leaven within to raise the whole man, to inform chaos and help a state of becoming towards one of being. The progress of the poem is a record of this human development, beginning in the first book with the discovery of faith itself and tracing in the subsequent ones the spread of the resultant inner virtue into area after area of human behaviour. We can trace the progress towards this Christian heroism in the gradual internalisation of Christ as the poem proceeds, manifested in the changing role of Arthur. In book I Arthur is primarily a figure of the external Redeemer descending through God's Grace to rescue Red Cross from the darkness of sin when all else is lost. Even here he does not come until Red Cross is capable of asking for him and fit to receive him; but the emphasis is primarily upon Grace and mercy and a redemption coming from without. In so far as Arthur plays the role of the human hero of holiness, he too is redeemed by Grace when fallen; it is his shield not his sword which destroys Orgoglio. Once, however, that faith has been established and the strength of the Redeemer made available to man, Arthur becomes less of an external figure and increasingly the symbol of the Christ within, the new man which the believer can summon from within himself to vanquish the old. In book II, as Miss Williams has suggested,[1] Arthur is almost as much a part of Guyon himself as are Pyrochles and Cymochles who oppose him; and by book VI Calidore has himself become the Christ-figure, raising Pastorella as Arthur raised Red Cross from Orgoglio's prison.

Yet, as we shall see, Calidore's Christ-like quality represents the poet's ideal of what man should be not the reality of what man is, and I do not think that Spenser would have gone as far as Hopkins's 'I am all at once what Christ is, since he was what I am'. The human hero may emulate the imperfect greatness of a Hercules but the moral perfection of Christ is beyond the reach of his fallen nature. Arthur is, after all, a figure of ideal and more than human virtue; and the fact that Guyon's encounter with Mammon is patterned on that of Christ with Satan only adds to the irony of his fall immediately afterwards. Where Spenser draws on the symbolism of Christ, he attaches it not to the hero himself but to the regenerate part of his nature: it is, for example, the Palmer, not Guyon himself, who stills the waters with his staff. Even the aspects of Christ's story which Spenser brings to mind most frequently in the episodes of the poem are those, like Arthur's own fall before Orgoglio's blow, which remind us of Christ's own mortality, and insist that the Christian victory will be through apparent defeat. The Christian struggle towards heroism is not an easy progress, and the characters of *The Faerie Queene*, though capable of redemption, are never without sin: the subtle and mutable elements of which they are made and among which they live confuse and trip them up continually; but the hero is the man impelled by inner necessity to pick himself up again, a little wiser for the time being. As Spenser presents it, life is God's rather rough mode of re-educating man in the virtues which he lost with the Fall: it is the pains of the Law preparing for the Gospels, the wanderings in the desert without which the promised land cannot be achieved.

[1] Kathleen Williams, *Spenser's World of Glass* (University of California, 1966), p. 63.

This is the Christian answer to sin which Spenser embodies in the progress of his heroes: there is no escape from it and no return to Eden, but there is profit by the way and final redemption for those who seek it. There is no comparable answer to the physical mortality which Adam brought into the world, only God's original creative Fiat

> the mightie word,
> Which first was spoken by th'Almightie lord,
> That bad them to increase and multiply: [III. vi. 34]

By this means the race though not the individual may 'enduren by successiouns'; and Spenser utters anew the traditional plea made by Nature's servant, Genius in *The Romance of the Rose*,[1] but in terms which are specifically Christian. Adam's original immortality is lost; but the dying generations of his sons, reproducing themselves within the framework of Christian marriage, save the species from falling into the maw of physical death while at the same time avoiding the spiritual death of sin to which sex of all the passions most easily leads. In this way Adam's seed replaces Adam as the new spring repairs the ravages of winter and the orderly cycle of the seasons replaces the original eternal summer.

The Faerie Queene is a Christian poem in its very essence, and Spenser could no doubt have embodied his theme in scriptural fable as Milton chose to do. His sense of historical issues, however, led him to draw on British history for the basic machinery of his poem, and the Biblical myth, therefore, is present but at one remove, running below the surface in the symbolism of the actions or the allusiveness of the language. The poem is full of double meanings and images which relate the individual conflicts back to the great central theme of the first and the second Adam. It may be a reference to Fidelia's 'Christall face', or to Red Cross's sword which bounces vainly off the dragon's hide 'As if in Adamant rocke it had bene pight'; or it may take the form of a pun, based on the Renaissance etymology which derived the Latin 'mulier' (woman) from 'mollis aer' (soft air). When Archimago frames his false Una 'of liquid ayre', it is

---

[1] *The Romance of the Rose*, trans. H. W. Robbins, New York, 1962, p. 413.

a figure of Eve he is creating. Double meanings of this kind run through the whole poem and form a pattern of moral touchstones which penetrates into every corner. They provide an important dimension of the allegory which must be mentioned at this point but may await for fuller illustration until the individual books are considered.

In a similar fashion, the Christian theology forces itself up and is reflected in some of the great image sequences of the poem. The Quest, itself made necessary by the Fall, must be achieved by means of fallen human nature; and the sweat of Adam's brow, at once the penalty of his sin and the source of his redemption, forms one of the most inevitable symbols in the poem as in 'Metaphysical' religious poetry. Belphoebe establishes the image in her opening speech:

> Where ease abounds, yt's eath to doe amis;
> But who his limbs with labours, and his mind
> Behaves with cares, cannot so easie mis.
> Abroad in armes, at home in studious kind
> Who seekes with painfull toile, shall honor soonest
> find...

> Before her gate high God did Sweat ordaine,
> And wakefull watches ever to abide:... [II. iii. 40–1]

The degree to which the characters sweat in the pursuit of virtue is a measure of their heroism: so Calidore 'yet sweating comes' to the shepherds in his pursuit of the Blatant Beast, and they, 'him seeing so to sweat/...Offred him drinke to quench his thirstie heat' [VI. ix. 5–6]: his acceptance marks the beginning of his fall. In the same way, the 'Wearie Traveiler' wandering into the Bower of Blisse is given drink to 'quench his thristy heat', and creeping slumber makes him forget his former pain and wipes away his 'toylsom sweat' [II. v. 30]. The word 'Traveiler' still carries something of its original association with 'travail', and is a pun very relevant to the context. The only labour and sweat in the Bower is that of Acrasia at her love-making:

> And yet through languour of her late sweet toyle,
> Few drops, more cleare than Nectar, forth distild,

That like pure Orient perles adowne it trild,

[II. xii. 78]

The comparison of the beads of sweat to pearls links them with the ruby and emerald grapes elsewhere in the garden and makes them all a part of the same evil artifice, just as the comparison to Nectar associates them with an even more than heavenly bliss. The natural imagery by which the sweat of Britomart is described in her fight with Artegall underlines the contrast between a virtue and a vice:

> With that her angels face, unseene afore,
> Like to the ruddie morne appeard in sight,
> Deawed with silver drops, through sweating sore,
>
> [IV. vi. 19]

Spenser's control of verbal detail is extraordinarily consistent, even in the most minor ramifications of a central symbol.

All the temptations of *The Faerie Queene* stem ultimately from Satan, who can be seen looking over the shoulder of every evil character, whether it is Mammon tempting Guyon as Christ was tempted in the wilderness,

> Wherefore if me thou deigne to serve and sew,
> At thy commaund lo all these mountaines bee;
>
> [II. vii. 9]

or Guyle with his 'great wyde net' [v. ix. 11], or, most explicitly, Archimago, the Lord of the Flies:

> And forth he cald out of deepe darknesse dred
> Legions of Sprights, the which like little flyes
> Fluttring about his ever damned hed,
> A-waite whereto their service he applyes, [I. i. 38]

Against this figure of Anti-Christ is set the Good Shepherd, whom Spenser consistently pictures as brushing away the flies that molest him. The image first occurs at the beginning of the poem when Red Cross, summoning all the strength of his faith, banishes the swarm of errors which crawl up his legs:

> As gentle Shepheard in sweete even-tide,
> When ruddy *Phoebus* gins to welke in west,

High on an hill, his flocke to vewen wide,
Markes which do byte their hasty supper best;
A cloud of combrous gnattes do him molest,
All striving to infixe their feeble stings,
That from their noyance he no where can rest,
But with his clownish hands their tender wings
He brusheth oft, and oft doth mar their murmurings.

[I. i. 23]

The comparison here is a diffident one, because Red Cross has
yet to learn the nature of the temptations which assail him and
also the strength which Christ has placed in his 'clownish'
hands. The image occurs again with more force when Arthur
and Guyon raise the siege of the House of Alma like shepherds
scattering the enemies of their flock before them [II. ix. 14], a
comparison which Spenser follows up two stanzas later with the
further simile of 'a swarme of Gnats' scattered by the north
wind. It occurs most significantly of all when Calidore in the
guise of a shepherd—a profession in which the brigands naturally
have little skill [VI. xi. 40]—breaks into the brigands' cave and
scatters the inmates as if they were flies:

How many flyes, in whottest sommers day,
Do seize upon some beast whose flesh is bare, . . .

[VI. xi. 48]

Through repeated metaphor of this kind a plain story of rescue
becomes an image of Christ harrowing Hell, and the particular
incident takes its place in the eternal struggle between the
servants of God and those of Satan. It is in this context that
Pyrochles, seeing death approaching at the hand of Arthur,
cries out 'Harrow and well away', like the devil in the old play.
[II. viii. 46].

Christ is very much a character in *The Faerie Queene* even
though he does not appear in person. Moreover, his unseen
presence throughout the poem and his successive incarnations in
the form of one or another hero draw attention to the human
vehicle through whom God took on human flesh; and though
Spenser makes little direct reference to the Virgin Mary, she too
adds her dimension to the total allegory. The whole poem is
after all addressed to and written around a Virgin Queen; and

33

although Spenser never attempts to equate the two or indulge in direct comparisons which would verge on blasphemy, he yet envisages Gloriana's role as an allegory of that of the virgin mother. As God used the Virgin Mary for the channel through which his mercy was made available to mankind, so he uses Gloriana to propagate the ideals of heroism, and the heroes come from her court of Maidenhead. She is the source of virtue as the other of faith. For this reason the proems addressed directly to the Queen speak of her in language with deeply religious overtones. In the proem to book IV, she is 'The Queene of love, and Prince of peace from heaven blest'. In that to book VI, Spenser asks his Muse to reveal to him the hidden source of virtue, lost since antiquity but found again in the mind of his 'soveraine Lady Queene':

> Revele to me the sacred noursery
> Of vertue, which with you doth there remaine,
> Where it in silver bowre does hidden ly
> From view of men, and wicked worlds disdaine;
> Since it at first was by the Gods with paine
> Planted in earth, being deriv'd at first
> From heavenly seedes of bounty soveraine,
> And by them long with carefull labour nurst,
> Till it to ripenesse grew, and forth to honour burst.   [5]

The silver bower in which divine virtue comes to birth calls to mind the womb-bower at the heart of the Garden of Adonis; and the whole sequence of images, so deeply suggestive of physical birth, brings together the virgin birth of Christ and the virgin source of courtesy. The title 'fruitfullest Virginia' can be applied to both sovereigns.

[3]

In its Christian mythology *The Faerie Queene* stands half way between a Morality play and *Paradise Lost*; but Spenser was writing a humanist heroic poem and was fully aware, as we have already seen, of the great heritage of pagan myth which went with the heroic tradition—a heritage too strong to be ignored even in a specifically Christian poem. Nor was there any need

to ignore it: Christian and pagan had learned to lie down together very peaceably, and classic mythology lent itself freely
to Christian purposes throughout the Middle Ages. Coming
before the myth of the dying God had been formulated,
Spenser had no precise counterpart in classical mythology for
the Crucifixion; but he had incarnation myths in plenty, and a
multitude of classical heroes already loaded with Christian
symbolism which fitted them perfectly to express a Christian
theme in a genre primarily associated with classical fable. Of
these, Hercules was the most useful, since he was at once the
generic hero of classical mythology and, in terms of Christian
symbolism, a literal son of God whose Labours had, from time
immemorial, been interpreted as a type of Christ's miracles.[1]
Spenser's brief description of the conception of Hercules can
accommodate a reference to the Trinity with absolute propriety
for this reason:

> But faire *Alcmena* better match did make,
> Joying his love in likenesse more entire;
> Three nights in one, they say, that for her sake
> He then did put, her pleasures lenger to partake.
>
> [III. xi. 33]

In terms both of Christian doctrine and humanist heroic tradition, Hercules had a central position in the mythology of *The
Faerie Queene*, and we have already seen something of his
labours within the poem. All the heroes in one way or another
play this common Christ–Hercules role.

Even Christ, however, is only a link in the whole story of
man's fall and redemption, and similarly Hercules forms a part
of a more comprehensive myth. Alastair Fowler has argued
convincingly that the formal structure of *The Faerie Queene* is
based upon the sequence of planetary deities associated with the
seven days of the week; but it seems to me that some of the
gods, at least, play a further and more complex role in the poem.
Spenser's theme is the Fall, and he turns, therefore, to the
great classical myth of the Fall, namely, the loss of the Golden
Age as a result of the deposition of Saturn by Jove. He draws his

---

[1] For an account of this, see, for example, D. W. Robertson Jr, *A Preface to
Chaucer* (Oxford, 1963), pp. 141–2.

materials from Greek and Latin sources alike, taking his names indiscriminately from both mythologies, but drawing heavily, as for so much else in his poem, on Ovid's *Metamorphoses*. He is less concerned with Jove's usurpation of his father's kingdom than with the resultant rebellions against Jove of the Titans and of the giants and monsters bred in revenge by Gaea, the earth. The mythological villains of *The Faerie Queene* are Typhon, son of earth, father of Cerberus and the Nemean lion, or the giants who tried to storm Olympus and whose fiery struggles beneath the mountains under which Jove crushed them produced volcanoes. The heroes, by the same token, are Jove's children, in particular Hercules and Minerva, who helped him in his struggle to maintain the order of his Silver Age.

The great myth runs below the surface of *The Faerie Queene* in imagery and allusion, only rising into the open in the *Mutability Cantos*. The Golden Age, like Eden, has passed away, as Spenser repeatedly insists:

> For that which all men then did vertue call
> Is now cald vice; and that which vice was hight,
> Is now hight vertue, and so us'd of all:
> Right now is wrong, and wrong that was is right; . . .

> For during *Saturnes* ancient raigne it's sayd
> That all the world with goodnesse did abound:
> All loved vertue, no man was affrayd
> Of force, ne fraud in wight was to be found:
> No warre was knowne, no dreadfull trompets sound;
> Peace universall rayn'd mongst men and beasts, . . .
>
> [v. proem 4–9]

The world of the ordered seasons which Jove is defending against Mutability is that of the Silver Age, but throughout the poem it threatens to run down and, losing its basic order, degenerate to a less admirable Age of Gold dominated by Mammon, or to reach the depths of Ovid's Age of Iron. Astraea is driven from the earth by human wickedness, leaving Talus, the iron man, in her place; and iron runs through the imagery of the poem as a symbol of all the forces of earth which have dragged man lower than he need be. The Blatant Beast [VI. vi. 9] and the dragon of sin [I. xi. 13] both have teeth of iron: there is the iron chariot of the Soldan [v. viii. 41] and the iron chariot of the Night, 'fild with rusty blood', which passes among the trembling ghosts of the underworld with their chattering iron teeth [I. v. 32]. Amoret is bound to Busyrane's brazen pillar with an iron band [III. xii. 30], and Mammon wears an iron coat all overgrown with rust but with the underlying gold showing through [II. vii. 4]. The reiterated image acts as a running commentary on the action of the poem, inviting us to see the fallen world in terms of the Iron Age as Ovid describes it, when the giants assailed the kingdom of heaven and, last of the immortals, the maiden Justice left the blood-soaked earth.

The eternal battle between Jove and the Titans, giants and monsters who threaten the order of his reign, is the classical myth which Spenser uses to embody man's fight with the vices and passions of the Fall; and the role of Gaea, the Earth, forms a link between the classical and the Christian, a prolonged pun uniting the two mythologies. Man's vices and rebellious passions spring from his fallen earthly nature just as the monsters and giants who challenge Jove are bred by Gaea, and she is the mother of a whole line of evil characters throughout *The Faerie Queene*. She bears Orgoglio to Aeolus, 'The greatest Earth his uncouth mother was' [I. vii. 9], and Disdain is of the same stock —'Like an huge Gyant of the Tytans race' [II. vii. 41]: she is the mother of Argante and Ollyphant by her own son, Typhon [III. vii. 47], and Maleger, like Antaeus, springs up again with his strength renewed each time he is cast down upon his mother earth, until Arthur, like Hercules, learns how to destroy him. In the light of this double background of classical myth and Christian metaphor, the many references to the earth throughout the poem contain a strong and punning irony. When Archimago first appears in the poem, we are told that 'to the ground his eyes were lowly bent' [I. i. 29], and the rich, ironic ambiguity of the line derives from Spenser's consciousness of this background, as it does in Cupid's taunt concerning Jove's love affairs that the Gods 'take me for their *Jove*, whiles *Jove* to earth is gone' [III. xi. 35].

Jove is the central figure of the myth and for the Elizabethans a rather ambiguous one. He is, of course, all-judging Jove, Jove the thunderer, whose battles with the Titans formed a favourite emblem of rightful force; and his image runs through Marlowe's *Tamburlaine*, Chapman's *Bussy D'Ambois* and Ben Jonson's tragedies with this significance. Not all the characters in these plays agree among themselves who is the figure of Jove and who is that of the Titan—is Tamburlaine, for example, a Titan rebelling against Jove or a successful Jove overcoming Saturn?— and the same question has to be asked about Bussy: yet all agree that Jove is the figure of justice. On the other side, however, Jove came in for the sort of Christian criticism which Chaucer had earlier levelled at the pagan gods, 'Jove, Appollo, of Mars, of swich rascaille!'. Marston, for example, sees Jove as the symbol of all the lawlessness afflicting the modern world, the figure who destroyed the Golden Age and brought sin and death to mankind:

> This thunderer, that right virtuously
> Thrust forth his father from his empery
> Is now the great Monarko of the earth...
> (*Certaine Satyres*, v, 65–8)

In the *Scourge of Villanie*, he castigates Jove for his amorous metamorphoses in the pursuit of his bestial lust:

> The sonne of *Saturne* is become a Bull
> To crop the beauties of some female trull...
> [viii, 153–4]

and Quarles makes the same point in the fifth emblem of his First Book, blaming Jove for the loss of the Golden Age and the expulsion of Astraea from the world:

> Until the wanton days of Jove,
> The simple world was all compos'd of love;
> But Jove grew fleshly, false, unjust;
> Inferior beauty fill'd his veins with lust;... [book I. v]

Spenser's attitude is more subtle than either of these alternatives and contains elements of both. Jove is certainly a figure of justice in *The Faerie Queene*: he is the patron deity of book v, as Alastair Fowler has argued, and justly engaged in the struggle with the Titans and monsters; yet the very rebellions he is fighting were caused initially by his own usurpation of Saturn's throne, and the monsters which his son, Hercules, is engaged in destroying are ultimately the result of his own lusts. Jove's first appearance right at the beginning of the poem is an ominous one: he sends the storm which drives Red Cross and Una into the forest of error, and the description is in terms unmistakably suggestive of sin and death:

> The day with cloudes was suddeine overcast,
> And angry *Jove* an hideous storme of raine
> Did poure into his Lemans lap so fast,
> That every wight to shrowd it did constrain, . . .
>
> [I. i. 6]

The first temptation which Red Crosse meets comes from Jove and, as we shall see, the rest follow logically from it. The hint contained in 'his Lemans lap' is developed in the tapestries of Cupid's triumphs which adorn the walls of Busyrane's castle, where thundering Jove is shown as roaming the world,

> Now like a Ram, faire *Helle* to pervart,
> Now like a Bull, *Europa* to withdraw:
>
> [III. xi. 30]

while Cupid seizes his throne like a successful Titan. The reference here is to Jove's love affairs and their repercussions in the world, but in books v and vi the emphasis falls upon his initial rebellion and the counter-rebellion it breeds among the Titans and their kin. We have seen how extensively the victories of Arthur and Artegall in book v are patterned upon those of Hercules, and yet the moment Artegall slays Grantorto, he is attacked by the Blatant Beast [v. xii. 41]. This is no accident, as the genealogy of the beast, which Spenser gives in some detail, makes clear. We are told that he is of the stock of Cerberus, 'This hellish Dog', begot of 'foule Echidna' by 'Cruell *Typhaon*, whose tempestuous rage/Makes th'heavens tremble oft' [vi. vi. 9–11]: but Typhon was born by the Earth to Tartarus in order that she might revenge herself on Jove for casting down the giants and Titans. In other words, the Cerberean Blatant Beast is the ultimate result of Jove's deposition of Saturn, and Jove's own acts bring about the evils which have to be conquered. His usurpation makes necessary his own justice which, in its turn, breeds the new rebellions which he and his offspring have to put down. It is Artegall's Herculean labours in book V which make necessary the final Herculean labour which faces Calidore in book VI, that of subduing Cerberus. The whole issue is made clear when Mutability, the Titaness, rises to avenge her brother Titans and depose the deposer of Saturn. In destroying the Golden Age, Jove let in Mutability and must justly face her challenge.

Jove's role in *The Faerie Queene*, therefore, is not that of the father of heaven, but of the father of earth: he is an Adam figure who brought about the Fall and let in the sin and mortality with which mankind has had to battle ever since. Like Adam, he has both strengths and weaknesses: his lightning may strike unjustly,

> Like as the lightning brond from riven skie,
>   Throwne out by angry *Jove* in his vengeance,
>   With dreadful force falles on some steeple hie;
>   Which battring, downe it on the church doth glance,
>   And teares it all with terrible mischance.   [IV. vi. 14]

but he also sets the sun in the sky to guide men's way:

> O lightsome day, the lampe of highest *Jove*
>   First made by him, mens wandring wayes to guyde,
>   [I. viii. 23]

He is the father of Helen by whom Troy fell, but he is equally the father of Venus by whose son, Aeneas, it rose again. In Cupid's tapestries we see him raping Leda in one stanza but seducing Alcmena, who bore him Hercules, in the next [III. xi. 33]. As all the sons of Adam are faced with the consequences of their forefather's action and are heroic in so far as they set things to rights, so Jove's sons may become heroes by maintaining his justice, and are venerated like Minerva or Hercules for doing battle with the rebellious giants, or like Bacchus for introducing the arts of civilisation.

Of all Jove's sons, Hercules is the greatest and the one who comes closest to the greatest of Adam's sons, the second Adam. Although Hercules is not a redeemer in the sense that Christ is, he represents the equivalent pattern of virtue, in terms of the classic myth, to that which Christ represents in terms of the Christian, and his labours are the answer to Jove's sins as are Christ's to those of Adam. For this reason, both are simultaneously present in most of the heroic actions throughout the poem. Everyman carries both Hercules and Christ within him and is free to fulfil or deny this heroic potential. The poem is full of references to Hercules's mortality and human weakness, to the shirt of Nessus or the service of Omphale, as well as to the achievements of his divinity. The choice is always there and the goal is the maintenance of Jove's Silver Age against all the threats of baser metal. Artegall inherits the sword which Jove wielded 'in that great fight/Against the *Titans*, that whylome rebelled/Gainst highest heaven:' [v. i. 9], although he does not always make proper use of it: Arthur's horse, Spumador, is of the heavenly breed which Hercules captured from Laomedon [II. xi. 19]. The human passions to be controlled are those of the angry giants crushed under the mountains, and the references to Aetna in the poem carry this symbolism. It is implicit in the 'hideous storme', thunder and earthquake heralding the Masque of Cupid which, as we shall see, is a great pageant of frustrated passion [III. xii. 2]: it is there more explicitly in Glauce's account of Britomart's incomprehensible grief at III. ii. 32, or in Spenser's description of the furious agonies of the Dragon of Sin, when Red Cross lops off the foot which is gripping his shield of Faith:

> For griefe thereof, and divelish despight,
>   From his infernall fournace forth he threw
>   Huge flames, that dimmed all the heavens light,
>   Enrold in duskish smoke and brimstone blew;
>   As burning *Aetna* from his boyling stew
>   Doth belch out flames, and rockes in peeces broke,
>   And ragged ribs of mountaines molten new,
>   Enwrapt in coleblacke clouds and filthy smoke,
> That all the land with stench, and heaven with horror
>   choke.   [I. xi. 44]

Here the Christian and Classic come beautifully together in the common image of Hell-fire and Titanic volcano.

The myth of Jove gave Spenser a vehicle with which to express his sense of the conflict at the heart of human nature, the enormous potentialities for good or for evil which lie in the human passions rightly or wrongly employed. I have traced it specifically in relationship to the problem of sin as raised by the Fall, but the simultaneous problem of mortality, though demanding a different answer, yet overlaps in innumerable ways. The 'hideous bellowing/Of many beasts, that roard outrageously' which Guyon hears as he approaches the Bower of Blisse [II. xii. 39] comes from the animal passions which are one with the animal roles so dear to Jove in his amorous conquests on earth. These, like any other passions, have to be mastered and tamed by the heroes, and Spenser's treatment of sex is always in relation to sin as well as to mortality. For this reason he chose as his framework for the treatment of sex a sequence of myth which was inevitable in view of the theme and, at the same time, inextricably involved with that of Jove, namely, the myths surrounding Venus. As Venus rising from the sea into which the seed fell when Uranus was castrated by Saturn or, in other accounts, when Saturn was castrated by Jove, she was the standard symbol for the union of form with first matter from which all creation arises. Spenser alludes specifically to this myth of creation which the ancient poets invented, after his account of the wedding of Thames and Medway:

> Therefore the antique wisards well invented,
> > That *Venus* of the fomy sea was bred,
> > For that the seas by her are most augmented:....
> > > > [IV. xii. 2]

This is the Venus who plays the role of great Nature in the Garden of Adonis, sending out forms to their union with chaos, and the role of Venus Genetrix in her own garden of love:

> Then doth the daedale earth throw forth to thee
> > Out of her fruitfull lap aboundant flowres;
> > And then all living wights, soone as they see
> > The spring breake forth out of his lusty bowres,
> > They all doe learne to play the Paramours; [IV. x. 45]

42

But the poets invented other myths about Venus for Spenser to draw on besides those of simple fruitfulness. She is, for example, Jove's daughter, the mother of Aeneas, and as such, relevant to the heroism which is the theme of the poem; yet at the same time she is the mother of the Cupid whose triumphs are celebrated in Jove's lustful amours, and the Venus whose erotic appeal conquered Mars and led to the destruction of Adonis. The boar which gave Adonis his fatal wound in the thigh is one with Gryll who prefers his hoggish form in Circe's garden, and is linked with the figure of Lust in book IV, 'With huge great teeth, like to a tusked Bore'. On yet another level, the two Venuses, Urania and Dione, clearly enter into the conception of the two sisters, Diana and Venus, and their respective wards, Belphoebe and Amoret. Indeed the endless variety of the forms of Venus afforded Spenser precise equivalents for all the distinctions he wished to draw between the heroic and the unheroic aspects of sex, and her very ambiguity made her an inexhaustible symbol for his purposes.

The essential activity of the hero is that of making the moral choice; and as Hallett Smith has pointed out,[1] the most pervasive of all the myths in *The Faerie Queene*, and one which is central to the Renaissance conception of the heroic poem, is concerned with this fact, namely the choice of Hercules. The image of Hercules at the forked way making his choice between the two ladies, Pleasure and Virtue, embodies the dilemma of every epic hero; and Belphoebe's manifesto at II. iii. 40 defines the traditional opposition between ease and toil in terms which derive by way of Tasso from the original statement of the heroic choice in Hesiod.[2] The choice between pleasure and virtue is one with which all of Spenser's heroes are continually faced, but the dilemma takes a great variety of forms and the answer is never a simple one. The preferability of Una to Duessa and of the ways of Belphoebe to those of Acrasia might seem obvious; yet for Spenser, virtue and pleasure never stand in complete and uncompromising opposition to one another; and the later books of *The Faerie Queene* present very sophisticated patterns of the choice, such as that between strict justice and gentle mercy in

[1] Hallett Smith, *Elizabethan Poetry* (Harvard, 1966), chap. VI.
[2] Ibid., p. 299.

book V, or between the heroic and pastoral modes in book VI. Here the choice is clearly between two kinds of good rather than between good and evil.

For Spenser the perpetual human dilemma seems to stem from what he regards as the two ultimate demands of our physical nature, the need to labour and the need to relax and have pleasure, the aggressive and the permissive instincts which Professor Nelson has identified as the 'forward' and the 'froward' passions.[1] These are personified in a whole spectrum of figures ranging from Pyrochles with his uncontrolled energy at one end of the scale to the hedonistic Acrasia at the other, with all manner of permutations, both good and evil, in between. Throughout the poem Spenser associates the two groups with Diana and Venus who are consistently there in the imagery of the poem even when they are not present in person, and whose quarrel offers a myth capable of expressing a wide variety of conflicts.[2] The sweat and labour of Diana is opposed to the ease and pleasures of Venus, the virginity of the one to the sexual pleasures of the other. In books III and IV, their opposition is that between the Platonic Venuses, Urania and Dione, and between the spiritual and physical loves associated with them; and we shall see that from time to time Spenser equates Diana's toil with the harsh justice of the Mosaic Law, and Venus's love with the kindliness and fruitfulness of the Gospels.

In whatever roles Venus and Diana appear, Spenser's point is that they are opposed to each other when they should be in harmony.[3] Before the Fall, pleasure and virtue were one, as they still are momentarily in the Garden of Adonis, or in the idyllic country of the shepherds, or as Acrasia would have us think they are in her Bower; but with the loss of primal innocence the two stand in ever-increasing conflict. Venus Genetrix is always in danger of forgetting her virtue of fruitfulness and sinking to the level of mere sensuality, the Venus Vulgaris of the Bower of Blisse: she has in her train not only the virtuous Amoret but

---

1 William Nelson, *The Poetry of Edmund Spenser* (London, 1963), p. 182.
2 For a different treatment of this theme, see Kathleen Williams, 'Venus and Diana: some uses of Myth in The Faerie Queene', *ELH* XXVIII (1961). Also C. S. Lewis, *The Allegory of Love*, chap. VII.
3 See Robertson, pp. 263–4, for an account of the traditional opposition between Venus and Diana.

the lustful and incestuous Myrrha. In reply, Diana is forced to
harden into total asceticism and turn into the fierce huntress of
the passions which have become merely bestial: Satyrane,
fighting the bestiality of his parent satyr, and Daphne who
broke her sacred oath to Apollo in order to keep her virginity,
exemplify the range of her following.

Yet both goddesses are necessary if virtue is to survive and the
world to continue, as Venus asserts at the meeting of the two in
book III, when she pleads with Diana to be more tolerant:

> As you in woods and wanton wildernesse
>> Your glory set, to chace the salvage beasts,
> So my delight is all in joyfulnesse,
>> In beds, in bowres, in bankets, and in feasts:
>> And ill becomes you with your loftie creasts,
>> To scorne the joy, that *Jove* is glad to seeke;
> We both are bound to follow heavens beheasts, . . .
>
> [III. vi. 22]

Amoret is as valid as Belphoebe, since she possesses the answer to
death as her sister the answer to sin; and both are in need of
each other to correct the excesses to which the Fall has made each
liable. The hero's task, therefore, is not to reject either but to
seek a reconciliation of virtue and pleasure, to select those
qualities of the two goddesses which are at once virtuous and
compatible with each other. There are wrong as well as right
forms of reconciliation, when harmony is achieved at the cost
of virtue, and Spenser uses the conquest of Mars by Venus as
his symbol of this: Phaedria's success in reconciling Guyon
with Cymochles is a case in point—'*Mars* is *Cupidoes* frend',
II. vi. 35. Virtue is the ability to choose the right combination;
to follow Diana for her energy and skill as a huntress rather than
for her virginity, and Venus for her fruitfulness more than for
the pleasure she gives. As a woman Britomart possesses literally
the power to combine the fertility of Venus Genetrix with the
idealism of the mother of Aeneas. She teaches Venus to fly
with Diana's wings in her arduous and earnest quest of love and
raises Acrasia's sexuality into an active, creative and moral
principle. The other heroes learn to combine the qualities of
Venus and Diana in ways which are appropriate to their sex.

We shall see that Red Cross and Guyon have to discover how to temper an ascetic ideal to fit the needs of human frailty, whereas Artegall and Calidore need to stiffen human gentleness with an infusion of the heroic.

The myths which I have been discussing derive from a variety of unrelated sources but are combined by Spenser into a coherent, interlocking scheme. Jove's battle with the Titans, the Choice and the Labours of Hercules, the quarrel of Venus and Diana, together with a host of minor myths which they draw into their train, provide the poem with an extended background of allegory wide and flexible enough to accommodate all the ramifications of his Christian theme. Spenser's unique quality as a myth-maker lies less in his ability to invent new myths than to recombine old ones and bring them into new and fruitful relationships. This syncretism was made possible by the enormous variety of interpretations which figures such as Venus and Hercules had collected over the centuries, and in this way the world of *The Faerie Queene* achieves a moral mythology which, as we shall see, is one with its topography and history.

3

Spenserean Allegory

[1]

Recent Spenserean scholarship has shown a healthy reaction against earlier criticism which reduced *The Faerie Queene* either to a series of moral precepts or to a gallery of historical portraits thinly veiled by allegorical characters. The last twenty years have seen a valuable attempt to rehabilitate the image itself in place of its content, and to bring the poetry back into the poem; but there are dangers even here of interpreting it in the not wholly appropriate terms of modern critical assumptions. The insistence that form and content are one has made it almost an offence to talk about the 'meaning' of the poem or to attempt an explication in prose of an allegorical sequence.

It is doubtful whether Spenser himself would have agreed with McLeish that 'A poem "is", not "means" '; nor was he aware of the heresy of separating form from content. He was writing a didactic poem and using allegory in its accepted rhetorical sense of an extended metaphor, as Puttenham defines it in a well known passage of the *Arte*:

when we do speake in sence translative and wrested from the owne signification, neverthelesse applied to another not altogether contrary, but having much coveniencie with it as before we said of the metaphore: as for example, if we should call the common wealth a shippe; the Prince a Pilot, the Counsellours mariners, the stormes warres, the calme and [*haven*] peace, . . .   [III. xviii]

Such allegory allows the poet to 'translate' his concepts into a pleasing fiction and so follow Horace's injunction to teach by delighting. It induces the reader to read on, drawn from his chimney corner by the attractions of the story, and at the same time it presents experiences in a form which engraves them more deeply in the memory and the mind. For Sidney the essential difference between philosophy and poetry was not one of content but of presentation: poetry activates the precepts of the philosopher by clothing them in fictions and images which take hold of the imagination and move men to virtue.

The Faerie Queene is composed of images and they are what we must deal with, recognising, however, that they are not ends in themselves but only means to an end. Spenser would not have equated the image itself with any prose 'meaning' which we may extract from it; but he would have recognized that the image began with a prose concept which the rhetorical 'colours' of poetry intensify and make universally applicable. It is the image of Phaedria's little boat which 'both from rocks and flats it selfe could wisely save' [II. vi. 5] which lingers in the mind, not any general precept about the capacity of mirth to melt opposition or chase away boredom; and yet unless the image reminds us of the precept, it fails to fulfil its purpose in the poem. Such epigrammatic images create a moral perception which would not otherwise come into existence: they are, in Elizabethan terms, the speaking pictures which voice precepts in terms applicable to all manner of situations and so provide the tools for moral discrimination.

The curiously logical structure of rhetorical extended metaphor entails an initial distinction between the idea and the image, the tenor and the vehicle, but an eventual convergence of the two after a sufficient period of parallel development. The metaphysical conceit works in this way, beginning with a simple comparison between dissimilars, such as lovers and compasses, but ending in a fusion as the logical development of each side reveals more and more points of contact. The pleasure lies to a great extent in observing this process of approximation and recognizing the aptness of tenor and vehicle for each other's purposes when the two are so initially different. Spenser's allegory works in the same way and delights by the endless and logical parallel which it establishes between the metaphorical world of romance and the real world of human moral values. At the same time, by forcing the reader to translate the one into the terms of the other, it fulfils its primary aim of fostering a process of continuous moral dissection.

At times, indeed, Spenser appears to be encouraging the very thing which modern Spenserean criticism cites as the chief heresy. We are warned against treating the poem as if it were a difficult code to be cracked; and yet it seems to me that the poem is full of enigmatic images whose main purpose is to tease the reader into thought. The Enigma or riddle was by definition merely a difficult form of allegory—'We dissemble againe under covert and darke speaches, when we speake by way of riddle (*Enigma*) of which the sence can hardly be picked out, but by the parties owne assoile' [Puttenham, III. xviii]. Many of George Herbert's emblematic poems are enigmas in this sense: his little poem, Hope,—'I gave to Hope a watch of mine but he/An anchor gave to me . . .'—must have set even the seventeenth-century reader, who was well versed in the language of symbols, an interesting exercise in interpretation not so very far removed from that of the crossword puzzle. Herbert can do this sort of thing in serious poetry because, as Dr Johnson recognised, it forces the reader to think and, in discovering the logic of the image, to define to himself more clearly than he would do otherwise the moral point at issue. This is something which Spenser does continually. When, for example, Arthur has killed Orgoglio, he finds Ignaro in charge of the prisoners, because it is ignorance of the nature of the faith which has led to their downfall [I. viii. 30]. He is an old man with a bunch of rusty iron keys—the keys of knowledge, rusty because unused, and iron because in his hands they belong to the age of iron; and Arthur proceeds to open the prison cells with them. When, however, he comes to Red Cross's door there is no key in the bunch to open it, and he has to break it down. The unexpected twist of the story, having almost the quality of a mixed metaphor, forces us to ask why, and to recognise the point of the riddle, namely, that although ignorance of the faith damns, knowledge by itself cannot save; only the Grace of God can do that. A central tenet of theology has been condensed into a witty image, as Herbert condenses the whole Christian system into his little parable, 'Having been tenant long to a rich Lord'. *The Faerie Queene* is full of such dark conceits which gain their effect by demanding an explanation. Why, for example, when he comes to the Bower of Blisse, does Red Cross go forward with his Palmer alone and leave behind the boatman who has done him such good service over the Idle Lake [II. xii. 38]? Why does not Talus rescue Artegall from Radegund, since he so easily routed her warriors earlier in the Book [v. v. 19]? Why is Phaedria's little boat a 'gondelay' with a little woody bower built into it [II. vi. 2]? The answers are always there in the context but they must be sought for, and posing the question is the mode of instruction. On one level, and by no means a negligible one, the poem is an enormous teaching machine programmed to its task by a technique of question and answer.

I would not for a moment claim that this is the whole or even the main method by which *The Faerie Queene* works, but it is an aspect of the poem which modern critical approaches tend to leave out; and it indicates a type of sensibility in the poem which differs from our own and makes Spenserean allegory especially difficult for the contemporary reader. There is, however, another reason for this difficulty, which springs not from the nature of the allegoric method but from the choice of the allegoric vehicle. The knights and giants and all the panoply of chivalry which charmed the Elizabethans by their fashionable novelty, and the Romantics by their nostalgic mediaevalism, have no such charm for the twentieth century. They fail, therefore, on the fictional level, and instead of leading us along by their own intrinsic interest, they tend to make us force our way through to the 'meaning' and, having reached it, to abandon the outward shell. Where, however, the vehicle still retains its interest as fiction, we are less apt to object to the method or reject the outer rind; and this is possibly why so much contemporary criticism of *The Faerie Queene* has been concerned with the role of classical mythology within the poem, which is agreeable to the contemporary fashionable interest in myth, rather than with the more strictly Romance sequences. Poetry which pursues the Spenserean method in terms of an acceptable fiction gives no difficulty. I can see no essential difference between many Spenserean sequences and such typical poems of Yeats as, for example, *Crazy Jane and Jack the Journeyman* or *Another Song of a Fool*. Both Spenser and Yeats offer a fiction which is capable of standing in its own right but which carries, for those who know the significance of the symbols from sources outside the particular passage, an additional meaning of which it is the metaphor; and it is this which shapes the logic of the metaphor itself. It so happens that Spenser's chivalric metaphors interest most modern readers less than Yeats's Fools, Irish journeymen and crazed beggar women which have for us the sort of romantic appeal that mediaeval fictions had for other ages. What passes in Yeats, therefore, is less acceptable in Spenser, although the basic methods are often identical. One can see an extreme example of this in Yvor Winters's[1] strictures on book I of *The Faerie Queene*:

The gentle knight encounters the dragon, and after many Spenserian stanzas he slays it. We eventually learn that the dragon represents Error. But the dragon in general and in all its details, and merely as a dragon, is a very dull affair; it is poorly described and poorly characterized. I do not, frankly, know what one might do to make a dragon more interesting, but it seems to me that unless one can do better than this one had better not use a dragon.

Winters's criticism makes explicit what is the unspoken assumption of many anti-Spensereans.

Allegory of Spenser's kind is always difficult to read, for it is not easy to keep the two levels, the literal and the allegorical, simultaneously present in one's mind. The tendency is to ignore one or the other side, or else to confuse the two and read as literal what is in fact metaphorical. The difficulty of the sequence concerning the unsocial witch and her lazy son, with whom Florimel has so much trouble, is a case in point. It is hard to accept the image of a mother and her son as a metaphor describing the way that prolonged virginity *breeds* uncouthness. On the merely verbal level it reads like a contradiction in terms, and when projected as personification, presents even greater difficulty. Only the dissociation of the literal from the metaphorical can in this case allow the underlying concept to come through. *The Faerie Queene* demands great and sustained powers of 'translation'; and even so skilled a reader as Miss Williams, who moves about within the metaphorical world of the poem with such sureness, yet seems at times to falter as when, for example, she says that Guyon faints because he has gone without literal food and sleep.[1]

[1] Yvor Winters, *The Function of Criticism* (London, 1962), p. 44.
[1] *Spenser's World of Glass*, p. 61.

[2]

The analysis of *The Faerie Queene* in the second part of this study will, I hope, always begin in the image itself; but I shall not hesitate to explore and define the underlying concepts which both govern and are revealed by the logic of the fiction. The prose 'meaning' is obviously not the poem, but it is nevertheless necessary to the poem as the two sides of a simile are necessary to each other. *The Faerie Queene* is an enormous extended metaphor of human life, so large and so complex in its ramifications that it grows into a complete, self-contained world of its own, parallel to the real world and embodying it metaphorically. To this extent, I agree entirely with Miss Williams's analysis of the poem as 'The World of Glass', but her conception of the relationship between the world of the poem and the moral world of man seems to me inadequate.[1] *The Faerie Queene* does more than present a world which reproduces in small the experiences of the larger world outside, though it certainly does do this; the relationship between the two is more precise and logical. The poem is a 'translation' of life: it relates to the real world as a metaphor to the concepts and experiences it embodies.

The sort of relationship I have in mind is exemplified at its simplest in Spenser's treatment of Red Cross's armour, itself a part of the larger metaphor of knighthood within the whole metaphoric world of chivalry. It is, of course, based on the traditional metaphor of the armour of the Christian man; and its 'old dints of deepe wounds' with which Red Cross begins his journey are those from Original Sin and schisms within the Church, of especial relevance to a knight whose quest is concerned with faith. It is his shield which both Error and the Dragon of Sin attack; and when he lays it aside and takes off his armour, he is no longer in a state of Grace and can be seized by Orgoglio. When redeemed by Arthur he is too weak from his long imprisonment in sin to support its weight again, and he has to go through the training of the House of Holiness with its penances and doctrines until he is strong enough to put it on. No sooner is it breathed on by the fiery breath of the dragon,

[1] Introduction, pp. xv–xviii.

however, than the armour becomes too hot to wear, as the Christian life becomes agonising in the presence of the terrifying fears of despair. But this time God does not allow Red Cross to disrobe, and Red Cross himself has access to the cooling balm so that all is well. The literal and the metaphorical develop side by side with parallel logic, and Spenser signals his pleasure in the wit of his own extended metaphor by uniting the two sides of the comparison within a pun:

> Whom fyrie steele now burnt, that earst him arm'd,
> That erst him goodly arm'd, now most of all him harm'd.
> [I. xi. 27

The armour is there for Guyon in the next book, but now, since faith is safely established, it is whole and perfect again, its dints removed, and ready to be used against a different set of foes.

This is a local example taken out of the larger comprehensive metaphor of the poem as a whole. The cosmography of the world of Romance in which Spenser's knights carry out their quests for honour is a simple one: 'In woods, in waves, in warres she wonts to dwell': it consists of the forest, the occasional plain, the mountain, the vale, the castle, the bower, the river, the great sea and, of course, the knights who fight their battles among them. These are Spenser's metaphors for human life, and he extends them with a logic which springs from their own nature but which yet is made to run parallel with the logic of the moral life which they express. The forest is the almost ubiquitous setting for the action and, in all its ramifications, the most sustained metaphor of the poem. It is a sinister symbol, drawing its significance from the primitive roots of our nature and figuring as a place of danger in the literatures of all ages, from the wild wood of folk and fairy tale, through the forests of Virgil and Dante, to such minor offshoots as the 'hertes forrest' of Wyatt's sonnet. We still talk with relief of being 'out of the wood'. It is the environment into which Red Cross plunges at the beginning of his quest, and Spenser uses it to define the nature of human life. He bases his long description of the forest trees upon Chaucer's in the *Parliament of Fowls* which, as the setting where Nature assembles all her creatures on St Valentine's day, provides a basic allegory for the mortal life of birth and death. Like all Spenser's pageants of life, this initial forest of the poem is an image of a fallen creation in which good and evil inextricably grow together. The Fall is the first thing we are reminded of:

> Whose loftie trees yclad with sommers pride,
> Did spred so broad, that heavens light did hide,
>
> [I. i. 7]

but the catalogue of trees which follows hints at the mixture of pleasure and pain, virtue and vice which compose the stuff of life:

> The Mirrhe sweete bleeding in the bitter wound,
> The warlike Beech, the Ash for nothing ill,
> The fruitfull Olive, and the Platane round,
> The carver Holme, the Maple seeldom inward sound
>
> [I. i. 9]

The Myrrh and the Olive, with their reminder of the gifts of the Magi and the Mount of Olives, are balanced by the Judas-like maple, the 'cedar prowde' and the 'Cypresse funerall': the forest, in fact, contains evil and the answer to evil, just as Archimago's cottage is 'Downe in a dale, hard by a forests side', but has also a 'Christall streame' playing by it [I. i. 34]; both lie in the path of man's fallen nature.

Those who, like Red Cross, enter the forest unaware of the moral choices it contains or indifferent to them, quickly find themselves in Error's den; and for this reason, Malecasta's castle is just at the edge of the forest, 'plast for pleasure right nye that forest side' [III. i. 20], and Britomart has only to fall asleep in the shade of a tree for Lust to run away with Amoret [IV. vii. 3]. The inhabitants of the forest are graded by the degree to which they give themselves up to the forest shades: Argante escapes to it for protection; Mammon has his cave there; Corceca, Care the Blacksmith, Slander, the witch who persecutes poor Florimel, all choose to have their cottages in the heart of it. Spenser feels none of our modern sentimentality about country cottages; they are squalid dwellings forming an appropriate allegory for the haunts of forest lovers. The only

exceptions are the hermits' cottages, since a hermit, by definition, has withdrawn from evil by withdrawing from life and so
can live in the heart of the forest unscathed by it. It is the home
of the lustful foresters who chase Florimel, and it is the very
element of the simple wood-folk who worship Una and use
Hellenore as their common mistress. They are capable of both
activities without discrimination because they are the embodiment of human instinct below the level of reason, and they are
innocent, therefore, although a rational human being who
descends to their unreason is guilty. Most important of all, the
wood is the home of the wild beasts, traditionally symbolic of
the uncontrolled human passions and associated in the poem
with Circe's swine and Adonis's tusked boar, both of which
figure largely in the mythology of *The Faerie Queene*.

On the other side, there are the hunters, Diana, Satyrane,
Tristram, Belphoebe with her boar-spear designed to kill Lust,
all of them embodiments of those aspects of human nature which
would tame the passions, and who live in the forest, therefore to,
subdue and civilise it. In such a context, the symbol of the
ultimate moral degradation is to be turned into a beast, like
Gryll, or to a tree, like Fradubio the doubter, sunk in despair
[I. ii. 43]. *The Faerie Queene* is full of allusions to characters
turned into trees, all of them carrying the stigma of some form
of sinfulness; and here in particular Spenser was able to tap the
rich vein of the *Metamorphoses* for his imagery. The guilty
lust of Myrrha, for example, who was turned into a myrtle for
her incestuous love of her father (*Met.* x), and the equally
guilty lack of passion of Daphne who was metamorphosed into a
laurel for breaking faith with Apollo (*Met.* I), are among his
favourite images of unvirtuous love. The long episode of
Morpheus in the first canto of the poem takes on another
dimension when we discover from the *Metamorphoses*, book XI,
that Morpheus himself was skilled in taking the shape of a man,
but that he had one brother who could turn himself into a
beast and another who could take on the appearance of trees. On
every level, therefore, he is a fitting ally for Archimago. At the
sight of Una, even Sylvanus, in name and nature the very god
of the woods, laments for Cyparisse who was turned into a
cypress tree [I. vi. 17]. In Ovid's account, it was Apollo who

wept at the metamorphosis of the boy (*Met.* x); and in echoing him Sylvanus, at the sight of Una's virtue, is lamenting for a moment his own woody nature.

The forest is only a single metaphor which, when extended in terms of its own logic, gives rise to a sequence of further images of beasts, hunters and arborisations, each with an inevitable moral significance in relation to that of the central metaphor. There are many others in the poem which ramify in this way and in doing so interweave themselves with the forest to form a common landscape. Sun and shade, light and darkness, day and night are archetypal images of good and evil in all civilisations and offer themselves in innumerable forms. Temptations normally occur when there is no sun—'Then with the Sunne take Sir, your timely rest' [I. i. 33], says Archimago to Red Cross, under a seemingly innocent suggestion tempting him to give up the joys of eternity for those of time. Whatever blots out the sun is a metaphor of evil in some form, whether it is the forest shade in which Red Cross and Duessa rest, or the darkness of the underworld in which Morpheus creates his deluding dreams, or the foggy mist which prevents Red Cross from killing Sans Joy and shrouds Guyon's boat on the way to the Bower. These images of light and darkness, day and night, release in their turn new clusters based upon sleep and waking, sloth and the active life. Arthur makes the connection most explicitly in his great lament in book III, when night robs him of the sight of Florimel:

> What had th'eternall Maker need of thee,
>   The world in his continuall course to keepe,
>   That doest all things deface, ne lettest see
>   The beautie of his worke? Indeed in sleepe
>   The slouthfull bodie, that doth love to steepe
>   His lustlesse limbes, and drowne his baser mind,
>   Doth praise thee oft, and oft from *Stygian* deepe
>   Calls thee, his goddesse in his error blind,
> And great Dame Natures handmaide, chearing every
>   kind.   [III. iv. 56]

and every impulse to rest in the shade or sleep at the wrong time heralds the onset of the most insidious of all temptations, the sloth of which Morpheus is once again the prototype.

This is the extended metaphor of the land of Faerie, but the sea too has its images and provides another great source of allegoric growth in the poem. Spenser draws upon its traditional association with fertility and Venus to make it his basic symbol for that ever-changing chaos which, as described in the Garden of Adonis, continually takes on new forms and so brings forth new creation. In this great sea of life, mortality, mutability and creation are different aspects of the same thing: its god is Proteus, and the rivers have their beginning and their end in it. Spenser uses it primarily, therefore, in association with his treatment of love and sex in books III and IV, and it becomes a touchstone in relation to fertility as the forest is in relation to sin. Marinell, whose name and nature are of the sea, yet prefers the sterile shore for his kingdom, and the virgin Florimell is forced most unwillingly into its embraces. Britomart mainly fights on land because, like all the other heroes, her quest is against the sins of the forest; but hers is a love story, and so she sets out upon the voyage of love even if only metaphorically:

> Huge sea of sorrow, and tempestuous griefe,
>   Wherein my feeble barke is tossed long,
>   Far from the hoped haven of reliefe,
>   Why do thy cruell billowes beat so strong, . . .
>
> [III. iv. 8]

It is a voyage which all must attempt if the world is to be kept alive, and to avoid its terrors is another form of sloth: Phaedria's little shallop has neither wind nor storm to cope with, since its journey is on the Idle Lake, not over the fruitful sea; but because it takes none of the life-giving sweat demanded of Guyon on the same voyage, it leads only to the sterile Bower of Blisse. That is why Phaedria's boat has a bower in it, 'That like a little forrest seemed outwardly' [II. vi. 2]: its 'boughes and arbours woven cunningly' are a miniature Bower of Blisse warning of the forest temptations it carries. For those who risk the voyage in the open sea, Aeolus, God of the winds and father of Orgoglio, is the chief enemy just as he sought to wreck Odysseus and Aeneas on their appointed journeys, although he never hinders

C   57

Phaedria's voyages. In this way, the relevant heroic myths are absorbed into the pattern of sea imagery as Hercules's fights with the beasts belong to the forest world, and the landscape of the poem takes on another allegorical dimension.

I have traced the way in which a few of Spenser's images develop and interlock with each other until a complete landscape emerges with a moral geography and a moral climate built into it. It has a moral history, too, in terms of the heroic line who inhabit it, and a moral mythology based, as we have seen, on the use of a few central myths and innumerable references to a very limited number of Ovidean tales. *The Faerie Queene* is not a learned poem demanding a knowledge of esoteric literary sources but a relatively popular one using a limited range of materials in a complex but self-defining way. In a world which is created out of these materials, everything that happens is necessarily allegorical: every move from plain to forest, by day or night, by land or sea, in sunshine or storm, has by its very location a moral significance derived from the logic of the central metaphors. Every reference to myth or history provides a touchstone of values. Spenser does not turn his allegory on and off; it is always inescapably there, built into the very structure of the romance setting.

This is not to say that Spenser's images are counters, fixed and rigid in their significance, and that to interpret them, therefore, is just a matter of mechanical translation. His method differs from that of Yeats, for example, who discovers different manifestations of a central symbol such as the gyre all around him—in the circling flight of the falcon, or the winding stair of his tower, or the swirling fabrics of Loie Fuller's dance—but sees them all as projections of an identical principle. Spenser's landscape, in contrast, is a mode of rhetoric which allows a single image to convey a wide range of different yet related meanings by means of distinctions in tone of voice, or choice of epithet, or by the juxtaposition of other materials; and one of his most characteristic methods is to use a 'loaded' image in such a way that it contradicts what we normally expect of it. Going into the forest, for example, can cover a wide range of human experiences, although all will in some degree be associated with entering into the presence of evil. The 'chearefull shade' of the

Bower of Blisse [II. xii. 71], is a startling expression, because 'shade', although metaphorical of a variety of activities in the poem from the positive commission of sin to the relatively innocent and necessary rest after labour, is always connected with the needs and frailties of our fallen nature. In terms of its normal usage it cannot with any truth be called 'chearefull'; and the choice of adjective, therefore, focuses our attention upon the context which can produce such a paradox and warns us of the sophistries of the Bower. Or consider Spenser's description of the arbour at the heart of the Garden of Adonis: it is a rich and fruitful place, belonging to Nature not Art, and yet its leafy shade is so dense

> That nether *Phoebus* beams could through them throng,
> Nor *Aeolus* sharp blast could worke them any wrong.
>
> [III. vi. 44]

At the simplest level, this is a description of the womb, secret and covered from the light of day, but the imagery implies a good deal more. The fact that it is a place of intense shade would lead us to expect it to be evil, a place of shame; yet the description of its natural wholesomeness in the previous stanzas contradicts this. Moreover Aeolus, usually hostile to all heroic endeavour, leaves it alone, which would normally be a proof of its unworthiness but is not so in this case because he cannot harm it if he would; it is beyond the reach of his power. The images pull in different ways and the whole description, if not quite a riddle, presents at least the paradox of something simultaneously virtuous and vicious.

This apparent ambiguity in Spenser's descriptive imagery is the basis of Professor Alpers's argument that Spenser passes no moral judgements in *The Faerie Queene* but presents instead a variety of possible and conflicting attitudes towards any issue, without attempting to resolve them. The aim of Spenserean rhetoric is not to persuade the reader to accept one point of view in preference to the rest, but to put him in possession of them all and so enlarge his moral consciousness.[1] My own approach is a

[1] Paul J. Alpers, *The Poetry of The Faerie Queene* (Princeton, 1967), pp. 148, 286–8, 296.

different one. I would interpret Spenser's paradox as his mode of asserting a fundamentally paradoxical conception of the nature of life. In his description of Adonis's Bower, for instance, he is describing the ambivalent nature of sex, at once the centre of our fallen animal nature—which is why Phoebus's light cannot reach it—yet at the same time the means of human regeneration, and so invulnerable to Aeolus. The same quality of paradox is apparent in the description of the Garden of Venus or the pageant of the rivers, as we have already seen, and it is something clearly central to Spenser's thinking.

To read *The Faerie Queene* is to be in the continuous presence of paradox and to be faced with a dilemma throughout the greater part of the poem. Good and evil are unmistakably there and the need to choose between them is inescapable; and yet the terms in which the enactment of the choice is described are often such as to blur the moral distinction for the reader, and hint that an apparently vicious choice is in reality a virtuous one, or that what is vice from one perspective is virtue from another. The moral code of *The Faerie Queene* is not a simple one of black and white, nor is it laid down explicitly from the beginning. It is something which emerges gradually from the cumulative effect of apparent contradictions which are only seen in their true harmony as our experience of the poem makes the pattern plain. The analysis of the books of the poem in subsequent chapters will attempt to trace this pattern through to the point where it is defined most explicitly in the *Mutability Cantos*.

[3]

A world of the metaphorical kind which I have been describing would either destroy or be destroyed by a set of inhabitants who existed on the simple, naturalistic level without any dimension of allegory. The chivalric quest itself, with all its knightly trappings, is an extended metaphor of man's struggle for virtue, and the knights themselves, therefore, must share in the nature of the world they live in. The central heroes of each book are real characters of flesh and blood, conceived in the likeness of their forerunners in Homer, Virgil, or Ariosto and, in the case of

Artegall, for example, possessing a necessary historical identity; but they are never merely that: each one is the generic human being, Everyman, engaged in the exploration of a particular aspect of human experience, and we should think of them in general terms as the human being discovering the nature of temperance or love or justice, rather than as the individuals, Guyon, Britomart or Artegall. The experiences which they encounter are appropriate to themselves as dramatic creations but are also shared by all mankind, including the reader and the poet himself; and Spenser moves in and out of his characters, from the particular to the general, as it suits his didactic purpose. Belphoebe, when she first appears in book II, is not so much a person as the voice of a profound human instinct expressing itself in terms of a traditional attitude. In her dealings with Timias in book IV, however, she is contracted into something much nearer to a historical character; and when she rescues Amoret from lust she has become, for the time being, the personification of an instinct in Britomart herself. These shifts are possible without destroying the narrative framework because Britomart and Queen Elizabeth alike are particular manifestations of the general nature of Everywoman. The action of the poem, therefore, can take place in a sort of no-man's land between the hero and the reader, common to both but limited to neither, while the poet stays outside, commenting. It is this possibility which makes the story of a Red Cross or a Guyon more than the mere biography of an individual, although based on biographical narrative.

There are very few personifications of abstract qualities in *The Faerie Queene*, and even Impotence and Impatience are the embodiments of common human experiences. As C. S. Lewis pointed out long ago, Spenser's basic method in the first three books of the poem, though not in the later ones, is that of psychological personification: the inner qualities and impulses of the human being are projected as characters who enact the inner drama in externalised form, so that a mental conflict becomes a battle between Arthur and Pyrochles, for example, representative of the warring aspects of Guyon's own nature. Alternatively, the struggle to resist impulses and temptations which spring from within may be shown as an external struggle between the character and the personification of the relevant part of himself, as Red Cross fights Sans Joy, or Florimel flees from the witch and resists the old man in the boat. This fragmentation of the human ego can be very difficult to follow, especially in book I, where it is extremely elaborate and where Red Cross himself often disappears behind the characters who act out his subtle and complex mental processes. In the first three books especially, the reader meets the inhabitants of the human mind as Guyon and Arthur meet them in the House of Alma:

> Some song in sweet consort, some laught for joy,
> Some plaid with straws, some idly sat at ease. . .
> This fround, that faund, the third for shame did
>   blush,
> Another seemed envious, or coy,
> Another in her teeth did gnaw a rush; . . .   [II. ix. 35]

There is this difference, however, that whereas in the catalogue of whims and moods in Alma's hall, the selection is random and the aim simply to indicate the variety of possible human impulses, the characters in the books at large follow each other with a logic which is that of human behaviour. Cymochles appears after Pyrochles because, in terms of the impulses which the two express, he is the result of his brother: Argante seizes Satyrane because the latter is no longer strong enough to hold down the spotted beast: Arthur comes to Una and to Guyon alike not by chance but because both are ready to receive him. In the allegory of *The Faerie Queene*, narrative sequence always implies cause and effect, and it is most important, therefore, to follow the details of the story. By means of the story line, Spenser anatomises the human mind and reveals with extraordinary penetration the physical and psychological springs of human action. As the hero goes on his uncertain way, surrounded by characters who act out his inner life in front of us, providing a dramatic commentary on his actions, we recognise the pattern of his behaviour, understand its sources and are forced to make a continual moral judgement.

Rosemond Tuve seems to me to pay too little attention to this aspect of the poem in her *Allegorical Imagery*. She identifies

Spenser's allegorical intention and method with that of the mediaeval allegorists such as Jean de Meun, and argues that the object of 'good' allegory, whether *The Faerie Queene* or *The Romance of the Rose*, is to examine the nature of general human qualities by the gradual unfolding of their properties. In this semi-philosophical context, psychological allegory and consecutive narrative will play a less important part than more discursive methods which allow the presentation of a central virtue in a variety of aspects and from a variety of different points of view. Miss Tuve's analysis of the structure of the *Romance of the Rose* is clearly true, but it is less adequate when applied to *The Faerie Queene*. She seems to me to ignore Spenser's more urgent didacticism: in contrast to Jean de Meun, his prime object is moral improvement rather than intellectual enlightenment—or, at least, the sort of intellectual enlightenment which results in immediate moral action. Spenser's allegory is essentially rhetorical; it is designed to persuade rather than to examine, and for this reason Spenser presses more insistently upon his reader and in a greater variety of ways than his forerunners in the Middle Ages. One of these ways is the unceasing analysis of human motive and action which has already been described: another is by means of the 'overt moral statements' which Miss Tuve finds incompatible with 'great' allegory. The fact that Spenser is 'much less daring about concealing his hand than is Jean de Meun' (p. 241), is not a sign of his failure to write good mediaeval allegory but evidence that he is attempting a different and more rhetorical mode.

Spenser's allegory is very much of its age: his subtle analysis of human psychology, as well as his mode of dramatic presentation, spring from the same national impulses which produced the drama of Shakespeare and the Jacobeans. It is important to recognise, however, that the allegory of *The Faerie Queene* is not all of a kind but changes with the changes of subject. As its intention is rhetorical, so it obeys the laws of rhetorical decorum. Psychological allegory of the type I have been describing is only possible where the conflicts are within the mind itself; and as the later books of the poem move increasingly from the world of the inner man to that of man in relation to society, other modes of allegory become necessary. Justice, for example, is largely concerned with the conquest of other people, and the inner personifications appropriate to the conquest of self are denied to it. Figures such as Acrasia have a peculiar resonance deriving from the fact that they literally find an echo in every bosom, but it is less easy to find symbols for injustice or communism or political treachery which move us in the same interior way. Spenser's method in book V, therefore, is to draw his symbols from the great and explosive issues of public life, capable of arousing violent sectarian and patriotic emotions. The Soldan, or Gerioneo and his monster under the idol, are such figures, and Spenser harnesses their emotive power to the general principles of justice with which he is concerned, and of which they provide particular illustrations. It is noticeable, however, that Arthur's victory over Gerioneo or Artegall's over Grantorto are very far from being transcriptions of contemporary history: Spenser's method is that of allegory, not example; he is writing an allegory about justice, not an allegory of the history of his own times.

In book VI we are back within the mind again, though not as in the early books of the poem. Courtesy is based on an idealistic vision which Spenser associates especially with the mind of the poet and which he projects, therefore, through the poetic genre of the pastoral idyll. Calidore's story is not designed to reveal Calidore himself so much as the poet's conception of his own craft, and book VI is an anatomy of poetry itself, using poetic genres as allegories of its strengths and weaknesses. In contrast, the *Mutability Cantos* make the least personal, most objective statement of the whole of *The Faerie Queene*, and offer no scope for subjective allegory. They owe their peculiar richness to the fact that they draw upon the whole corpus of the poetry which has gone before: every character, incident, and myth in the cantos has already been used in a variety of forms in the six books, and here they rise out of the depths, bringing with them the wealth of association and complexity of meaning which they have acquired on their journey. It is as if all the fictions of the poem become articulate in a final fiction which speaks for them all. The cantos are literally an allegory to end allegories, as Spenser unites all the parts of the poem in this final, most literary of his allegoric statements.

[4]

No character or place or action in *The Faerie Queene* is merely
literal, and the total structure of the poem depends on the
maintenance of the metaphorical level throughout. Without
this consistency, the distinction between literal and allegorical
would break down, letting in a host of extraneous reactions
which would destroy the intellectual and moral pattern of the
whole. Once the reader begins to confuse the allegorical with
the literal, he finds himself feeling sorry for Duessa when she is
so ruthlessly stripped by Arthur, or blaming Guyon for being a
Puritan, or reading the Garden of Adonis canto as if it contained
a philosophical statement about reincarnation, when it merely
uses reincarnation as a metaphor to express the continuity of the
type. There is always the danger of this confusion when human
action itself is the metaphor to express human action, and Spenser takes great pains to keep the necessary distance between the
allegorical world of romance and the world of reality which it
expresses. If ever an episode appears in danger of turning from
allegory to realistic example, he is careful to transpose it back
into the unmistakable key of metaphor. In this way the long
account of the unhappy affair of Phaon and Claribell is rescued
from the level of example when Phaon, chasing the maid
Pryene with intent to kill her, suddenly finds himself seized by
Furor:

> Feare gave her wings, and rage enforst my flight;
>   Through woods and plaines so long I did her chace,
>   Till this mad man, whom your victorious might
>   Hath now fast bound, me met in middle space,
>   As I her, so he me pursewd apace, . . .   [II. iv. 32]

Similarly Amyas and Aemylia, having arranged an assignation
in a grove, find when they get there not each other, but
Corflambo and the monster, Lust. The naturalistic metaphor has
been made unmistakably metaphorical, and at the same time
Spenser is able to make a moral comment on the action by
forcing the reader to analyse the implications of the change.

The world of *The Faerie Queene*, though arresting enough in
its varied detail, is nevertheless a transparent world and has to

be so to get its effect; the moment it becomes opaque and halts
our vision at the surface metaphor so that we cease to look
through it to what is behind, the whole *raison d'être* is lost. It
must at all costs remain metaphorical and never be mistaken for
the literal. There were many factors in the sensibility of Spenser's age which helped him to maintain this transparency over
the enormous range of the poem. One of these lies in the very
nature of the rhetorical extended metaphor which demands and
encourages the capacity to keep vehicle and tenor apart yet
both simultaneously present in the mind—like watching someone posturing in front of a distorting mirror. A modern reader
would probably watch only the image in the mirror, but an
Elizabethan would watch both the figure and the image and
be conscious of the relationship between the two. There is still
some trace of this type of sensibility left in Addison's conception
of the pleasures of art which derive, he believes, from the act
of comparing the image with what it represents. This idea is a
part of the whole conception of art as an 'Imitation' of nature,
and lies behind the discussions throughout the seventeenth and
eighteenth centuries concerning the distinction between true
and false wit, which depends on the truth of the likeness between the object and the thing to which it is compared within a
simile or a metaphor. One remembers Addison's bundles of
heterogeneous materials tied together in his Temple of False
Wit. The Elizabethans were more flexible in their conception
of what could properly be compared, but they were as acutely
conscious of the relationship and the pleasures to be got from its
recognition. It is this fact above all, I think, which allows
Spenser to keep his two levels so truly parallel without ever
actually meeting.

Perhaps, too, the very chivalry from which Spenser drew his
metaphor was of a nature to help him. We know that there was a
genuine revival of interest in chivalry at the court of Queen
Elizabeth, and yet the magnificent armour which Sidney or
Blount wore at the barriers to celebrate the Queen's birthday was
not that which Launcelot carried, nor were the battles the
same. The ethics of chivalry were real enough, but the trappings,
the tinsel armour and the knightly combats were themselves
only a kind of allegory, the expression through a romantic

metaphor of the living values of Elizabethan courtesy. Malory, though living long after anything which could be called the age of chivalry, cared too strongly about the realities of knightly combat to be able to use them as Spenser did; for him the jousts were of such intrinsic interest that even the most conventional accounts have the gusto of realism: he has no wish to see beyond them or make allegories of them. It is because the Romance, for Spenser, was unashamedly a romance that it lent itself so readily to the expression of contemporary ideas: the national taste and impulse which prompted Sidney and his friends to dress up as the Four Foster Children of Desire enabled Spenser to use his knights as the medium of allegory. *The Faerie Queene* is built upon the foundations of Tudor Court chivalry.

A further and final point which must be stressed is the language of *The Faerie Queene*, which plays a vital part in the success of the poem. Ben Jonson's complaint that Spenser writ no language is in one sense true: the language of the poem is neither contemporary Elizabethan nor is it good Chaucerean, as Spenser obviously knew. He was very familiar with his Chaucer and shows himself acutely aware of the changes in language since Chaucer's day. The poem uses a purely literary language, a unique version of the High style which is geared to the particular needs of the allegoric method. It does occasionally slip for brief moments into colloquialism, as in the description of Hellenore among the satyrs, where its function is to establish a particular comic tone, or in Tristram's account of the knight 'pounching' a lady with the butt-end of his spear, where the intention is to administer a shock. The normal tone of the diction, however, is one of studied remoteness, achieved by the careful avoidance of all that is colloquial and naturalistic. It is this fact more than any other which has aroused critical opposition to the poem in the twentieth century. Dr Johnson's criticism of Shakespeare for his metaphor, 'the blanket of the dark', is pedantic in respect of a play which presents human behaviour in essentially realistic terms, but the criticism would have some validity if the image occurred in *The Faerie Queene*. Such a phrase would shatter the unity of tone and force the reader's attention from the allegoric to the literal statement by giving too great an immediacy to the image. What rightly serves to rivet the attention on the literal fact in a satire or a drama may merely obscure the view in an allegory.

For this reason, I think, Spenser uses his artificial diction and reiterates the romance clichés, the stock comparisons of battling knights to lions and tigers, and all the standard rhetoric of challenging, reviling and wading in blood to the ankle. The adjectives are a part of the time-honoured ritual—'That all his garments and the grass in *vermeil* dyde', 'And into a deepe *sanguine* dide the grassie ground'. This is heraldic language which removes the descriptions from the level of naturalism as the lions on a shield are remote from the real animal. The realism of *The Faerie Queene* is not a literal one: we look through the transparency of the language and the actions to the reality of the experience behind them. In Spenser's Faerie world, we walk about within the human mind and meet ourselves face to face with frightening frequency; we see our own actions thrown back at us from the society around us, or reflected in the mirror of history; but the poem is never a simple mirror. It is all kept at one remove by means of the sustained unity of action, image and style. Such sustained allegory ceases to be a mode of presentation as C. S. Lewis defined it and becomes, like symbol, a mode of thought.

4

Fashioning a Gentleman

[1]

At the most basic level, the extended metaphor of *The Faerie Queene* works like any other image: in the words which T. E. Hulme used to describe poetry in general, 'It is a compromise for a language of intuition which would hand over sensations bodily.'[1] The units of communication in Spenser's poem are extended sequences not single metaphors or metaphoric phrases such as one finds in Shakespeare, and the scale is one appropriate to epic rather than drama: there is none of the sudden brevity of the 'sublime' in Longinus's sense of the term. Nevertheless a Spenserean sequence illustrates very precisely T. S. Eliot's definition of the 'objective correlative' as 'a set of objects, a situation, a chain of events which shall be the formula of that particular emotion'.[2] The description of Britomart's journey through the castle of Busyrane, for example, with the empty rooms, the enigmatic mottoes over the doors, the silent Masque which she watches without wholly understanding, embodies with great vividness the sensation of exploring strange, half frightening, half attractive experiences all on one's own. Britomart's exploration of the emotions to which her newly awakened sexual instincts give rise finds its precise equivalent in external terms.

The experiences being communicated are at once particular and general: they are those appropriate to Britomart at this specific stage of her quest, but they are also part of the common stock of human experience. The mottoes over the doors, for example—'Be Bold', 'Be Bold', 'Be not too bold'—are, as will appear, the sort of deterrent we should expect from Busyrane, but also embody the universal sequence of excitement and fear which belongs to the initiation into sex. This fact is the basis of

---

1 T. E. Hulme, *Speculations* (Routledge Paper Backs, 1924), p. 134.
2 Essay on *Hamlet* (1919).

Spenser's rhetorical method, as Professor Alpers has rightly analysed it when he describes the aim of *The Faerie Queene* as that of 'evoking and manipulating our responses'.[1] There can be no doubt that the primary aim of the poem is rhetorical, and that the gentleman whom Spenser hopes to fashion is the reader himself, by means of the sweet violence of poetry. Spenser's object is to move the reader to virtue rather than to tell him a story, yet I cannot see that the rhetorical and the narrative approaches to *The Faerie Queene* are as opposed to each other as Professor Alpers claims. Because the narrative itself is extended metaphor, it is the medium of rhetoric, the means by which the experiences of the poem are defined and communicated. The fiction has its own validity and cannot be ignored or chopped up into isolated episodes, for to do so is to lose all sense of sequence and of purpose in the experiences to which Spenser wishes to subject his reader. Professor Alpers would, I think, deny that the sequence matters, or that Spenser has any aim other than to make his reader aware of the variety of moral attitudes possible in any given case. My own conception of Spenser's rhetoric is as something altogether more traditional. Spenser had at his disposal the two great resources of the art of persuasion, the open palm of elocution and the closed fist of logic; and Spenserean allegory exploits both, providing the pleasing fiction by which the reader's interest is maintained and his emotions are involved, and at the same time the logical definition which is inherent in the very nature of rhetorical allegory, by means of which the reader is instructed.[2] Spenser's frequent method, as we shall see, is to exploit the tensions which exist between the two aspects of rhetoric, between the emotions which an image arouses and the moral definition of those emotions which it simultaneously implies, so that the reader is forced to experience a miniature conflict in himself between reason and passion, and undergo the experiences of life at one remove.

An examination of a few passages in detail will provide the best evidence of the way in which Spenser's rhetoric works, and we may begin with the opening description of Mammon's

---

[1] P. 28 and *passim*.
[2] See Rosemond Tuve, *Elizabethan and Metaphysical Imagery* (Phoenix, 1968), *passim*.

cave. This is in the tradition of the memory locations, to which
further reference will be made, and it provides a very concentrated pictogram of a life spent exclusively in the pursuit of
riches:

> That houses forme within was rude and strong,
>> Like an huge cave, hewne out of rocky clift,
>> From whose rough vaut the ragged breaches hong,
>> Embost with massy gold of glorious gift,
>> And with rich mettall loaded every rift,
>> That heavy ruine they did seeme to threat;
>> And over them *Arachne* high did lift
>> Her cunning web, and spred her subtile net,
> Enwrapped in fowle smoke and clouds more blacke then
>> Jet.

> Both roofe, and floore, and wals were all of gold,
>> And overgrowne with dust and old decay,
>> And hid in darkenesse, that none could behold
>> The hew thereof: for vew of chearefull day
>> Did never in that house itselfe display,
>> But a faint shadow of uncertain light;
>> Such as a lamp, whose life does fade away:
>> Or as the Moone cloathed with clowdy night,
> Does shew to him, that walkes in feare and sad affright.
>> [II. vii. 28–9]

This passage is typical of *The Faerie Queene* in its capacity to
make its point simultaneously at literal and allegorical levels.
Literally, it gives a picture of darkness, smoke and sweat
entirely appropriate to a creature whose sole interest is making
money. The foul smoke and black clouds would have suggested
to Spenser's readers the new furnaces of the Elizabethan in-
dustries, about whose chimneys with their dark Satanic smoke
there was already much feeling. At the same time its allegory
describes, analyses and evaluates very completely a life lived
exclusively in the service of Mammon. Caves throughout the
poem are associated with barbarous and uncivilised values, and
Mammon's den belongs with those of Despair and Jealousy,
although it is not actually a cave but a house built like a cave. In

other words it represents a deliberate debasement of civilised values in return for the crude and brutal strength which lies in money, and the nature of this debasement is defined by the details. It is of gold throughout, even in the floors and ceilings where timber would serve better, for the heavy bosses hang over the owner's head like a sword of Damocles. Spenser is not, in fact, attacking money as such but the pursuit of money to the exclusion of everything else, which results in a perpetual burden of fear that it may all be lost—a fear of ruin created by the mind itself, for it only 'seems' to threat. The spiders' webs which cover everything suggest that the gold is never used; but the reference to Arachne also recalls her ill-fated spinning match with Athena, which provided the Elizabethans with one of their commonest emblems of the fall of pride. This lifts the description to another level by establishing Mammon both where Milton placed him, among the fallen angels, and among the rebellious giants with whom Athena/Minerva did battle. The darkness and reflected light of the moon link the picture with the central image of the poem and turn the house with its 'faint shadow of uncertain light' into a type of Plato's cave, the symbol of the world of illusion. By means of literary references, or by images which derive their significance from the larger pattern of symbols throughout the poem, Spenser is able to combine economy of statement with an extraordinary comprehensiveness.

Here the imagery works all in one way to give a picture which is at once emotionally repellent and intellectually reprehensible, and the rhetoric arouses feelings which reinforce the effect of what it defines. This is Spenser's normal method of presenting evils which are basically unattractive; but if evil always appeared in its true colours, the Quest would be an easy matter. Spenser understands very clearly that not everything evil seems so; and he is at pains, therefore, to present it not only as defined by the philosopher but as experienced by the average man, the tempting illusion as well as the loathsome reality. Often the two are placed side by side and the reader is left to make the connection himself: Phaedria is happy in the apparently innocent occupation of watching the 'water worke, and play/About her little frigot, therein making way' [II. vi. 7], though even here her impartial interest in work and play alike is a clue to the nature of her own folly. The point, however, is made without ambiguity a few stanzas later, when the same ripples are described as 'The slouthfull wave of that great griesly lake'.

In the same way, the five troops of temptations which are given objective description when they make their attack on the five fortresses of the senses in the House of Alma, are described more subjectively when they assail Guyon in the Bower of Blisse. The House of Alma, as its name implies, is a set piece defining the nature of the residence of the soul under the government of temperance; and its temptations, therefore, are described in their essential quality as excesses of the senses, each one embodied in a creature notorious for its possession of a particular sense in an extreme degree. The temptations of sight are in the form of owls and lynxes, each with a bow and arrows symbolic of the darts which Cupid shoots from and into the eyes [II. xi. 8]: those of touch are, at one extreme, hedgehogs painful to the touch, and at the other, snails whose tender horns are excessively soft and sensible. All are made to seem repulsive since evil in its true nature is repulsive, and together they form a collection of monsters reminiscent of the temptations which assail St Anthony in Grünewald's picture. As the perfect knight of temperance, Arthur can see them for what they are and fight them in their true guise.

Guyon, however, has less clarity of vision, and the same forces appear in a more insidiously tempting form when they besiege his senses in the Bower: there are the naked girls to assail the sight, the lulling melodies of birds and streams, which Spenser suggests with such onomatopoeic mastery, to tempt the hearing; there are the temptations of taste and smell in the grapes that press themselves upon the lips, and in the ever-blooming flowers; and lastly, the appeal of touch in the description of Acrasia's amorous labours and the memories and desires which the descriptions awake. Spenser works through all five senses, using his enormous powers of pictorial imagery and soporific prosody to create an image which is essentially pornographic in its appeal; and for this reason he has been accused of hypocrisy, and charged with posing as a puritan when his most effective verse proves him to belong, in reality, to the devil's party.

73

Criticisms of this kind are based on a failure to understand Spenser's rhetorical method, which is that of arousing pleasurable emotions while simultaneously indicating that they are evil. The descriptions make a deep appeal to the senses but at the same time, by drawing on the great patterns of image or myth throughout the poem, they have built-in moral signposts which force the reader to recognize and evaluate truly the experiences. By the fact of reading the sequence at all, we experience what the Bower of Blisse stands for and are invited to use our own inner Palmers to control our reactions; and if at the end of canto xii we condemn Guyon for smashing up so much beauty, we have in fact identified ourselves with Acrasia and all that she represents. The stock Renaissance phrase about the bee gathering honey from the same flower from which the spider extracts poison has a very real meaning in relation to *The Faerie Queene*.

A few instances will make the method clearer, and it is important that it should be clear, for the Bower of Blisse exemplifies one of the basic rhetorical techniques of the whole poem. We first encounter the Bower in canto v when Cymochles is found there; and at this stage, the description is normally accompanied by an explicit moral condemnation, for we are only beginning to learn about the nature of the place, and the time to test our knowledge has not yet come. The account of Cymochles lying surrounded by the naked girls gives an extraordinary impression of the sensuous appeal they exert and of the perverted nature of his reaction to it:

> He, like an Adder, lurking in the weeds,
> His wandring thought in deepe desire does steepe,
> And his fraile eye with spoyle of beautie feedes;
> Sometimes he falsely faines himselfe to sleepe,
> Whiles through their lids his wanton eies do peepe,
> To steale a snatch of amorous conceipt,
> Whereby close fire into his heart does creepe:
> So, he them deceives, deceiv'd in his deceipt,
> Made drunke with drugs of deare voluptuous receipt.
>
> [II. v. 34]

Spenser's condemnation is explicit in the last two lines, but it would carry no weight if it had not already been justified by the nature of the experience as the description defines it throughout. The initial reference to the adder links the situation with the temptation of Eve, with Cymochles in the dual role of tempter and tempted, the temptation, however, involving that of sloth as well as lechery. The over-sweet, cloying quality of the language with its reiterated vowel sounds insists on the excess and ultimate monotony of life within the Bower; while the verbal repetition, accompanied by a sudden change of rhythm—'So, he them deceives, deceiv'd in his deceipt'— forces us to pause while we disentangle the meaning, and ponder the nature of the experience.

By canto xii, however, both Guyon and the reader are ready to face temptations which are less explicit and less obviously vicious, and Spenser includes less overt moral commentary, therefore, leaving the reader to come to his own conclusion in the light of his understanding of the poem to date. Much of the garden appears innocent on the surface:

> The joyous birdes shrouded in chearefull shade,
>> Their notes unto the voyce attempred sweet;
>> Th'Angelicall soft trembling voyces made
>> To th'instruments divine respondence meet:
>> The silver sounding instruments did meet
>> With the base murmure of the waters fall:
>> The waters fall with difference discreet,
>> Now soft, now loud, unto the wind did call:
> The gentle warbling wind low answered to all.
>
> [II. xii. 71]

The initial impression is one of happiness and harmony: the description implies a comparison between the song of the birds and the human voices and instruments on the one hand, and the music of the heavenly hierarchies around the throne of God himself, on the other, beginning with the joyful notes of the birds, ascending to the angelical voices and culminating in the divine respondence. The extension of the harmonic metaphor into the punning word, 'base', however, brings us tumbling down with the 'fall', and there is built into this little sequence a reminder of Satan's rebellion which destroyed the harmony of both heaven and earth. The over-formal rhetoric of what Puttenham calls Clymax or the Marching figure—'notes... voyces; voyces...instruments; instruments...waters'—takes us up a set of steps only to precipitate us on the other side, and the whole description becomes emblematic of vaulting ambition. There are other warning signs, too, such as the slightly ridiculous and stagey 'warbling wind', the ominous 'shrouded' coupled with the 'chearefull' shade. The passage, in fact, condemns the harmony of the garden even in the act of describing it and suggests that it is counterfeit and sinister.

Hints such as these should be enough to put the careful reader on his guard against the very real beauty of the Bower and force him to analyse what is wrong with it; and as the sensuous appeal becomes more intense, so the need to evaluate it in moral terms is thrust upon us with simultaneous and corresponding intensity.[1] The climax of the Bower lies in Acrasia herself, and we are spared no sensuous detail:

> Her snowy brest was bare to readie spoyle
> Of hungry eies, which n'ote therewith be fild,
> And yet through languour of her late sweet toyle,
> Few drops, more cleare than Nectar, forth distild,
> That like pure Orient perles adowne it trild,
> And her faire eyes sweet smyling in delight,
> Moystened their fierie beames, with which she thrild
> Fraile harts, yet quenched not; like starry light
> Which sparckling on the silent waves, does seeme more
> bright.   [II. xii. 78]

She lies there on her bed of roses, with all the adulterous associations of the Rose tradition, covered only by her transparent veil of 'scorched deaw' whose symbolic associations we have already met in the cave of Mammon—'More subtile web *Arachne* can not spin'. Her slothful languor itself seems to produce the pearl-like drops of sweat which, as we have seen earlier, are linked with the emerald and ruby grapes of the garden. Her 'snowy brest' will be echoed in the sterility of the snowy Florimel, and the 'fierie beames' of her eyes will be defined by

---

1 A. C. Hamilton, *The Structure of Allegory in The Faerie Queene* (Oxford, 1961), p. 7.

the 'contagious fires' of Corflambo in book IV. Her combination of fire and ice recalls the stock Petrarchan cliché of the sonnet, and suggests the paradox of an unyielding sonnet mistress who yet has given herself to a lover. It is a picture in which sterility, lust, sloth and artifice are all rolled into one, and the final image shows that it is only a reflection of a reflection, like Plato's Cave once more. The inferior light of the stars sparkles on the silent waves and produces a reflection brighter than itself, just as the animal spirits, flowing from the eyes, kindle a reciprocal flame in the partner in lust which in its turn rekindles the originator: thus the cycle of unquenchable hunger goes on, and Acrasia creates a carnal desire which, as Spenser insists twice in the stanza, can never be satisfied.

This is a sequence which taps the basic images of the poem in innumerable ways and produces its own critical commentary even as it describes. By this means Spenser intends that his reader shall experience the force of temptation and at the same time discover why he should resist it, so that he may go through the Bower as Guyon does, and feeling its power, yet refrain. More than any other poem in the language, *The Faerie Queene* converts the experiences of life into art and subjects the readers to them. It is strenuous reading designed, in the words of Shelley, to strengthen the moral limb; and it makes more credible the common Renaissance assertion made by both Elyot and Ascham that the experience of books can teach as much, and with less pain, than the experience of life itself. The poem is a rehearsal for the temptations of life as Spenser visualised them; and in a sense, *The Faerie Queene* is one long temptation, a temptation into which the Romantics only too eagerly fell, to enjoy the poem as a sensuous romance and ignore the allegory.

[2]

One further aspect of Spenser's rhetoric may be considered; namely, Memory, traditionally the fourth part of the art of persuasion. Miss Yates's recent book on the art of memory[1] has drawn attention to the hitherto unsuspected importance of

[1] Francis A. Yates, *The Art of Memory* (London, 1966).

the ancient techniques of memory training, and traces the art from its origin in Simonides through to the Renaissance, where it had its last and most extraordinary efflorescence at the hands of Bruno and the Hermeticists. The traditional art of memory is based on the association of concepts with memorable visual images which, in their turn, are related to some familiar location—the inside of a building or the length of a well-known street; so that the orator has only to take a mental stroll to recall first the location, then the images placed in it, and by this indirect route, the concepts he wishes to hold in his memory. The technique throws very interesting light on the sensibility of centuries of orators who found it easier to memorise enormously elaborate sequences of visual images than to remember a logical sequence of abstract ideas, and with its aid were able to achieve the enormous feats of memorising which were necessary before books offered a less cumbersome system of artificial memory. Its importance was such that it had been transferred by the Middle Ages from the province of rhetoric to that of Prudence, as an aid to memorising large schemes of moral virtues and vices;[1] and Miss Yates points out, in this context, the debt which both mediaeval iconography and renaissance emblem owe to the art of memory and the sort of striking image which it fostered.

Miss Yates is concerned with the history of the art and does not explore in any detail its relevance to the techniques of literature and oratory. There is much research to be done into the relationship between poetic imagery, for example, and the image sequences of the memory systems, and perhaps even more into the effects of the art upon modes of literary presentation. For the art of memory offered more than just a set of techniques for memorising: it also conditioned the ordering of knowledge into patterns which lent themselves most readily to the techniques of artificial memory; and it influenced the ways in which writers organised the knowledge which they wished to imprint firmly in the memories of their audience. This is most clearly illustrated in the techniques of sermon, homily and didactic poetry. A homily such as *Jacob's Well*[2] is a case in point, where the various scoops and shovels with which the mud of sin is

[1] Pp. 20–1.
[2] *Jacob's Well*, EETS, 115 (1900).

removed are not so much metaphors of the Christian virtues as mnemonics to remind the listener of them.

The techniques of the sermon show the same tendency and for the same reason. God himself is visualised as a divine rhetorician, imparting his revelations through the memorable parables and images of the Bible, and the human rhetorician, therefore, may use the same techniques. Tyndale, in his *Obedience of a Christian man*, advises the preacher to use the Bible itself as a location for artificial memory, and having chosen a familiar episode, to associate with the landmarks of the story whatever points of doctrine he wishes to implant in the minds of his congregation. Tyndale takes as an example the story of how Peter smote off Malchius's ear and Christ healed it again, and uses it as an image-sequence to impress upon the congregation the relationship of the Law to the Gospels:

Then come I when I preach of the Law and the Gospel and borrow this ensample to express the nature of the Law and of the Gospel and to paint it unto thee before thine eyes . . . And of Peter and his sword make I the Law and of Christ, the Gospel, saying 'As Peter's sword cutteth off the ear, so doth the Law: the Law damneth, the Law killeth, the Law mangleth the conscience; there is no ear so righteous that can abide the hearing of the Law. But Christ, that is to say, the Gospel . . . healeth the ear and conscience which the Law hath hurt.[1]

Writing of this kind is not quite allegory, since there is no real parallel between the logic of the story and of the meaning it is made to embody. The connection between the image and the doctrine is an arbitrary one, and the story reminds by association rather than expressing through extended metaphor, though Tyndale makes valiant efforts to justify his use of Peter's sword as a metaphor for the Law at the end of the passage. The distinction between mnemonic and metaphor is always a very fine one, and the special skill of Donne or Herbert is to convert one to the other by establishing logical connections between two sets of terms which appear initially to have little in common. The striking memory-image slips easily into the far-fetched metaphor and in doing so becomes all the more effective as an

[1] Writings of Tyndale, 'Four Senses of the Scriptures', Parker Society, p. 306.

aid to memory. Tyndale, in the passage quoted, is primarily concerned with memory, and he sees his Biblical story as a means of impressing ideas upon his congregation by associating them with something which they know very well:

This allegory proveth nothing nor can do so. For it is not the Scripture but an ensample or a similitude borrowed of the Scripture to declare a text or a conclusion of the Scripture more expressly and to root it and grave it in the heart. For a similitude or an ensample doth print a thing much deeper in the wit of man than doth plain speaking.[1]

The art of memory was inevitably of special importance to the preacher, and Herbert, in the seventeenth century, still seems to apply it in the traditional way. The framework of *The Temple* is a walk around the church, beginning at the porch, crossing the threshold and passing by the altar, the windows, the monuments. This is a time-honoured memory location, and the places on the tour are associated with relevant images from the scriptures and relevant doctrines of the Church, so that the familiar structure becomes impregnated with the aspects of Christian experience to which Herbert wishes to draw attention. The little poems in the shape of altars and Easter wings add their quota by reminding the reader more forcibly of the visual basis of the whole in the church itself.

It is against a background of such practice that we must consider the image sequences of *The Faerie Queene*. As a didactic poet, Spenser was concerned to impress his message in terms which would remain in the memory of the reader and be available for application whenever the relevant circumstances occurred. His basic instrument, therefore, is the familiar, the striking, or the monstrous image which springs to consciousness and illuminates our daily experience by providing a touchstone of moral values: the reader will carry round with him for ever a set of archetypes offering guidance in every moral or intellectual dilemma. We think inevitably of Ate with her discordant features, or Impotence with her crutch which she yet uses as a club, or of the Graces dancing in all their naked beauty. Often a sequence of such images is associated with a series of memory

1 Writings of Tyndale, 'Four Senses of the Scriptures', Parker Society, p. 306.

places, so that the journey brings to mind the sequence of ideas associated with the images placed on them. Guyon's journey through the cave of Mammon is the most traditional memory sequence of this kind, where a series of temptations is conveyed by a sequence of images set in memorable places along the way —the broad highway, the gates of Hell, the second room with the devils labouring at the furnaces, the great Hall of Philotime with its pillars, crowns and diadems, all of them in the tradition of mediaeval memory schemes.[1] The journey across the sea to the Bower of Blisse is organised in the same way: the reader has only to recall Odysseus's various ports of call and the creatures he encounters at each one to have in his mind a set of images epitomising the whole range and logic of temperance and its opposite.

The Faerie Queene is full of journeys of this kind performing an obvious mnemonic function but this is, of course, by no means their whole purpose. Spenser's places are not merely aids to memorising something other than themselves but form part of the statement of what is to be memorised: the journey itself is an allegory of the exploration into the nature of temptation which is Spenser's subject. This is especially true of Britomart's journey through Busyrane's castle to which allusion has already been made. The location itself is a perfect instance of a setting for artificial memory—the inside of a building with its successive rooms, its symbolic arras on the wall, its altar and statue, its doors with their mottoes; yet it is not these which remind us of Britomart's emotional Odyssey but the emotional sequence which dictates the nature and order of the places and makes them memorable. The traditional memory places provide Spenser with sequences of action well known to his readers which can be used for allegory. Often, indeed, he does not bother to develop his places, even where they would seem to be most obviously available. The House of Holiness, for example, could easily have been developed as a powerful source of artificial memory, with the significant images firmly placed in their topographical niches, so that the tour of the building would have brought the whole of Christian doctrine to mind. In fact the topography of

[1] Yates, chap. IV.

81

the House is scarcely indicated: there is a locked door and a 'streight' way, as we should expect; but the spacious court inside, the goodly lodge, the chamber where Charitas resides and the cellar where Red Cross undergoes penance are too slightly indicated to form memorable locations for the concepts associated with them. Even when Mercy takes Red Cross to the holy Hospital 'by a narrow way,/Scattered with bushy thornes and ragged breares,/Which still before him she remov'd away' [I. x. 35] she is not taking us through the house but going the way of Christ to Calvary. The whole sequence of theology is made memorable not by the place in which it is established but by the innate logic of the scheme. In this episode at least, Spenser's dependence on logic rather than on memory suggests an affinity with Erasmus and the line of humanists who had little use for the traditional art of memory.

It is interesting and by no means irrelevant to speculate whether Spenser was involved in the curious developments in the art of memory at the end of the sixteenth century which Miss Yates traces to the influence of Hermeticism.[1] Camillo's Memory Theatre was still talked about in Spenser's day, and Bruno, whose visit to England had created a considerable stir, had published his *Shadows* and his *Seals* in 1582 and 1583. Bruno used as the basis of his memory system a large number of traditional Hermetic images supposedly deriving talismanic powers from the stellar bodies of which they were the symbols. The thinker, therefore, who committed these to memory and organised human knowledge in terms of them could absorb into himself the magic powers of the stars; and Memory thus became the supreme source of greatness, the means by which a human being could make that ascent to divinity which Pico claimed, in his *Oration on the Dignity of Man*, to be within the reach of human powers. It is unlikely that Spenser shared this belief: his strong, orthodox conception of the Fall and his preoccupation with human weakness would seem to forbid any ascent to divinity other than through the orthodox channels of Grace; and the House of Alma, where we should expect to find evidence of such Hermeticism if any existed, reveals no trace. Memory

1 Chaps. VI–XII.

in the third chamber is an old man possessing none of the magical powers with which Bruno endowed memory; and the human microcosm of Alma's castle and its inmates is not shown as embodying the macrocosm of the whole universe but only that of society. The warder teeth, the porter tongue, the kitchen digestion and the bower and common room of whims, moods and impulses suggest a less hyperbolic conception of human greatness than that of Bruno and Pico.

Spenser's debt to Camillo's Memory Theatre, however, is another matter. The little wooden Theatre with its seven gangways and gates seems to have been designed as a location for memory images based on the seven planets and the seven cabbalistic Sepiroth which formed their Intelligences; and the orator, therefore, who organised his material around these places and expressed them by means of the seven forms of good oratory could harness the force of the stars to his pleading and speak with magic tongue.[1] Such a conception is a long way from Spenser's mode of thought; and yet Alastair Fowler has produced strong evidence to suggest that Spenser organised his poem around the seven planetary deities, and that each book is permeated with the symbolism of its patron planet. There is a real affinity of method between the Memory Theatre and *The Faerie Queene*, though it is improbable that the two had the same object in view. Spenser must have been familiar with so widely publicised a project as Camillo's, and possibly he found in it a convenient way of organising his poem along lines already familiar to the average reader. It is conceivable that with his immense powers of syncretising he drew upon Hermeticism as upon everything else, as a necessary part of the total microcosm of his poem. Some aspects of Hermeticism certainly appealed to him, in particular its claim to transcend the discords of jarring religions and religious sects. It was the most syncretic form of Renaissance religion, since it claimed to be the original source from which all subsequent religions sprang, pagan or Christian alike, and *The Faerie Queene* has the same all-embracing quality. The ultimate villain of the poem is Ate, the goddess of Discord, and the ultimate creator of Concord is Cambina who, it will be

[1] Yates, chap. VI.

remembered, imposes peace upon the battling knights by means of Hermes's magic wand [IV. iii. 42]. The symbolism of Cambina will be discussed later in connection with book IV. As far as the present argument is concerned, it is possible that Spenser's tolerance of the religious ethics of Hermeticism made him more sympathetic towards those aspects of the cult which were incompatible with his own Christian beliefs. It is doubtful whether he himself believed that a poem embodying stellar images would persuade with the magic of celestial power, but he may well have felt that it might do so for those who were believers.

Wherever he stood in relation to the debate about Hermeticism, Spenser was certainly familiar with the traditional art of memory and conscious that without its aid, all other parts of rhetoric would be ineffective. The sort of memorability which the poem possesses stems from the visual quality of the ancient memory systems rather than from the normal methods of rhyme and rhythm by which poetry stimulates the verbal memory. As Professor Alpers has argued,[1] and as one's own experience of the poem suggests, *The Faerie Queene* is not easy to remember in verbal detail and extremely hard to quote from: the sequence of the story eludes the memory, in part, I think, because the final alexandrine of the stanza stops progression and turns the attention back upon the preceding lines, in contrast to the great verse paragraphs of *Paradise Lost* which hurry the reader along as in seven-league boots. At the same time, this very process which forces one to linger over each stanza does not have the result of imprinting lines and phrases upon the memory but ensures that we look through these to the meaning behind. To follow verbal echoes through the poem, or to look for running images as we seek them in a Shakespeare play, is to falsify the experience of reading.

Yet *The Faerie Queene* is supremely memorable as a system of locations, as a visual world comprising the plain, the wood, the river, the cottage, the castle, and the sunshine or storm that affect them. Spenser uses the world of the popular Romance as a gigantic set in which all the time-honoured properties and

[1] P. 125.

inhabitants have their meanings riveted to them by association and by the logic of metaphor. The basic constituents are very few, but they ramify with such interlocking logic that to recognise the function of one is to be able to deduce that of any other. It is because the metaphorical world of the poem is such a logically coherent one that it remains in memory and provides the principle of organisation within the poem.

For this reason *The Faerie Queene* is a poem to which the techniques of modern practical criticism are after all appropriate in that any stanza, line, or even single image, is dependent for its effect on its relationship to the canto, the book in which it stands, and ultimately to the context of the poem as a whole. When Artegall unlaces Radegund's helmet, her face appears 'Like as the Moone in foggie winters night' [v. v. 12], and the force of the comparison depends upon the use of day/night, winter/summer, sun/moon images throughout the poem, although it is not necessary to recall other specific instances where they are repeated or varied, since each is self-defining in relation to the total moral landscape. Spenser does not demand that his reader shall have a mind like a computer with an infinite capacity for cross-referencing but that he shall carry a location in his memory and be capable of extending it logically. In this way, Spenser's metaphors provide a concentrated form of shorthand which harnesses the force of the whole poem to every individual statement.

PART II

The Books of the Poem

5

Holiness

[1]

Book I of *The Faerie Queene* is the book of faith. Spenser's holiness is not a state in which there is no sin, for that has been impossible since the Fall: it is a state in which one sins and is forgiven, so that no fall need be final and the Christian can resume his quest after each lapse, as Red Cross 'up lightly rose againe' when the dragon knocked him down. For this reason holiness is at the head of the virtues, for without its sanction there could be no virtue at all: 'Works done before the grace of Christ and the Inspiration of his Spirit', says Article XIII of *Articles of Religion,* 'are not pleasant to God, for asmuch as they spring not of faith in Jesus Christ, neither do they make men meet to receive grace...but they have the nature of sin'.[1] If Red Cross were not rescued from Orgoglio by Arthur there would be no point in any subsequent quest, for Guyon and the rest start in the strength of Red Cross's Justification and explore those virtues which his achieved faith alone has made possible.

Because holiness is so far-reaching in its consequences, book I is peculiarly multiple in its allegory, embracing a wide variety of simultaneous levels of human experience and, more than any other book of the poem, conforming to the complex pattern of allegory which Harington describes in his well-known *Preface to Orlando Furioso.*[2] Through his association with the patron saint of England, Red Cross invites a historical interpretation throughout concerning England's lapse into the toils of Rome and her subsequent liberation by the Elizabethan settlement. In his role of defender of the faith, he evokes a multitude of traditional scriptural interpretations, as Professor Northrop Frye has

---

[1] *Of Works before Justification,* Articles of Religion, The Book of Common Prayer.

[2] Sir John Harington, *A Preface, or rather a Briefe Apologie for Poetrie,* in Gregory Smith, vol. II, pp. 201–3.

pointed out.[1] Una searching for Red Cross derives one level of
her meaning from the Song of Solomon which was interpreted
as an allegory of the yearning of the Bride of Christ for her
spouse; while at the other extreme, Archimago and Duessa
draw on the mythology surrounding anti-Christ and the fantastic lore concerning the Beast of Revelation and the Whore of
Babylon. The names Una and Duessa encourage all manner of
interpretations concerning unity and division, whether in terms
of the original Christian church which, according to the Protestant view, had been divided against itself by the Roman Catholic
schism, until the Anglican settlement restored the original
unity again, or in terms of the individual and his fall from
singleness into duplicity. There is an allegory of the individual
Christian who wanders into error but eventually recovers his
faith with a fuller understanding of its nature; and above this,
an allegory of the whole history of mankind, in which the human
race loses its pre-lapsarian innocence but struggles back, through
pagan virtue, to the new innocence of Christian redemption.
Most insistent of all, perhaps, is the psychological level of
allegory in which the individual man destroys that hierarchy of
his inner powers which alone makes virtue possible, but succeeds
through bitter experience in achieving a final reintegration.

The list is not exhaustive, nor can it be so, for Spenserean
allegory consists of archetypal images, and the cap is meant to
be put on wherever it may be made to fit. That is what Harington means in his Preface to *Orlando* when, after finding a whole
variety of meanings embodied in the myth of Perseus, he
concludes, 'The like infinite Allegories I could pike out of other
Poeticall fictions, save that I would avoid tediousnes' (p. 203).
Such allegory is not the statement by the poet of one particular
thing in terms of another but the statement of a general pattern
which the reader is invited to discover for himself in any field of
human experience where the details of the allegory can be
applied. It is a matter of applying principles rather than digging
out meanings, and for this reason Professor Hamilton's parody
interpretation of book I as an allegory of Russian Communism
would not have seemed as ridiculous to Spenser as it might to a

---

[1] Northrop Frye, *Anatomy of Criticism* (London, 1957), p. 194.

modern reader.[1] All levels of meaning are simultaneous and parallel, since all are different aspects of the same process, namely, the Fall and the Incarnation, as it is manifested in different areas of human life.

The struggle to achieve or maintain faith is an inner one and the greater part of the action, therefore, occurs within the mind of Red Cross himself. The faculties which govern his behaviour are personified and accompany him on his quest, in this way demonstrating the springs of his actions and providing a moral commentary upon them. We move about within the mind of Red Cross as in a sort of Yeatsean 'Dream-back' where the experiences are at once lived through and understood.

The famous opening has an extraordinary concentration made possible by the fact that Spenser was able to draw on so many traditional symbols which provided him with a sort of short-hand of expression—St Paul's armour of a Christian, Una's lamb, Plato's horses, the forest itself. Red Cross is the young man baptised into the Christian faith but not yet having tried out his new weapons, so that he has 'his new force to learne', and his quest is to be his education. Spenser varies slightly the details of the metaphorical armour which St Paul gave to the Christian (Ephesians 6:11-17), since the approach of book I is psychological as well as theological. Red Cross's faith lies in his heart so that he wears the bloody cross, 'The deare remembrance of his dying Lord', upon his breast, and the same cross upon his shield, therefore, not as a symbol of faith but of the hope which springs from faith and protects it from assault. It is this which his enemies attack first of all, knowing that it is more vulnerable than faith itself and that its destruction will plunge the knight into the most damning of all sins, despair. The third of the trinity of Christian virtues, love, is not directly mentioned, but it is implied in the conventional description of Red Cross as the faithful lover in the next line—'Right faithfull true he was in deede and word'. He is thus the inevitable target for the three anti-Christian vices, Sans Foy, Sans Joy, and lastly Sans Loy, whose lawlessness is a denial of God's love for his creation. He is able to kill Sans Foy, but not Sans Joy, and that this will

[1] A. C. Hamilton, *The Structure of Allegory in The Faerie Queene* (Oxford, 1961), p. 9.

be so is already hinted at in Spenser's initial description of him as 'too solemne sad', even though he has the strength of the Gospels at his disposal. It is clear that Red Cross does not yet fully understand the happiness and power which lies in his faith.

He is accompanied by Una and the dwarf. In her role of rescuer, truth-bearer and guide both to the House of Holiness and to the Hill of Contemplation, Una is Spenser's symbol of right-reason, the channel of grace, the spark of divinity remaining in Everyman even after the Fall. Since the tragedy of her first parents in Eden, however, she is veiled and in mourning, and can neither see nor be seen as clearly as she once could; and in this she shares the nature of Error in her forest darkness, 'Where plaine none might her see, nor she see any plaine' [I.i.16]. The two are complementary aspects of the Fall. Una's palfrey, though white and docile like the good horse in the *Timaeus*, is slower and less forceful than Red Cross's 'angry steede' of the passions which is never under complete control. Nevertheless, she is the agent of divinity in man and is conceived, therefore, both as the 'heavenly virgin', source of the faith, and the 'royal virgin', its defender.

The dwarf, who bears 'her bag/Of needments at his backe' [6], is the third of the trio of human elements, the rational soul which, in terms of Elizabethan psychology, acts as mediator between the spiritual understanding and the fleshly body. He should be the instrument by which understanding governs human action, but in fact he is lazy and lags behind: indeed the whole procession is in the wrong order, with the passions in the lead bearing Red Cross far ahead of understanding and the soul, whereas ideally Una should go first, the dwarf second, and Red Cross's horse a well-controlled third. Spenser shows us, however, the normal state of fallen man, and such a perversion of the ideal hierarchy inevitably leads to error. When the storm comes they hasten into the forest and 'led with delight' quickly forget the quest in the variety of the daily life around them. The beaten track leads to Error's den and Red Cross, with the characteristic zeal of inexperience, rushes in, 'full of fire and greedy hardiment' to encounter heresy which, since he already has faith and is concerned only with his own salvation at this point of the poem, he would have been wiser to leave alone. Human instinct drives him forward, however, against the advice of both Una and the dwarf. The nature of Error is indicated by the books and papers which she vomits, and by the quality of her offspring, black as ink, who drink their mother's blood in dreadful parody of the means of Christian redemption, 'Making her death their life, and eke her hurt their good' [25]. It is a blood, of course, which kills instead of saving. Spenser's description of her as half woman, half serpent makes her a figure of Eve, and the sexual pun implicit in her 'taile' pointed with 'mortal sting' hints at the appeal of the senses by which Adam fell and Red Cross is to fall later. She attacks his shield and enwraps his body in her 'endlesse traine', but he is saved when his understanding invokes his faith—'Add faith unto your force' [19]. He escapes and the trio laboriously retrace their steps by the way they came: there are no short cuts for Spenser, no sudden and miraculous illuminations, only a hard and persevering effort to undo what has been done which 'at last out of the wood them brought'. As we can see from Red Cross's painful rehabilitation in the House of Holiness, Spenser believed in the hard way of penance and the Law more than evangelical conversion.

Such a struggle weakens man's energy and control, and so inevitably Archimago is waiting for them when they come out of the wood. Archimago is one of the many personifications in the poem of the weakness of the flesh and the corruption of our fallen nature. He is in his activities a type of Satan; he has, like Proteus, the power of metamorphosis and is thus one with chaos against form; he is a magician, like Acrasia and Busyrane who in their different ways embody the power of the passions to blind the eye of reason and make the worse appear the better. At this point of the story he speaks with the voice of reason itself, pointing out the need for rest; there is a wrong to be righted but it is 'Far hence...in wastfull wildernesse' [32], and in the meantime his little cottage offers an 'In' of irresistible appeal—'Then with the Sunne take Sir, your timely rest' [33]. Red Cross sleeps and has dreams conjured up by Archimago from the Underworld, the ordinary erotic dreams of our physical nature which yet hint at his desire for a less stringent rule of life than that imposed by his faith and his understanding. He dreams of a Una, unveiled and naked, who pleads with him that as he is fallen he should be content to accept a discipline appropriate to his fallen nature; to renounce carnality now is to aim too high:

> Your owne deare sake forst me at first to leave
> My Fathers kingdome, . . .   [I. i. 52]

Red Cross awakes horrified at his own backsliding but full now of the doubts which his desires have suggested to him and angry at the thought of the pleasures which he is missing and other men enjoy. This is the meaning of the vision which Archimago sends of Una and the squire in bed together, and the thought is too much for him; his 'eye of reason was with rage yblent' [I. ii. 5], and disowning Una, he rushes away. He is now wholly in the grip of angry passion instead of under the government of understanding, and for this reason Archimago takes on the guise of Red Cross—'*Saint George* himself ye would have deemed him to be' [I. ii. 11]: his lower nature has in fact taken over.

Archimago is delighted to see his guests so 'divided into double parts' [I. ii. 9] with the understanding turned against the passions, and Red Cross's self-division is reproduced by a division of stories which gives a graphic impression of his loss of inner unity. On the one hand we see Una committing herself to the company of a Red Cross whose falsity she does not recognise until it is too late to do anything but utter a sustained yet impotent protest. On the other is Red Cross following a false Una, striving to destroy the unhappiness which is inseparable from his state of error and which is the voice of Una within him. The two stories add up to a very subtle portrait of the Christian in the grip of his passions, half knowing the best but driven to pursue the worst and struggling, like Macbeth, to silence the voice of his own conscience. In this conflict the dwarf reason at first leaves his proper place with the understanding to follow the passions, but later, by the Grace of God, returns to the true service of Una and so makes regeneration possible. The two stories alternate but are, of course, complementary to each other, forming together the total account of the motives and behaviour of the same person.

Red Cross does not fall into complete infidelity; the habit of faith is strong in him and his new companion masquerades as Fidessa. The very violence of his fight with Sans Foy represents the over-emphatic zeal with which he insists to himself that he is still one of the faithful; but Spenser makes the battle a slightly comic one, full of echoes of the old folk-play of St George and the paynim with its slapstick and mock killing—'Who well it wards, and quyteth cuff with cuff'—until the paynim is finally sent to the place 'Whither the soules do fly of men, that live amis' [I. ii. 19]. It is only shadow-boxing, for Red Cross cannot tell the difference between a true faith and an adulterate one, and the enemy he kills is little worse than himself. At this stage he is zealous in the service of a laxer, more easy-going faith, and one more agreeable to the demands of his fallen nature than that of Una. Duessa, however, is not yet wholly identical with the Roman Catholic church, nor does she become so until Orgoglio takes full possession of Red Cross and sets her up on the beast of *Revelation* with the triple tiara on her head [I. vii. 16]. She can claim, like Una, that 'Her dearest Lord' fell into the hands of his 'accursed fone'; but there is great irony in her complaint that

> His blessed body spoild of lively breath,
> > Was afterward, I know not how, convaid
> And fro me hid: . . .   [I. ii. 24]

It is very like the one-eyed merchant with something on his back which T. S. Eliot's Madame Sosostris is forbidden to see.

Red Cross is still capable of moments of clear vision which startle him but are not of sufficient strength to make him change his course. The episode of Fradubio and the shrieking, bleeding, branch embodies most vividly such a moment of truth and the pang of fear to which it gives rise: Fradubio, the doubter, has become one with the forest itself, in the grip of despair and prey to all three fatal brothers, without faith, hope or that sense of God's love which would give him strength to break out of his wooden prison:

> Time and suffised fates to former kynd
> Shall us restore, none else from hence may us unbynd.
> > > [I. ii. 43]

This is the state of which Red Cross has a momentary and horrifying glimpse, but Duessa distracts him, and with typically Spenserean symbolism he banishes it by thrusting the bleeding bough into the ground and stopping the wooden wound with clay. His fallen earthy nature is strong enough to enable him, at this point in his descent, to crush his fears and continue on his inevitable way to the Palace of Pride where he will have to meet them again in the person of Sans Joy.

Having taken Red Cross so far on his downward path, Spenser now turns to Una and the unavailing struggles of the understanding to free the hero from the grip of his passions. After the first shock of desertion Una sets out in search of her errant knight with a love great enough to forgive and forget everything: indeed Spenser suggests that she goes further than this and, in finding excuses for his backsliding, falls into his own blindness and for a time even helps him on his downward way. This is the point which seems to be made by the episode of Una and the lion. In the Palace of Pride, wrath rides upon a lion, 'loth for to be led', the same wrath which blinded Red Cross's eye of reason in the first place and is the mainspring of his energies in the fight with Sans Joy. As the habit of virtue asserts itself, his wrath is tempered to become its near and equally unseeing neighbour, zeal, with which he serves Fidessa and fights Sans Foy: the lion is a part of him as much as the fiery horse of his passions from which it is metaphorically born.

Una, too, finds herself carried along by the ramping lion, and though her virginity, both royal and heavenly, can tame it, its devotion is blind as well as benevolent. When the pair take shelter with Corceca, Una herself takes on the blind devotion of her hostess, and the destruction of Kirkrapine, however justified, is an act not of reason but of blind zeal. An article by Mother Mary Falls makes clear the nature of the abuse which moves Una to so violent and uncharacteristic an action.[1] Abessa would seem to be not only the catholic abbess but, as her name implies with its pun on 'abesse', the new protestant absentee holder of church benefices who, with the acquiescence of the queen, grew

---

[1] Mother Mary Robert Falls, 'Spenser's Kirkrapine and the Elizabethans', *Studies in Philology* 50 (1953), 457–75.

rich on the plunder of the church. Kirkrapine pillages the church and gives his stolen riches to Abbessa, daughter of Corceca—in other words, he robs the church and makes his zeal for the new faith the justification of his actions. It is a subject which Spenser had treated earlier in *The Shepheardes Calender*,[1] and one about which he felt deeply. In the context of book I, he sees it as an example of bigotry in the new religion which produces an equally dangerous reaction in favour of the old, as Una's initial fervour in the rescue of Red Cross turns to a justified anger against the church he has abandoned which makes her excuse his backsliding. In terms of the central character, Red Cross's unworthy inclinations towards the catholic faith are stoked by his disgust at the abuses of the protestant, so that he can go on his way and fight Sans Foy with a sense of righteousness. Under the pressure of his desires, his own understanding seems to sanction his transference of allegiance to Duessa. It is all part of the same blindness of passion, and Una's action, therefore, puts her in the company once more of the false Red Cross who has been directed to her by Corceca [I. iii. 25]. The relief which she feels when she thinks her true knight is with her again has a slightly hysterical quality:

> Much like, as when the beaten marinere,
> That long hath wandred in the *Ocean* wide, . . .
> Soone as the port from farre he has espide
> His chearefull whistle merrily doth sound,
> And *Nereus* crownes with cups; his mates him pledg
>   around.
> Such joy made *Una*, when her knight she found; . . .
>   [I. iii. 31–2]

It corresponds to the 'foole-happie' relief which Red Cross feels when he escapes from the Palace of Pride and deludes himself that his trials are over:

> As when a ship, that flyes faire under saile,
> An hidden rocke escaped hath unwares,
> That lay in waite her wrack for to bewaile,
> The Marriner yet halfe amazed stares

---

[1] Paul McLane, *Spenser's Shepheardes Calender* (Notre Dame, 1961).

> At perill past, and yet in doubt ne dares
> To joy at his foole-happie oversight:. . .   [I. vi. 1]

The use of the same metaphor in both cases draws attention to the identity of the two.

But Una is to have a rude awakening: she has mistaken Red Cross's ignoble motives for noble ones, and in encouraging him on his way, has put herself into the power of his passions. The arrival of Sans Loy who kills the noble lion and reveals the Archimago in Red Cross's armour represents her horrified recognition of where her zeal has led her, when it is too late to resist. She is swept away by the anarchy of the passions and is powerless to do anything but protest. In other words, Red Cross, though aware of his errors, can do nothing to correct them and goes on his downward way to the Palace of Pride haunted by the protests of his conscience which he can neither destroy nor obey.

He is still not wholly corrupted, and struggles confusedly against what he takes to be evil; but passion has blinded his eye so that he can no longer distinguish it clearly from good. The reader can see Lucifera in all her presumption, 'like *Phoebus* fairest childe' [I. iv. 9], but Red Cross can only see her upward look—'Looking to heaven; for earth she did disdayne' [I. iv. 10]; and the 'dreadfull dragon' which lies beneath her 'scornefull feete' might appear to be conquered, when it is in the position of a faithful hound. Even the deadly sins have a dual aspect, inevitable to one whose vision is coloured by Duessa, which can be mistaken for virtue or at least serve to confuse his sense of values further. Sloth, for example, claims that his inactivity is really contemplation [I. iv. 20]; and Envy, taking advantage of the debate over the nature of justification by faith or merit, accuses those who do good deeds of a lack of faith:

> And who with gracious bread the hungry feeds,
> His almes for want of faith he doth accuse;   [I. iv. 32]

The Una within is still making her cries heard, however, and for this reason Red Cross has to face the third brother, Sans Joy, the unhappiness which is the inseparable companion of Duessa. This unhappiness is to be his ultimate salvation, and Spenser compares Duessa's visit to Aesculapius, therefore, with that of Diana when she sought to save the virtuous Hippolytus [I. v. 39]. As we shall see, Spenser associates Diana's rigorous discipline with the punishment of the Law, and in preserving Sans Joy, Duessa is preserving the force by which Red Cross will be painfully educated into salvation: all unwittingly she is doing God's work.

Red Cross's fight with Sans Joy is 'all for prayse and honour' [I. v. 7] and wrath not virtue gives force to his winning blow; but when it is over, he vacillates from the anger of Pyrochles to its opposite in Cymochles. The 'most heavenly melody' [I. v. 17] which beguiles him of grief and agony after the uncompleted battle is, however, only a temporary respite, the relief that the bad mood has been put down for the present; and although he has the sense to escape from the Palace of Pride, it is through the merely prudential advice of the dwarf who reminds him of the lessons of history, not through any principle of ultimate truth derived from his understanding. Inevitably, therefore, the sadness and the self-division return:

> Yet sad he was that his too hastie speed
> The faire *Duess'* had forst him leave behind;
> And yet more sad, that *Una* his deare dreed
> Her truth had staind with treason so unkind;
> Yet crime in her could never creature find, . . .
>
> [I. vi. 2]

and inevitably, too, Duessa is still waiting for him. Disheartened by the misery he can never overcome, wearied by the perpetual moral dilemma, he sits down by the fountain of sloth and, taking off his Christian armour, seeks to lose himself in sensual pleasures. It is for his own salvation that he is not successful even in this: the experience is fraught with the irrepressible pangs and fears of conscience,

> Till crudled cold his corage gan assaile,
> And chearefull bloud in faintnesse chill did melt,
>
> [I. vii. 6]

Una is still protesting, Sans Joy still vigorously alive, and sin never has any real pleasures to offer him; but hope and faith have gone and he is crushed by the burden. Orgoglio's name suggests the original sin of pride, and his genealogy reminds us of the earthy nature of his mother and the hostility of his father, Aeolus (the god of winds), to the heroic Aeneas. The triumph of the giant symbolises that insurrection of the lower nature by which Adam fell and all his sons after, and marks Red Cross's total abandonment of his quest for the time being.

It is significant that his final capitulation takes place by and through the fountain of the nymph who has fallen out of Diana's favour [I. vii. 4–5]: in forsaking Una for Duessa, Red Cross has faced Hercules's choice between virtue and pleasure but, unlike the hero, has followed the path of Venus instead of that of Diana. Yet even in this instance, when the choice seems to be the wholly traditional one, Spenser blurs the issue and avoids an uncompromising opposition between black and white. The state of sloth into which both the nymph and Red Cross have fallen is not entirely a sinful one, as Professor Alpers has shown by drawing attention to the surprisingly 'unloaded' imagery of 'cooling shade', 'breathing wind' and 'trembling leaves' in terms of which the fountain makes its appeal [I. vii. 3].[1] In consequence of this, Red Cross's relaxation by its waters seems less a sinful relapse from Christian virtue than an inevitable necessity of the human state since the Fall. Such pleasure, because natural to man cannot be totally evil, and the 'sacred nymph' will be forgiven: she is out of Diana's favour only for the time being, 'as it then befell', and the fountain will regain its eternal and life-giving properties—'the bubbling wave did ever freshly well,/Ne ever would through fervant sommer fade' [I. vi. 4]. At this moment of decisive error, the verse is full of hope, not of condemnation, and contains paradoxical hints that the ways of Diana and Venus will not always be in conflict.

[2]

The note of hope embodied in the imagery of the episode has already been anticipated in the previous canto, and the theme of regeneration introduced even before Red Cross has fallen.

---

[1] Pp. 142–3.

Sans Loy and Orgoglio are complementary to each other, the impotence of the understanding which coincides with the domination by the lower nature; and the seizure of Una by Sans Loy is the inevitable precursor of Orgoglio's victory. But Una is not raped, and Spenser carries on her story and shows her release by the Grace of God before Orgoglio even enters the story. The adventures of Una among the wood-folk is a subtle allegory in psychological and theological terms of the beginnings of regeneration; and in making this precede the fall itself, Spenser demonstrates the love of God which anticipates and provides for the sins of man even before they occur. In the same way Milton makes his God foretell both the Fall and the possibility of redemption in book III of *Paradise Lost* before Adam is created.

The source of regeneration lies in that divine Grace which restored to Adam a remnant of his original uncorrupted understanding so that the Fall was not in effect a total one. Milton's God states in explicit terms what is the underlying assumption of *The Faerie Queene*:

> Man shall not quite be lost, but saved who will,
> Yet not of will in him, but grace in me
> Freely vouchsafed: once more I will renew
> His lapsed powers, though forfeit and enthralled
> By sin to foul exorbitant desires:...
>   ... for I will clear their senses dark,
> What may suffice, and soften stony hearts
> To pray, repent, and bring obedience due...
> And I will place within them as a guide
> My umpire Conscience, whom if they will hear,
> Light after light well used they shall attain,
> And to the end persisting safe arrive.
>   *(Paradise Lost.* III, 173–97)

The agents of this Grace are, in canto VI, the 'rude, misshapen, monstrous rablement' of the wood-folk [I. vi. 8], who, through 'Eternall providence', scare Sans Loy away from the helpless Una. They comprise the half-human satyrs though not the non-human wood-nymphs and Naiads whose only feeling is of envy towards her [I. vi. 18]; and they symbolise the vestige of innocence still remaining in human instinct. Although they rescue Una 'From Lyons claws' [I. vi. 7], they themselves are compared a few stanzas later to a lion which saves an innocent lamb from the greedy wolf [I. vi. 10], and the simile contains all manner of relevant allusions to the lion lying down with the lamb, as opposed to what is represented by the 'grim wolf with privy paw'. The difference is between the ramping lion who first rushes at Una and the lion made mild by the royal and heavenly virgin. Providence has metaphorically raised Una's lion from the dead and set in motion a process which exactly reverses that of the Fall. The wood-folk, though half bestial, have nobler instincts than the 'lustfull heat' and 'beastly sin' of Sans Loy and share the instinctive reverence and blind devotion of the lion earlier; they 'kisse her feete, and fawne on her with count'nance faine' [I. vi. 12], while Sylvanus and his satyrs begin as we have seen earlier, to 'scorne their woody kinde'. As the simple primitive inhabitants of the first age of the world, they stand for the small but sufficient spark of prelapsarian virtue in the heart of Everyman, and because of it Una is never overcome. Even in the very depths of sin, Red Cross is never totally fallen, and his unhappiness which is the symptom of this fact preserves the moral life within him.

The symbol of this instinctive stirring of the moral will is Satyrane, born of a Satyr but himself human, who spends his life subduing the symbolic beasts. He carries Una out of the forest into the plain again [I. vi. 33], and the moral will which he embodies is sufficient to hold Sans Loy at bay while the understanding escapes from his clutches. The proper inner hierarchy of the faculties can now be restored, and the dwarf, therefore, leaves the scene of the fight with Orgoglio and takes up his place beside Una again. The understanding is not yet in full control, and Una swoons three times and thrice is lifted up by the dwarf [I. vii. 24], reminding us of Christ's rising from the dead which will enable Red Cross to rise from spiritual death. The dwarf's long and very specific catalogue of all the stages of Red Cross's fall,

> The subtill traines of *Archimago* old;
> The wanton loves of false *Fidessa* faire,

Bought with the bloud of vanquisht Paynim bold:
The wretched payre transform'd to treen mould;
The house of Pride, and perils round about;
The combat, which he with *Sansjoy* did hould;
The lucklesse conflict with the Gyant stout, . . .

[I. vii. 26]

is Red Cross's clear-eyed recognition of his own errors, born in
upon him by the force of his suffering; while Una's grief at the
tale, arousing in her the resolution to find him, 'resolving him
to find/Alive or dead' [I. vii. 28], expresses his consciousness of
guilt and determination to do better. Red Cross has now transcended the blind instinct towards virtue which has kept him
morally alive throughout and has risen to a state of humility and
self-knowledge. He is once more fit to receive the faith, and so
Arthur appears [I. vii. 29]. The concentrated little dialogue
between Arthur and Una at I. vii. 41 recapitulates all that has
gone before. Una, invited to tell her grief, finds it difficult to do
so, for to define it clearly to oneself is to recognise its full
implications and to be plunged in despair. This was the dilemma
of Red Cross who sought, accordingly, to suppress his unhappiness rather than to face it in the open. Arthur counters that
there is no despair where there is faith, but Una replies from
sad experience that faith is easily impaired by the flesh.
Arthur's answer, 'Flesh may empaire (quoth he) but reason can
repaire', brings the whole matter down to Una herself: 'goodly
reason' is the first step on the ladder of faith, as demonstrated by
the fact that Arthur has come at Una's call, and we have followed
the whole process in detail. Spenser is summing up and offering
a comforting assurance to the reader that redemption is within
the power of every one.

The sequence of cantos VI and VII has described the stages of a
moral and psychological regeneration so fundamental to Spenser's whole concept of virtue that he embodies them in images
embracing all human history. Red Cross's private progress from
the wood-folk by way of the Roman Satyrane to Arthur is an
epitome of human development from the primitive through the
pagan civilisation to the Christian revelation; and within the
terms of Christianity itself, Arthur suggests both the Old Law

and the New. His helmet, which 'Both glorious brightnesse, and great terrour bred', looks in both directions. The old dragon, carved in gold, sprawls upon it, his paws enfolding the crest, his wings covering the top and his head resting upon the beaver, giving a fearsome appearance to the whole:

> his dreadfull hideous hed
> Close couched on the bever, seem'd to throw
> From flaming mouth bright sparkles fierie red,
> That suddeine horror to faint harts did show,
>
> [I. vii. 31]

yet from the centre of this vision of hell-fire springs the gay and happy crest which Spenser describes in perhaps the most famous simile of the poem:

> Like to an Almond tree ymounted hye
> On top of greene *Selenis* all alone,
> With blossomes brave bedecked daintily;
> Whose tender locks do tremble every one
> At every little breath, that under heaven is blowne.
>
> [I. vii. 32]

The impression of fruitfulness, release and holy joy is overwhelming; but the symbolism is made more specific by the reference to Aaron's rod which budded and yielded almonds (Numbers, 17:8), a traditional symbol of the Old Testament foreshadowing the New.[1]

Arthur is a figure of very complex meaning in book I, deriving from the fact that he is at once redeemer and redeemed. At the most obvious level, he suggests Christ who comes at man's need and liberates those who believe in him. Like Christ, he wins the battle by losing it, for it is not until he has fallen before Orgoglio's blow that his shield of diamond loses its cover and reveals its power:

> And in his fall his shield, that covered was,
> Did loose his vele by chaunce, and open flew:
> The light whereof, that heavens light did pas, . . .
>
> [I. viii. 19]

---

[1] Kathleen Williams, p. 22.

It is this which makes Orgoglio quite unable 'For to have slaine the man, that on the ground did lye'. We have here the image of Christ crucified and then resurrected and the suggestion, too, that as the Fall serves to reveal the shield, so the first Adam inevitably leads to the second. But Arthur is also the perfect knight of Holiness, the hero who has specifically put on the body of Christ, and in this role his perfect faith gives him the strength to rise again without any danger of the despair which besets Red Cross throughout so much of his quest. Arthur provides simultaneously an example of the perfect Christian, a definition of Christian faith, and an allegory of divine Grace working within the heart of Red Cross himself.

Red Cross's physical passions were the prime cause of his fall but his ignorance of the true redeeming power of faith is what keeps him down, and Arthur's next task, therefore, is to rescue him from the prison of this ignorance. He breaks down the doors, and throughout the whole episode there runs the symbolism of the Gospel redeeming man from the prison of the Law. The sight of Red Cross's wasted body, we are told, 'Could make a stony hart his hap to rew' [I. viii. 41]; and the reference is the common one to Moses's tablets of stone.[1] The victory of Orgoglio over Red Cross, as Professor Heninger has argued,[2] embodies not only the Fall of man but the judgement of God and the wholesome sufferings under the Law which it inflicts. Sin itself purifies by its own intrinsic painfulness, and the way to Arthur has to be through Orgoglio's prison. In this way Red Cross is saved; and the drops of Christ's blood in a box of the same diamond as the shield, which Arthur gives, and the Testament offered by Red Cross in return [I. ix. 19], round off the lesson of redemption offered through the sacrament and faith pledged in the Word.

Although Red Cross's sins, original and acquired, are now forgiven and his burden removed, he has yet to demonstrate his reborn capacity for virtue. He is especially vulnerable, because the deep knowledge of his own past guilt which his adventures

---

[1] Rosemond Tuve, *A Reading of George Herbert* (London and Chicago, 1965), part I, pp. 27 ff.

[2] S. K. Heninger, 'The Orgoglio Episode in *The Faerie Queene*', *ELH* 26 (1959), 171–87.

have taught him is masked by a superficial confidence in his new found faith; and at this moment, when he is fresh from the prison of ignorance, when his faith is largely based on emotion and has no backing in knowledge, Despair, the final sin of all, attacks him on the rebound. As of old, he rushes into the fray, 'With fierie zeale he burnt in courage bold' [I. ix. 37], but his over-confidence is quickly punctured by the memory of his guilt and his sense of the justice of Despair's charge that 'he should die, who merites not to live'. Despair holds out death as an infinitely appealing escape from the never-ending struggles of living,

> Sleepe after toyle, port after stormie seas,
> Ease after warre, death after life doth greatly please.
>
> [I. ix. 40]

and at the same time confuses him from another direction with the fear of eternal damnation. Like Marlowe's Faustus quoting Jerome's Bible, Red Cross remembers the Law but not the Gospel—'Is not he just. . ./Is not his law, Let every sinner die': he is bemused by the ambiguities of the word 'die'—'Die shall all flesh'—and by scraps of half-remembered theological argument:

> Shall he thy sins up in his knowledge fold,
> And guiltie be of thine impietie?   [I. ix. 47]

Only just in time can Una prompt him to remember that God is not just but merciful—'In heavenly mercies hast thou not a part' [I. ix. 53].

This is enough to banish Despair; but faith based on emotional needs is not adequate, and Red Cross's theology is clearly rusty. Una leads him, therefore, to the House of Holiness to be trained in the doctrines of the church, 'Of God, of Grace, of Justice, of freewill', doctrines which, based as they are on revelation, are beyond the reach of understanding by itself:

> And heavenly documents thereout did preach
> That weaker wit of man could never reach,   [I. x. 19]

—but towards which the understanding inevitably directs him. The house of Holiness is a house of Christian theology, beginning

in Faith, leading into the Hope which gives strength for the
Patience to undergo Penance, after which—and not until
then—the good deeds of Charity are possible. To conclude the
sequence, Spenser draws attention to the source of it all, not in
the understanding but in the vision of the hill of Contemplation
to which Una leads Red Cross but which is beyond the scope of
her powers. He sees his mystic vision alone while Una awaits his
return 'with pensive mind' [I. x. 68].

At last Red Cross is ready to start out on his quest once more,
armed only as he was in canto I in his battered armour, but
aware now of its true nature and of the snares which may tempt
him to forget its powers. The dragon lying asleep on 'the sunny
side/Of a great hill' is an emblem of both pride and sloth; and its
blazing eyes, 'As two broad Beacons, set in open fields', give
it a topical quality in terms of the Armada. Red Cross falls before
it as he fell at the beginning, and as Arthur himself fell; but
now he has the certainty of faith to succour him—the well of
Christ's blood which 'unto life the dead it could restore', the
tree of life, Christ's cross, which answers Adam's tree [I. xi. 46]
—so that even when the dragon's sting penetrates his shield, he
can rise again with 'baptised hands' and slay it on the symbolic
third morning.

Such is the Christian victory, and as Red Cross has put on the
body of Christ, so Una takes off her veil. Once more she is
described in terms of Diana,

> As faire *Diana* in fresh sommers day
> Beholds her Nymphes, enraung'd in shadie wood,
> Some wrestle, some do run, some bathe in christall flood.
>
> [I. xii. 7]

In rejecting Duessa for Una, Red Cross has corrected the wrong
choice which he made at the beginning of the poem; yet it does
not turn out to be a simple choice between the Diana of virtue
and the Venus of pleasure. The Diana of the simile has forgiven
her lazy nymphs and is allowing them to rest in the shade and
bathe in the fountain which, from being 'as cleare as cristall
glas' when Red Cross drank of it [I. vii. 6], has now developed
into the 'christall flood' with its more emphatic Christian
allusion. In the same way, Una herself has changed from the

ascetic virgin whom Red Cross abandoned for metal more attractive to a more fruitful virgin who, like Britomart, is on the threshold of marriage. On the level of theology, she has become the bride of Christ who is truest and most pleasing when open to most men. Fidelia is on the way to becoming one with Charitas. In other words, for Spenser the Christian way is that in which pleasure and virtue meet, and Una herself must allow for the human need which gives Duessa her eternal appeal.

This is only canto XI, however, and Archimago is to appear again: the battle has been won this time, but the very assumption of holiness is that the same battle will have to be lost and won again and again, and there is fine irony in the description of the children playing round the body of the dead dragon while the anxious mothers wonder whether there might yet remain

> Some lingring life within his hollow brest,
> Or in his wombe might lurke some hidden nest
> Of many Dragonets, his fruitfull seed; [I. xii. 10]

The structure of the poem, however, is schematic, not dramatic, and once the way to Holiness has been charted, it does not have to be explored again. Although the subsequent heroes all fall in their respective ways, none of them has to face despair, and all start in the basic security of faith. In a sense all the heroes of *The Faerie Queene* form one hero who, beginning in holiness, goes on to explore and learn the nature of virtue in area after area of human life. One should remember, in the face of what might seem to be the cynicism of book V, that the facts of faith are laid firmly down at the beginning of the poem and that the rest must be read in the light of this.

The unique quality of book I springs from the extraordinary psychological detail in which Spenser examines the processes of Christian hope and despair. As a study of someone wanting to have his cake and eat it, to do what he wants and yet retain a clear conscience, book I presents the whole cycle from redemption to deadly sin and back again, the cycle of which Macbeth demonstrates only the first half, for he never escapes from Orgoglio's dungeon. The mainspring of Red Cross's progress is the unhappiness which accompanies the state of sin and is the means of his education in virtue. In tracing this process,

Spenser takes his reader through a full-scale analysis of the nature of the Christian faith, both in terms of abstract theology in the House of Holiness and in the terms of human drama through the story of man. He has energised doctrine by projecting it through the normal experiences of human life and evoking the memories of temptation, despair and relief which most Christians have undergone. He has, moreover, analysed the logic of temptation and held up for inspection the apparently harmless minor rebellions which yet lead so inevitably to the major ones, the hair-breadth escapes which, in breeding over-confidence, lead to a fall. Book I makes a plea for unceasing self-awareness and mental vigilance; virtue demands above all that we use our brains. Although Spenser speaks to anyone who for any reason has ever suffered from a guilty conscience, his rhetoric is aimed specifically at the Christian, and is designed not to establish the efficacy of faith for the unbeliever but to remind the believer what it feels like to be without it. The reader of this kind should come out at the end of book I more knowledgeable in the nature of his faith, more able to answer his doubts, and with greater confidence, as a result of his vicarious passage from faith to unfaith and back again.

6

Temperance

[1]

St George bears the cross of Christ upon his shield but Guyon, carrying the image of Gloriana, is the knight of the Quest par excellence, the first for whom strictly heroic virtue is possible from the start. Red Cross becomes both the patron saint of England and one of the glorious company of saints who are justified by their faith:

> For which enrolled is your glorious name
> In heavenly Registers above the Sunne,
> Where you a Saint with Saints your seat have wonne:
>
> [II. i. 32]

and in this justification the separate heroes who follow, and who together make up the collective Everyman of the poem, are able to explore their special fields of virtue. Faith makes virtue not only possible but obligatory and provides the motive for the Quest, and for this reason book II and all the subsequent books come down from the plane of belief to that of virtuous action. Una, conceived in the image of the Virgin, accompanied by Christ, the lamb, has her eyes turned upward towards the source of light and is motivated by love: Guyon's Palmer, in contrast, always has his eyes upon the road—'Still he him guided over dale and hill'—and personifies the same right-reason as Una, though directed downwards now to the rational control and conduct of life. Guyon has to meet and overcome the same enemies as Red Cross, the blind energies of aggression and the seductive impulse to relax; but where, in book I, these were analysed as obstacles in the path of faith, they are now presented as basic energies to be mastered and used in the pursuit of active virtue.

The proem marks the change of direction and the descent from matters of eternity to those of time. Book II, with its chronicle of Briton kings, is set in the world of history and begins with a justification of that 'famous antique history' for whose authenticity there is no proof. Spenser's defence of his land of Faerie is based on what must have seemed very valid grounds to an age in which equally improbable countries were continually found true:

> Who ever heard of th'Indian *Peru?*
> Or who in venturous vessell measured
> The *Amazons* huge river now found trew?
> Or fruitfullest *Virginia* who did ever vew?
>
> Yet all these were, when no man did them know;
> Yet have from wisest ages hidden beene: [proem. 2–3]

Virginia was much in the news at the time and of special interest to Spenser in view of Raleigh's connection with the colony; but the paradox of 'fruitfullest Virginia' applies both to the riches of the new country and to the virgin queen herself after whom it was named and whose fruitful reign it celebrated. Spenser is associating the world of active virtue in which his poem is set with the active life and the expanding political enterprise of the Elizabethan age. He is doing more than this, however: the paradox of 'fruitfullest Virginia' leads us to a deeper level of Gloriana's mystery, to the Virgin Mary, whose literal fruitfulness has provided the theme for book I and is the justification of the virtue of book II. In this context, the apparently otiose adjective, 'living', in the first stanza of the proem takes on a very literal truth:

> Sith none, that breatheth living aire, does know,
> Where is that happy land of Faery,

and the reference to the 'antiquities, which no body can know' which have been hidden from 'wisest ages' and are still not believed by 'witlesse' man, all become covert references to the truths only accessible to faith. Faerie is the place where heaven and earth meet in the virtue incarnate, and active virtue has its basis in a lively faith. The concept of the 'fruitful virgin' is central to *The Faerie Queene*, finding its embodiment, in one way, in the virgin Britomart whose quest is to win a father for her child and, in another, in Gloriana or Belphoebe whose fruits are in their deeds. The term itself implies the paradox of the fusion of Venus and Diana, which is Spenser's formula for virtue, and for which the holy virgin provides both emblem and sanction. It is appropriate that Spenser should introduce his 'fruitfullest Virginia' in the proem to the book of Temperance, the virtue specifically concerned with the nature of the mean.

[2]

The heroes have to achieve their quests in the fallen world, a fact which Spenser underlines by opening the second book not with Guyon but with 'That cunning Architect of cancred guile', Archimago, who escaped the moment Red Cross departed out of 'Eden Lands' and is now on the lookout for his next victim. A few stanzas later, Duessa, too, reappears on the scene, a fallen Eve,

> Lurking in rockes and caves farre under ground,
> And with greene mosse cov'ring her nakednesse,
> To hide her shame. . .   [II. i. 22]

In between is sandwiched the description of Guyon, setting out on his journey with the complete armour and impeccable horsemanship of firm faith and academic temperance. His vulnerability, to which Spenser quickly draws attention, lies in the very violence of his virtue: the rigorous self-control which he exercises and the self-repression it demands breed a passionate reaction which, even in a good cause, can itself be a form of intemperance. The salacious tale of the maiden's rape told, inevitably, by Archimago, moves him as it could only move a repressed personality; and at once laying aside his 'sober mood', he rushes off 'with fierce ire/And zealous haste', all 'inflam'd with wrathfulnesse', to execute justice. It is the same dangerous zeal which carried Red Cross into Error's den, and Guyon is in constant danger of being betrayed by his passion for truth and right. On this first occasion of temptation, the first demonstration of the sinister nature of the hag Occasion, who appears in canto IV, Guyon has sufficient temperance to control his horse in time, and it is St George who 'his steede could stay uneath';

but Guyon is to have little chance to use his excellent horse-manship throughout his quest.

Temperance is a general quality of rational self-control which enters into the nature of all virtue, and for this reason book II opens with a series of great emblematic tableaux of relevance not only to Guyon but to all the subsequent heroes. The first of these is the episode of Mordant and Amavia which has, at its centre, the very puzzling riddle of Acrasia over her charmed cup:

> Sad verse, give death to him that death does give,
> And losse of love, to her that loves to live,
> So soone as Bacchus with the Nymphe does lincke:

[II. i. 55]

Although allegory itself is by rhetorical definition akin to the enigma, there is nothing else in the poem of the same deliberate obscurity, and it must be assumed, therefore, that in setting it at the forefront of the book, Spenser is establishing the riddle form itself as a part of the total allegory. He is drawing attention to the fact, perhaps, that the world into which Guyon has just entered is a confusing and ambiguous place in which virtue itself can become a vice and vice a virtue, and the most necessary human instincts are the most dangerous. Guyon will be faced with a number of moral dilemmas which will demand all his intelligence to cope with, and even that will not be enough. Neither he nor the reader is expected to know the answer at the beginning: that is something which will only emerge gradually through the trials and errors of experience and will not be wholly plain until the end of the poem. One can guess at the start, however, that because the charm is Acrasia's, it will be deceitful; that what she calls a 'sad verse' will not turn out to be so, and that her promise of death will, rightly apprehended, be revealed as a promise of life.

There have been many attempts to interpret the oracle, most of them involving some reference to theology. Professor Hamilton, for example, has drawn attention to the unmistakable references to Original Sin and the Fall, in the blood which the child gets upon its hands from the sin and death of its parents.[1]

---

[1] A. C. Hamilton, 'A Theological Reading of *The Faerie Queene*, Book II', *ELH* 25 (1958), 155–62.

On the other hand, Alastair Fowler has interpreted it in terms of baptismal regeneration.[1] He argues very cogently that the waters of the nymph are those of baptism and penance; that Mordant is the flesh, Amavia the soul which would rescue him from sin; and his death from drinking of the water, therefore, after his escape from Acrasia, signifies the death of the old Adam. The child accordingly is the new man he puts on with the death of the old, and its hands remain bloody because regenerate man still carries the stain of Original Sin in his nature, even though he is free of the burden of guilt. In taking up the child and making its cause his own, Guyon shows himself to start his quest where Red Cross left off, in a state of Christian regeneration.

Dr Fowler's exposition certainly explains more of the details of the episode than any other and leads also to a conclusion which seems to me incontrovertible: Guyon begins his quest in the possession of faith, which is why, when the occasion comes, he does not fall into despair. My own route to this conclusion would, however, be a very different one. The virgin waters of the nymph in their cold purity bear no resemblance to the life-giving waters as they appear in book I, in the Well of Life:

> For unto life the dead it could restore,
> And guilt of sinfull crimes cleane wash away
>
> [I. xi. 30]

and I find the general tone of the interpretation untrue to the text. The death of the old Adam, although a painful process for the flesh, should still presumably fill the soul with some degree of hope and joy, yet Amavia dies in despairing love of the flesh, 'As heaven accusing guiltie of her death' [II. i. 49], and it is Mordant who dies with so cheerful a smile upon his ruddy lips.

Mordant, as his name defines him, is clearly to be identified with 'him that death does give', the mortal, fallen flesh—'For he was flesh: (all flesh doth frailtie breed)'; And Amavia, by the same token, must be 'her that loves to live', although her name would suggest equally the way of love. I would interpret her love of life, in contrast to Dr Fowler, as a love belonging to

---

1 Alastair Fowler, 'The Image of Mortality: *The Faerie Queene*, II, 1–2', *The Huntington Library Quarterly* XXIV (1961).

body not soul: she gives birth to the child; and when she describes her rescue of Mordant from the Bower of Blisse, it is in a series of sexual puns which suggest an escape from one kind of physical love to a better kind rather than from the physical to the spiritual:

> Him so I sought, and so at last I found,
>   Where him that witch had thralled to her will,
>   In chaines of lust and lewd desires ybound,
>   And so transformed from his former skill,
>   That me he knew not, neither his owne ill;
>   Till through wise handling and faire gouvernance,
>   I him recured to a better will, . . . [II. i. 54]

The ambiguities of 'will', 'that me he knew not', point in this direction, and suggest that in giving him back his former skill she is removing him from the sterile embraces of Acrasia to her own more fruitful ones. Amavia kills herself for grief at the loss of this sexual love, and her action expresses the traditional tragedy of love when it attaches itself wholly to whatever is mortal, ephemeral and corrupt. Mordant lying there, beautiful, death-giving and himself dead with Amavia beside him, presents an emblem of human mortality and intemperance, as Guyon defines it in his speech over the dead bodies:

> Behold the image of mortalitie,
> And feeble nature cloth'd in fleshly tyre,
> When raging passion with fierce tyrannie
> Robs reason of her due regalitie,
> And makes it servant to her basest part: [II. i. 57]

The cryptic last line of Acrasia's prophecy, however, 'So soone as Bacchus with the Nymphe does lincke', suggests a further dimension to the allegory. At this point of the poem, Bacchus clearly anticipates the values of Acrasia: it is his wine which fills Excesse's cup at the gate of the Bower, and his boat which takes Phaedria and her servants there. In popular iconography the god of wine was depicted in a boat with a vine growing at one end very similar to Phaedria's little bower. As he represents sensual excess at one end of the scale, the Nymph, fleeing all contact with human sensuality, represents the other extreme; and we have here again the confrontation between sensuous pleasure and ascetic virtue, between Venus and Diana. Acrasia and the nymph alike are forms of excess, the one in her complete acceptance of sensuality, the other in her refusal to sully her waters with any stain of Original Sin. The virgin fountain of the nymph would certainly destroy Mordant in destroying all flesh, but she is as sterile as Acrasia, and her answer to sin is no more adequate.

Once more, Spenser's choice of Hercules is not the simple one between the ladies of pleasure and virtue but between two opposed forms of intemperance, which demands a greater degree of moral discrimination and a fine perception of the point when virtue itself becomes a form of vice. Guyon acknowledges the inadequacy of the two extremes represented by Bacchus and the Nymph: in picking up the child with its bloody hands, he shows an acceptance of the sinful human state of which the nymph is incapable; and in taking it to Medina, he seeks a temperance alien to Acrasia. His task is to find a middle way between the two excesses of sensuality and asceticism, to discipline the fallen flesh without denying it altogether. Temperance is in the most general terms the virtue designed to solve the human dilemma and heal the unnatural division into extremes which the Fall has brought about, but it is a lesson which all the subsequent heroes have to master in their own specific fields of virtue: Britomart has to steer her way between virginity and lust; Artegall between the letter of the law and indiscriminate mercy; Calidore between idealism and the claims of the real. Each of Spenser's virtues is itself a specific Golden Mean between Bacchus and the Nymph in one form or another. The marriage and fusion of the two would destroy all extremes of intemperance and be a recipe for virtue, which is one reason why Acrasia calls the charm a 'sad' verse, and warns her devotees not against the nymph but against her union with Bacchus.

The linking of Bacchus with the nymph, however, is more than a definition of temperance; it is, after all, a mixing of wine with water, and as such, it brings to mind the mixture of wine and water in Fidelia's cup in the House of Holiness which, deriving from the miracle of Christ's turning the water into wine, forms part of the emblem of faith:

> And in her right hand bore a cup of gold,
> With wine and water fild up to the hight,
> In which a Serpent did himselfe enfold,
> That horrour made to all, that did behold;
> But she no whit did chaunge her constant mood;
>
> [I. x. 13]

This could be a description of Acrasia's riddle which, while seeming to imply death, yet carries a promise of life to the eye of faith able to comprehend such 'darke things...hard to be understood'. The faith which is unafraid of the old serpent within the cup is the same which gives 'death to him that death does give', not only in the sense of the mortal body but of the ultimate giver of death, Satan himself. Temperance and faith, for Spenser, go hand in hand, both springing out of the same rational instinct; and for this reason the actions of the Palmer in subduing the passions are often modelled on those of Christ.

If we accept this theological level of meaning above, yet parallel to, the ethical one, we shall find that the other episodes of the sequence drop into place along with Acrasia's charm. The nymph, as we have seen, is Diana's maid, and her story is based ultimately on that of Arethusa's escape from Alpheus in *Metamorphoses*, V, but Spenser describes her in terms which suggest a further level of interpretation. The most curious thing about his description is the reference to stones which occurs four times in a very few lines:

> The goddesse heard, and suddeine where she sate,
> Welling out streames of teares, and quite dismayd
> With stony feare of that rude rustick mate,
> Transformed her to a stone from steadfast virgins state.
>
> Lo now she is that stone, from whose two heads,
> As from two weeping eyes, fresh streames do flow,
> Yet cold through feare, and old conceived dreads;
> And yet the stone her semblance seemes to show,
> Shapt like a maid, that such ye may her know;

> And yet her Vertues in her water byde:
> For it is chast and pure, as purest snow, . . .
>
> [II. ii. 8-9]

Alastair Fowler has drawn attention to the traditional symbolism of baptism and penance which the nymph carries, but he has ignored the reference to the tablets of the Law which Spenser and his age so commonly include under any reference to stones: the world of Justice in book V, for example, is described as one of stone, instead of the iron which we should expect in the context:

> For from the golden age, that first was named,
> It's now at earst become a stonie one; [proem. V. 2]

It would seem that Spenser is identifying the harsh remedial discipline of Diana with the rigours of the old Law, and that the waters which slay Mordant when he drinks of them are those of the Divine Justice to which Despair has already alluded in book I:

> Is not his law, Let every sinner die:
> Die shall all flesh? [I. ix. 47]

In this sense, Acrasia can legitimately call her charm a 'sad verse' as opposed to the joyfulness of the Gospels: she is, in fact, warning sinners who look like escaping from her clutches of the divine and terrible justice which awaits them, and so tempting them to despair as we should expect her to.

But the old Law has a dual nature: it slays but it also saves, in that it both prepares for and foreshadows the Gospel. Spenser acknowledges this when in book I he compares the blood flowing from the wound which Arthur gives to Orgoglio to the water which flowed from the rock when Moses struck it (Numbers, 20:11):

> Large streames of bloud out of the trunked stocke
> Forth gushed, like fresh water streame from riven rocke.
>
> [I. viii. 10]

The waters flowing from Moses's rock had long been interpreted as a prophecy of Christ's redeeming blood,[1] and Spenser's

---

[1] Rosemond Tuve, *A Reading of George Herbert*, part I, pp. 27-9.

description of the nymph's fountain seems to hint in the same way at the traditional sense of the relationship between Old and New Testaments. The waters suggest the grief and sufferings under the Law, 'through feare and old conceived dreads', and yet the stones from which they flow remind us of the form of the maiden:

> And yet the stone her semblance seemes to show,
> Shapt like a maid, that such ye may her know;
>
> [II. ii. 9]

It seems to me that Spenser's only purpose in including such a detail is to draw upon the tradition of Biblical exegesis in order to suggest the form of the blessed virgin-to-come within the stony image. Even the cold waters of the fountain contain a promise of regeneration, and what slays will be the ultimate means of redemption.

If we turn now to the child who is the survivor of the whole sad relationship, we shall find the same ambivalent quality. As an image of mortality and the Original Sin inherited from the Fall, he fulfils Acrasia's prophecy of death to the letter; yet as a new-born child he embodies that eternity by succession which is the flesh's answer to mortality and, in opposition both to Acrasia and to the nymph, leads on to Britomart's mission to be the mother of a line of kings. He symbolises life as well as death, and in more ways than the merely physical. The child dips his hands in his mother's blood because she sins and dies, and he does so very joyfully:

> Als in her lap a lovely babe did play
> His cruell sport, in stead of sorrow dew;
> For in her streaming blood he did embay
> His little hands, and tender joynts embrew;...
>
> [II. i. 40]

There could be an allusion here to the Christ child who, through the Fall of Adam, takes on human corruption and, bearing on his hands the stigmata of sin, carries thereby the promise of redemption which his Incarnation makes possible. The very blood on his hands becomes the justification of his mother's innocence,

But let them still be bloudy, as befell,
That they his mothers innocence may tell,   [II. ii. 10]

and attaches a new level of meaning to Amavia, whether we
translate her name as the love of life or the way of love. The
child himself embodies a riddle, like Southwell's 'Burning
Babe', or even more, like the bloody child in *Macbeth* who also
points towards death or life according to the way you read him.
One wonders how much Shakespeare owed to Spenser's
episode both here and in the hand-washing scene.

We must bring to this section of the poem the same sort of
awareness that we bring to the poetry of George Herbert, and
recognise that Spenser's initial use of the riddle is his hint that
we should look below the surface. If we do so, we find a very
concentrated statement both of the nature of virtue and of the
faith which dictates the form that virtue must take. In giving
the child to his Palmer to carry, Guyon is giving rational
assent to Christian theology, and in carrying Mordant's bloodied
armour he accepts as his lot the burden and the hope of man's
fallen state. His avoidance of the way of the nymph and his
acceptance of the quest to destroy Acrasia will ultimately
transform Mordant into Verdant and turn the Bacchus of
Acrasia's charm into Bacchus, the Law-giver of v. i. 2. Faunus,
too, will undergo a metamorphosis between his attempted rape
of Diana's nymph in book II and his second encounter with
Diana in the *Mutability Cantos*, where he plays the more
innocent role of Actaeon. The difference between the grief and
tears of the first episode and the laughter and tolerance of the
second is very marked, and demonstrates the fulfilment of
Acrasia's riddle through the intervening book. Faunus, as
Dr Fowler has shown, is the symbol of concupiscence, the embodiment of fallen human nature which in its flesh sins, and in its
lusts begets. In so doing he provides the channel by which the
mortal escapes mortality, and so he is spared: Diana's nymphs
neither kill nor geld him, for the Wood-Gods' breed 'must for
ever live' [VII. vi. 50]. Physical desire makes possible the
Incarnation and is in turn made holy by it. Spenser's answer to
Faunus and the nymph is the marriage of Thames and Medway,
an Alpheus and Arethusa who in due time come together in

holy union, no longer left asunder as in Ovid's myth. The point is made more explicitly in the *Mutability Cantos*, where Molanna finally marries her Fanchin.

[3]

The temperance which Guyon seeks is not Aristotelean but Christian, based on the assumption of the Fall and having, as a necessary addition, the faith to fall back on when the need inevitably arises. As soon as Guyon takes up the child and accepts the quest associated with it, he discovers that he has lost his horse—'his loftie steed with golden sell,/And goodly gorgeous barbes'—and this follows logically: there is no place for his splendid and perfect horsemanship on the quest he has to follow, and it is appropriate, as we shall see, that Braggadocio is the thief. Medina, with whom he leaves the child, has little of the Aristotelean magnanimity: with her golden locks at first 'roundly uptied' but soon dishevelled in her attempts to keep peace between Sans Loy and his fellows, she offers a rueful picture of idealism beset by the pressures of human irrationality. This is the state of things for which Belphoebe offers a remedy.

The sudden and isolated appearance of Belphoebe in canto III has aroused much controversy. Professor Berger,[1] for example, sees her as the epitome of classical as opposed to Christian temperance: Miss Williams[2] finds her chilling, inhuman and slightly ludicrous, the embodiment of those splendid qualities which Guyon rightly abandons when he loses his noble horse. Neither of these interpretations strikes me as being tenable, if for no other reason than that Spenser establishes her through a great tableau, and raises her to so great and striking a stature. The fact, which has often been pointed out, that he models her on Venus as she appears to Aeneas to direct him on his heroic way at the beginning of the *Aeneid*, is a guarantee of her especially sacred significance. Throughout the long description, Belphoebe is systematically built up into the embodiment of an idealism at once Christian and Platonic. Her face is a 'heavenly

---

[1] Harry Berger, *The Allegorical Temper. Vision and Reality in Book II of Spenser's Faerie Queene*, Yale Studies in English, CXXXVII (New Haven, 1957).
[2] *Spenser's World of Glass*, pp. 49–52.

pourtraict of bright Angels hew' [II. iii. 22]; her eyes are living lamps

> Kindled above at th' heavenly makers light,
> And darted fyrie beames out of the same,
> So passing persant, . . .   [II. iii. 23]

in contrast to the 'fierie beames' of Acrasia, which are mere star-light on water in comparison [II. xii. 78]. Her forehead is like a table for love to engrave his 'loftie' triumphs upon, and her legs resemble two marble pillars 'Which doe the temple of the Gods support' [II. iii. 28]. It is a sustained, deeply religious icon, a 'glorious mirrhour of celestiall grace', which derives to a considerable degree from the *Song of Solomon* and at times seems to evoke the image of Christ, 'Hable to heale the sicke, and to revive the ded' [II. iii. 22].

She is the virgin servant of Diana, but it is essential to recognise that she is in no way identical with the virgin nymph of canto II or with Florimel in the next book. Hers is an active virginity which does not flee from the impurities of the world but goes into the midst and hunts the evil passions. She embodies, in fact, the aggressive instinct, tending towards asceticism, which the Fall has made necessary to defeat the ever-present temptation of sloth; and though she does not represent the whole of morality or the final ethic of the poem, she expresses the primary essential discipline without which a complete temperance is impossible. Spenser's description emphasises not only what she is, but what she leads on to, in terms of both Christian and Platonic morality. I would argue, against Dr Ellrodt,[1] that the penultimate stanzas of the description establish her in the role of the Platonic Venus Urania whose spiritual contemplation of the divine forms breeds the desire to propagate them in her younger, carnal but equally sanctified sister, Venus Dione. The relationship of the two sisters is, I think, alluded to in the curious sequences of stanzas, numbers 29 and 30:

> Her daintie paps; which like young fruit in May
> Now little gan to swell, and being tide,
> Through her thin weed their places only signifide.

[1] Robert Ellrodt, *Neoplatonism in the Poetry of Spenser*, Travaux d'Humanisme et Renaissance, XXXV (Geneva, 1960).

Her yellow lockes crisped, like golden wyre,
About her shoulders weren loosely shed . . .
And low behinde her backe were scattered:
And whether art it were, or heedlesse hap,
As through the flouring forrest rash she fled,
In her rude haires sweet flowres themselves did lap,
And flourishing fresh leaves and blossomes did enwrap.
[II. iii. 29–30]

The earlier reference to the 'loftie' triumphs of love proper to
Belphoebe is appropriate to the Venus Urania; but the breasts
beginning to form, and even more, the flowers in her hair,
suggest that her mode of spiritual love leads on to the procreative love of her sister. The flowers recall the Flora towards
whom Botticelli's Venus moves as she rises from the sea, or the
nymph transformed to Flora by the divine breath in the
Primavera, as Professor Wind interprets it.[1] Like Guyon,
Belphoebe herself has no time for love but she makes love
possible.

The final and very puzzling stanza of the description uses the
central myths of the poem to make what seems to me the same
point in more specifically Christian terms:

Such as *Diana* by the sandie shore
Of swift *Eurotas*, or on *Cynthus* greene,
Where all the Nymphes have her unwares forlore,
Wandreth alone with bow and arrowes keene,
To seeke her game: Or as that famous Queene
Of *Amazons*, whom *Pyrrhus* did destroy,
The day that first of *Priame* she was seene,
Did shew herselfe in great triumphant joy,
To succour the weake state of sad afflicted Troy.
[II. iii. 31]

Professor Berger recognised that the two similes pull in different directions, the triumphant Diana contrasting with the
tragic Penthesilea, and suggested that they embody the contrast

[1] Edgar Wind, *Pagan Mysteries in the Renaissance* (Peregrine Books, 1967),
chaps. VII and VIII.

between the classical and the Christian definitions of temperance, the one based on human self-sufficiency, the other on human weakness and the need for Grace.[1] This is an over-simplification, in that Diana is shown as a lonely figure deserted by her nymphs, while Penthesilea's tragedy involves an element of triumph; and the interpretation ignores, moreover, the significance which Spenser attaches to both the goddess and the amazon throughout the poem. I have suggested, in connection with Mordant and Amavia, that Spenser associates the rigorous austerities of Diana with the discipline of the Old Law; and the reference to succouring the weak state of sad afflicted Troy suggests that he is at this point associating Penthesilea with the mercy of the New. She is on the heroic side in the Trojan story, and is quoted among the heroines of love in the next book [III. iv. 2]. Her heroism lies in her sacrifice, as Diana's in the unflagging labours of the chase, and together they make up the full circle of salvation. Spenser's juxtaposition of the two forms a parallel to his reference to the two Venuses in stanzas 29 and 30, and suggests again that Belphoebe's labours prepare the way for Grace and for love.

Since she is so important in the scheme of the book and of the poem, one must ask why she makes her appearance not to Guyon but to the wholly unworthy Braggadocio. There are several possible reasons for this. In the first place, although Belphoebe is at this point modelled on Virgil's Venus, Guyon is not primarily a figure of Aeneas, in spite of the occasional echo, as when, for example, he tells his story to Medina 'From lofty siege' in imitation of Aeneas with Dido. Guyon in his pursuit of self-control has no desire to found a line of kings, and the pattern of his quest is that of the wise Odysseus: there are others in the poem for whom the pattern of Aeneas is more strictly appropriate; in particular, Arthur and Artegall who are of the line of Aeneas and more directly concerned with the founding of the third Troy. In book II the truly Virgilian exploit is that of Arthur when he kills Maleger in imitation of Aeneas's fight with Turnus. Furthermore, Guyon does not derive the source and inspiration of his quest from Belphoebe as Aeneas derives his

[1] Pp. 123 ff.

from Venus. The motive of Guyon's quest springs from the Christian faith and has already been dealt with at the beginning of the book in his meeting with Red Cross. Belphoebe's function is not so much to express the motive of the quest—though that is implied in the imagery by which she is described—as to define the nature of the action necessary for its achievement. To bring this definition into greater prominence, therefore, Spenser confronts her with her opposite, Braggadocio. If her code is based on the acceptance of the Fall and the possibilities of amendment which human nature still possesses, his code, like that of Acrasia, denies the Fall altogether and the need of labour to repair the ruins. Braggadocio seeks the results without the labours, and his confrontation with Belphoebe anticipates that of Guyon with Acrasia, the harsh, sweating realism of the one faced with the delusive fantasy of the other. That is why Braggadocio is the proper person to have Guyon's splendid horse and is prepared to take Arthur's sword [II. iii. 18]; they offer an apparent short cut to Fame which the nature of the fallen world makes illusory. Though a comic figure he is an important one, since representative of a human instinct at once common and very dangerous, and Spenser makes out of the meeting, therefore, a great set piece.

Throughout book II, Belphoebe provides the touchstone for values and the norm from which all the other characters are the variants. Pyrochles has her energy without her controlling vision, while the cave of Mammon shows that energy applied to the wrong purposes: the labour and sweat of the devils as they toil at their furnaces forms an infernal parody of all that Belphoebe stands for—'And every one did swincke, and every one did sweat' [II. vii. 36]. There is no sleeping or sloth in the presence of self-consuming care, but such labour, for Honours not for Honour, has no virtue in it. At the other extreme are the characters who do no work at all, such as Cymochles who lies in the bed of lilies, and Phaedria who makes the symbolism of this fact clear by referring to the lilies of the field [II. vi. 16], and blurs the distinction between the lily and the rose. Her little boat goes without the need of oar or pilot, whereas Guyon has to cross the Idle lake by the sweat of his boatman and the unceasing vigilance of his Palmer.

[4]

Guyon's task is to emulate Belphoebe's rigorous virtue, and before sending him on his way, Spenser gives a warning of the special dangers in the path of his ardent moral idealism. Battling with vice can exhaust the powers of rational control and make the virtuous man subject to the passions which he is opposing; and once these have a hold, they are uncontrollable by reason, as we have already seen from Una's ineffective struggle to escape from Sans Loy. The episode of Occasion, therefore, contradicts the usual assumption about the need to take her by the forelock and suggests that, whenever possible, she is better left alone. The motto of book II could be 'Lead us not into unnecessary temptation'. There is such a thing as intemperance even in virtue, and a main lesson which Guyon has to learn is to husband the limited stock of moral energy which a mortal man possesses. He has to know when to avoid as well as to attack, and to discover that the way to defeat Acrasia is by making judicious allowance for the human weakness from which she draws her strength.

His journey lies between the extremes of Pyrochles and Acrasia, and his special problem is to avoid the way of Cymochles who, although partaking of both, represents an alternation, not a golden mean between the two. Cymochles swings from one to the other, an outbreak of bellicosity being followed by a retreat into the languors of the Bower; and his essential nature, as his name implies, is to fluctuate and waver between Impatience and Impotence. He represents the innate quality of human passion to flag when it has spent itself and then to flare up anew on the next occasion. His ebb and flow is the most insidious enemy to the controlled and steady effort which Belphoebe demands, the surest way to fall into one or the other extreme. Once in his company, Guyon swings between the extremes of violent action and slothful relaxation; and in over-compensating for what he recognises as the error of the latter, he drives himself too hard until he is reduced to impotent exhaustion. The page, Atin, runs from one brother to arouse the other and so presumably represents the unthinking impulse or the movement of the animal spirits by which we change from one to another mood. He has no thought or fear of the consequences and is described, therefore, by the very pithy emblem of a man bearing his shield on his back [II. iv. 38], in contrast to Fear, for example, who bears it on his right arm, instead of his sword [III. xii. 12].

Guyon first becomes aware of the insurrection of these passions after the Palmer has demonstrated the proper way to deal with Occasion. Atin immediately arrives and, announcing the approach of Pyrochles seeking Occasion [II. iv. 43], taunts Guyon with cowardice for being afraid of a 'silly weake old woman'. The consciousness of possessing self-control can breed complacency, and Guyon, out of a mixture of curiosity and over-confidence, is tempted to try out his newly discovered powers and prove that his self-mastery is equal to any occasion. He conquers Pyrochles by the wisdom he has learned from his reason, letting his angry impulses exhaust themselves by never grappling with them in direct ascetic opposition, as hunters kill the wrathful Unicorn by avoiding its charge. He now feels very confident of his ability to control his passions whose first insurrection he has so capably dealt with; and so, in a gesture of over-confidence, he frees Occasion, feeling that this particular battle is now permanently won and he need have no 'needlesse trouble of renewing fight/Already fought' [II. v. 25]. In this, he is already beginning to relax too soon and swing over to the quality of the other brother; and Atin accordingly hurries off to find Cymochles who is pleasantly slumbering in the Bower of Blisse underneath a stately tree:

> That dedicated is t'*Olympicke Jove*,
> And to his sonne *Alcides*, whenas hee
> Gaynd in *Nemea* goodly victoree;   [II. vi. 31]

The Nemean lion which Hercules slew is one with the lion which Wrath rode upon, and in conquering Pyrochles, Guyon feels he has deserved the same meed of victory as Hercules, even though his real battle has only just begun. That is why he steps into Phaedria's little boat upon the idle lake, leaving his Palmer behind him. The little bower at one end of it

> With boughes and arbours woven cunningly,
> That like a litle forrest seemed outwardly.   [II. vi. 2]

is a warning to the reader, though not to Guyon: it suggests both the dangerous art of the Bower of Blisse to be revealed later, and the general dangers of the forest.

Though wavering a little, Guyon has not yet fallen into intemperance, and he dislikes Phaedria's 'light behaviour, and loose dalliaunce'; but lacking his Palmer, he lacks the ability to recognise the dangerous temptation which her holiday mood presents—unlike the later occasion when he meets her on the way to the Bower and his Palmer abuses her roundly. Building, therefore, on the lesson he has already learned about the need to avoid Fury, he restrains his feelings and, only 'half discontent', he finally 'to that Damzell thankes gave for reward' [II. vi. 38]. He fights Cymochles when he meets him, but is quickly persuaded to a peace by Phaedria's sonnet talk of love. In this he has, after a brief moment of resistance, taken on Cymochles's own wavering nature, and Spenser underlines the point by so interweaving the stories of Guyon and Cymochles throughout the episode that it is difficult to tell at any one moment about which character he is talking. In literal terms, Guyon has swung from a mood of self-repression to one of self-indulgence which in its turn provokes the next mood of energy and action; and to mark this, Atin at once rushes away to arouse Pyrochles, whose enforced inactivity during Guyon's holiday from action is vividly portrayed in the burning agonies he suffers when plunged in the Idle lake. It is a curiously modern picture of repressed passions boiling within because lacking an outlet. Pyrochles is not to die, however: Archimago heals him [II. vi. 51], and in doing so asserts the permanence of these uncontrollable passions in Guyon's lower nature which, in due course, will have their turn again—'And dying daily, daily yet revive' [II. vi. 45].

Because he is now following the fluctuations of his passions and not guided by reason, Guyon finds no Palmer awaiting him when he comes to shore. Spenser is at pains, at the beginning of canto VII, to define the state which Guyon is in, like that of a pilot who, when his north star is hidden by cloud and storm, tries to steer by his card and compass, 'The maisters of his long experiment' [II. vii. 1]. Lacking the moral certainty which his right-reason once gave him, Guyon is now forced to steer his course by the knowledge which he has gleaned from his own previous experience, just as Red Cross pushed blindly and by habit towards a virtue which he could no longer clearly recognise in the absence of Una. He is not without self-confidence, and 'evermore himselfe with comfort feedes,/Of his owne vertues, and prayse-worthy deedes' [II. vii. 2], but the description is both pathetic and ominous. On this wrong course, he naturally finds no adventure 'Which fame of her shrill trompet worthy reedes', and instead wanders into the gloomy shade shut off from 'heavens light', where Mammon has his den.

The account of Mammon is perhaps the most controversial section of this controversial book. Professor Berger sees Guyon's passage through the cave as an exercise in idle curiosity for which he pays the penalty;[1] Professor Kermode interprets it as a triumphant saga in which like Christ in the wilderness he perfects his virtue;[2] Miss Williams takes it as an experience which, as a human being, Guyon had at some time to face, and from which he emerges triumphant even in his failure.[3] Spenser does not blame Guyon for going through the cave or fainting after it: like other heroes, Guyon is only human and bound to make mistakes; and these, indeed, are the means of his education and the only way he can learn the nature of virtue. The important thing for him is to discover exactly what the cave of Mammon has to teach. As a virtue relevant to every aspect of life, temperance has to come to terms with the thing of the world, and Mammon, the lord of wealth and worldly success, must presumably be faced in some guise, therefore.

The significant thing is that Guyon enters the cave without his Palmer—and indeed, he would never have entered it at all if his Palmer had been there, but would have given it a wide berth as he avoids both Phaedria and the great treasure ship on the way to the Bower. He enters it not by rational design but on an impulse, the swing of the pendulum which takes him from his sojourn with Phaedria and Cymochles over to the opposite extreme of moral activity: because he has relaxed into sloth, he

---

[1] Part I, section 1.
[2] F. Kermode, 'The Cave of Mammon', *Elizabethan Poetry*, chap. VIII, Stratford-upon-Avon Studies, no. 2 (London, 1960).
[3] Pp. 55–62.

over-corrects by an excess of active virtue and challenges something which need not have been challenged. Mammon does not, after all, represent the normal temptations of worldly success but an excess of these, the life devoted exclusively to material affairs which is never a serious temptation for Guyon. His whole journey is, in a sense, an academic exercise in virtue. He enters the cave, not because the gold tempts him, but out of curiosity to find where it all comes from and whether it is 'well got'; and he confirms what he already knows, that it is got in corruption. The vision of the fiends all fighting for the gold and Mammon's cynical comment:

> Loe here the worldes blis, loe here the end,
> To which all men do ayme, rich to be made:
> Such grace now to be happy, is before thee laid.
>
> [II. vii. 32]

explains why he sees the fruit of Proserpina's garden in its true colours.

Mammon lets him see the gold rather unwillingly and shows him the truth about it in a cynical way, scarcely bothering to tempt him; and he is certainly never moved as he is, for example, in the Bower of Blisse: he knows all the traditional answers to the traditional temptations. Guyon is very much a type of the idealist who enters the world of big business to see what it is all about, although conscious from the start that his own values are nobler ones. He lives in it, despising what he sees and showing that he is not to be bought, until by the end, big business scarcely offers to buy him. It is a waste of virtue upon something irrelevant to it, for the proper virtue there would be not temperance but justice, as Artegall demonstrates when he razes Munera's castle to the ground. In the meantime, Guyon's energies and his life are being wasted, and this vindication of a virtue which was never in doubt exacts a price in a roundabout way. Any sojourn in thoroughly alien surroundings takes its toll in draining the physical energy and weakening self-control; but more than this, the fact of being in such an environment blunts the sensibility and corrupts it to its own level, making it unfit to cope with any other. Having fed on smoke and darkness for the symbolic three days, Guyon is no longer fit to 'sucke this vitall aire into his brest' when he comes out [II. vii. 66]: Spenser describes him as 'feeding his eyes' on the sights within the cave, and there is a pun on 'vitall' and 'vittles'. The food and sleep without which he has gone are, of course, not literal but allegorical, the proper sustenance of his virtue; and what was once his natural element now overcomes him, therefore, with its 'too exceeding might'.

His faint, also an allegorical one, represents his descent into a state of intemperance in which he can no longer exercise rational control over his passions, and Atin, followed by Pyrochles, Cymochles and Archimago at once gallop up to seize the helpless knight. What Guyon has to learn from Mammon's cave has nothing to do with riches but concerns, instead, the limitations of his own mortal nature. By neglecting right-reason he has demonstrated the truth of what right-reason told him about the necessity of avoiding Occasion, and it is this wisdom which later enables him to keep straight on his way to the Bower of Blisse and not be side-tracked by irrelevant temptations.

This is Guyon's fall, stemming from over-confident virtue. At the time of his faint he has been 'three dayes of men' [II. vii. 65] underground, and the reference reminds us that he is not only a man but a Christian able to rise again. The account of Guyon's regeneration emphasises the external grace of God poured down upon fallen Adam and all his sons. It is significant that the angel appears and summons the Palmer before Guyon has been seized by his rebellious passions, although he is 'slumbring fast/In senselesse dreame' [II. viii. 4]. God's prevenient Grace anticipates the Fall here, just as in book I Una is already well out of Sans Loy's clutches before Red Cross falls under the blow of Orgoglio. The Angel of Grace who descends to Guyon's aid is at once a Christian angel and a Platonic Higher Cupid, servant of Venus Urania; and Spenser describes him in paradoxical terms; as

> flying Pursuivant,
> Against foule feends to aide us millitant?
> They for us fight, they watch and dewly ward,
> And their bright Squadrons round about us plant,
> And all for love, and nothing for reward: [II. viii. 2]

The actual pursuivants of Spenser's day, whose job was to inform on and hunt out Catholic recusants, had a less savoury reputation which Spenser must have been aware of, and the comparison, therefore, underlines the gulf between God's love and man's zealous undeserving—'O why should heavenly God to men have such regard?' [II. viii. 2].

The subsequent action represents dramatically the theological and psychological sequence which has already been worked out more fully in relation to Red Cross. The angel does not himself raise the fallen Guyon but restores to him his Palmer who, being too weak himself to drive off the enemy once they have a hold, calls upon Arthur to save. By Grace fallen man regains his right-reason; by reason he can reach to faith, and in the regeneration of faith he can conquer. The debate and battle between Arthur and the two brothers assert this theology and the subsequent fight exemplifies its working.

The battle, as Miss Williams has suggested,[1] is within the mind of Guyon himself, between his regenerate and his unregenerate parts, though it is only possible because of the historical fact of Christ. Arthur, therefore, is at once the symbol of the inner Christ and a reminder of the outer one on whom the Palmer calls for aid. This is made clear in the opening debate, when Cymochles insists that the wages of Original Sin is death— 'The trespasse still doth live, albe the person die' [II. viii. 28]; and Arthur is forced to agree that we are all sinners and deserve to die:

> Indeed (then said the Prince) the evill donne
> Dyes not, when breath the bodie first doth leave,
> But from the grandsyre to the Nephewes sonne,
> And all his seed the curse doth often cleave,
> Till vengeance utterly the guilt bereave:
> So streightly God doth judge...   [II. viii. 29]

He pleads for mercy, however, and Cymochles all unwittingly provides the answer when he accuses Arthur, 'How that thou art partaker of his crime' [II. viii. 30]. Pyrochles tries to use Arthur's sword, to 'carve with this inchaunted brond/His

1 Pp. 63.

Lords owne flesh' [22]; but Mordure will not turn against its master nor Guyon's regenerate nature deny Christ. In this state of self-division, however, Guyon's passions assail his Christian temperance, and Pyrochles wounds Arthur deeply in the right side with Guyon's own sword:

> Wyde was the wound, and a large lukewarme flood
> Red as the Rose, thence gushed grievously;   [39]

The shedding of this symbolic blood is the turning point of the battle, for at this point, and not until then, the Palmer gives Guyon's sword to Arthur who has so far been without one; and with it he rises in his wrath to kill the two brothers. In other words Guyon, at the moment of his crisis, shakes off his fears of judgement and turns to the security of the redeeming blood in the memory of which he can draw once more upon the strength of Christ within him. As soon as the two are dead, Guyon wakes from his swoon, a temperate man in rational control of his passions, and the energies which in excess have threatened his temperance are now, in moderation, his faithful servants. He has been saved by Grace from Pyrochles and Cymochles for the time being, but Archimago and Atin are always there, and there will be other battles to fight. In the meantime Guyon acknowledges the part which right-reason has played in leading him to the strength of faith, thanking his Palmer—'Firme is thy faith, whom daunger never fro me drew' [53]—and paying tribute to Arthur, and to Christ for the Grace shown to him:

> And to the Prince bowing with reverence dew,
> As to the Patrone of his life, thus sayd;
> My Lord, my liege, by whose most gratious ayd
> I live this day, and see my foes subdewd,
> What may suffise, to be for meede repayd
> Of so great graces, as ye have me shewd,
> But to be ever bound . . .
>
> [II. viii. 55]

Because of his Christian victory, the House of Alma in the next canto can be a joyful and exuberant place. Though only built of earth and slime like the Tower of Babel [II. ix. 21], it yet rises towards heaven in dazzling tiers of extended metaphor;

and the virtuosity of its ramifications, from watch-tower to privy, are only possible because it is held in God's hand. It is as flimsy as a house of cards, yet secure because built on the rock and having Arthur within and without. Spenser's enormous and challenging elaboration represents in linguistic terms the expression of an act of faith and the reminder that all depends on Grace. It is appropriate that its chronicles should deal with human heroism, actual and potential.

[5]

The episode of Arthur and Maleger in canto XI seems almost like an afterthought, and one reason for its inclusion may have been to fulfil the promise in the Letter to Raleigh that Arthur should embody the perfection of each virtue. In canto VIII he has played a role appropriate to holiness rather than temperance, and demonstrated a strength which, though necessary to temperance, is not an intrinsic part of it. In canto XI, therefore, Spenser presents him in the specific role of the hero of temperance, emphasising the quality of the virtue itself and merely alluding to the strength of faith which underpins the whole. The fact that Maleger is besieging the House of Alma defines the nature of his challenge: unlike faith which is attacked through the lusts of the flesh, temperance is threatened primarily through the weakness of the physical body; and Maleger, though obviously involving sin, is essentially the symbol of mortality. With his death's-head helmet and his ghost-like appearance, 'as pale and wan as ashes', he embodies all the mortal weakness from the Fall, the sickness, weariness, age which sap rational control and produce first the Impotence, then the Impatience which are the parents of intemperance. His strength naturally springs from the source of human weakness, namely, man's earthly nature, and Arthur at first fails to make allowance for this just as Guyon did: Maleger fights by running away so that Arthur, the 'greedy knight', as Spenser calls him, exhausts himself with his zealous chase, and trying to prevent Impotence from restoring to Maleger his arrows, is seized first by her and then inevitably by her fellow. Only Grace can save him— 'That had not grace thee blest, thou shouldest not survive'

[II. xi. 30]—and it comes in the form of Timias who gives Arthur time to collect himself and get himself under control again, so that he rises like Guyon rising from his swoon:

> As one awakt out of long slombring shade,
> Reviving thought of glorie and of fame,
> United all his powres to purge himselfe from blame.
>
> [II. xi. 31]

When, therefore, Maleger himself comes to finish off the work of his harbingers, Arthur is able to face him with the controlled energy of virtuous anger. Mortal weakness cannot, of course, be finally destroyed in this life and only gains power from its contact with the earth, so that Arthur is constrained to carry him off-stage 'Above three furlongs' and drown him in the lake. What the waters symbolise, whether they are those of the Well of Life or those of the great sea from which new life perpetually springs, Spenser gives no clue: he is not concerned for the moment with the final answer to mortality but only with the best way of evading its power to undermine human virtue. For this reason the 'standing lake' may indeed be the Idle lake which, properly used, is the means of restoring the tired body. Whatever may be the meaning of the final detail of the sequence—and the last interpretation seems to me the likeliest—it is of no relevance to the final stage of Guyon's quest, and so Spenser treats it very briefly, as a means of disposing of Maleger. It is relevant to the total concept of temperance, but not to those aspects of it which Guyon will be in need of on his way to the Bower.

The Maleger episode makes explicit what was implied by Guyon's fall after the cave of Mammon; and its central importance to the book as a whole can be gauged by the way in which Spenser tied it in with the central myths of the poem. Arthur's fight with Maleger recalls both that of Hercules with Antaeus and that of Aeneas with Turnus. The 'huge great stone' which Maleger hurls at Arthur echoes the stone which Turnus throws in the final battle of the *Aeneid* (book XII, line 896):

> An huge great stone, which stood upon one end,
> And had not bene removed many a day;

Some land-marke seem'd to be, or signe of sundry way.

[II. xi. 35]

The description, though very close to Virgil, could well be designed not only to evoke the obvious heroic parallel but to recall, yet again, the tables of the Law; in which case Arthur's victory, like that over Pyrochles and Cymochles, would be that of the Gospels. Spenser's 'signe of sundry way' in place of Virgil's 'to ward dispute from the fields' would seem to point in this direction.

[6]

At last Guyon is ready to put his temperance to the final test; and as his fall began with the Idle lake, so his quest must be completed by crossing it again and overcoming the insidious temptations of sloth to which it is the highway. He has to help him the energies which, in excess, produced Pyrochles and Cymochles but, temperately governed by the Palmer, are personified in Alma's boatman who labours unflaggingly at his oars as Belphoebe ordained:

> So forth they rowed, and that *Ferryman*
> With his stiffe oares did brush the sea so strong,
> That the hoare waters from his frigot ran,
> And the light bubbles daunced all along, . . .

[II. xii. 10]

It is a fine brisk beginning to the journey, full of confident energy and health able to transform the sluggish waves of the Idle lake. The ultimate temptation is in sexual form, and the setting, therefore, is the symbolic sea, though one from which Acrasia, the creator of counterfeits, will arise instead of the true Venus. Circe's power to turn men into swine had long been received as an emblem of the transforming powers of lust, and Acrasia obviously carries this primary symbolism; but there are other beasts in her bower besides Gryll, although they all take their source from the same carnal blindness. For Ascham,[1]

---

[1] Roger Ascham, *The Scholemaster*, English Works, ed. William Aldis Wright (Cambridge, 1904).

for example, Circe's court is a symbol of Italy which meta-morphoses the English traveller into an Italianate–English monster:

If *Scylla* drowne him not, *Charybdis* may fortune swalow him. Some *Circes* shall make him, of a plaine English man, a right *Italian*. And at length to hell, or to some hellish place, is he likelie to go: from whence is hard returning, although one *Ulysses*, and that by *Pallas* ayde, and good counsell of *Tiresias* once escaped that horrible Den of deadly darknes.   (p. 225)

He goes on to give a 'trewe Picture of a knight of Circes Court' who brings out of Italy:

the Religion, the learning, the policie, the experience, the maners of *Italie*. That is to say, for Religion, Papistrie or worse: for learning, lesse commonly than they caried out with them: for pollicie, a factious hart, a discoursing head, a mynde to medle in all mens matters. . . . These be the inchantementes of *Circes*, brought out of *Italie*, to marre mens maners in England.   (p. 229)

The earlier reference to Phaedria's 'litle Gondelay' [II. vi. 2], takes on a new significance in the light of this, for it, too, is of Italy, leading the Englishman by way of pleasure to the Italian Circe's court, and bringing him back all set to enter Mammon's cave. The infections of the Bower are not only sexual but involve matters of relevance to both Duessa and Dolon. Even the separate obstacles which Guyon has to face on his Odyssean journey have, as well as their obvious and primary allegorical meaning, further levels of significance in terms of the Circe myth and the general patterns of reference throughout the poem. Charybdis, for example, was a child and Scylla a grandchild of Gaea, the Earth, so that the temptations they embody are defined in relation to the primary metaphor of the Fall. Another Scylla, in Ovid's account, was turned to a monster by Circe (*Met.* XIV), and she forms, therefore, a sort of mythological pun, uniting the corruptions of sex with those of greediness and vile reproach, all of them deriving from man's fallen nature. The Sirens, Spenser tells us [31], were deprived of their beauty because they chal-lenged the Muses in song. As figures of corrupt art, therefore, they have their logical place in the allegory of a journey to uncover the corrupt art of the Bower of Blisse.

Guyon's ordeal is in two stages, beginning with the journey over the Idle lake and leading logically on to the Bower. The lake is primarily a test of Guyon's control of his moral energy and his ability to sustain the 'painfull toile' which Belphoebe demands of her followers; and it entails not only using but saving that energy by the avoidance of temptations which do not have to be met. There is no need to try out gluttony or prodigality, for example, to prove that one can give them up, and the journey through Mammon's cave has shown the dangers of over-exercising one's moral strength. By constant vigilance Guyon reaches the land, but is faced in Acrasia's Bower by a final range of temptations to which the ardours of his journey have made him vulnerable.

The temptations of the Idle lake, beginning in sloth, arise in the traditional order—gluttony, lechery, prodigality, leading on to ruin and the horrors of fantasy in an Elizabethan Rake's Progress. They cunningly follow the natural rhythms of the passions, a challenge demanding energetic resistance being followed by the insidious impulse to relax; and Guyon's task is to avoid his previous fluctuations, the 'wandring to and fro' which led to his downfall before. He must steer his course along the straight line of the golden mean; and for the sake of the metaphor, Spenser makes him sail between pairs of obstacles which masquerade as Aristotelean extremes, though in the case of Scylla and Charybdis, for example, they are really cause and effect.

The success of the voyage depends primarily upon the boatman but the Palmer, too, is necessary; and Spenser distinguishes very precisely between the functions which each performs, pointing out at the same time the way they protect and support each other. The boatman, embodying the habit of temperance, can avoid such traditional and recognisable forms of temptation as gluttony and prostitutes, but he cannot deal with the more subtle kind which, emanating from Acrasia, would confuse the distinction between intemperance and its opposite; and here the vigilance of the Palmer is needed. At first all is easy: the trio pass between the Charybdis of Greediness and the Scylla of Vile Reproach: on the one side the whirlpool presenting the traditional mediaeval image of drunkenness brilliantly crossed with the metaphor derived from the *Odyssey*:

> Which having swallowd up excessively
> He soone in vomit up againe doth lay,
> And belcheth forth his superfluity,   [II. xii. 3]

On the other, the perilous rock covered with 'carcasses exanimate', not physically dead but having lost their divine spirit, and now preyed upon by the 'Cormoyraunt' money-lenders upon whose coasts they are wrecked. The boatman advises the Palmer to leave these severely alone: they repel the temperate instinct and are for justice to deal with and temperance to avoid. In the same way, he rows firmly past the wandering islands, though Guyon wishes to land, thinking it is the Bower [XII. 10]. But these offer less subtle temptations than Acrasia, and decked in their 'blossomes dyde in white and red', they suggest not only casual pleasures of any kind but more specifically those associated with prostitutes. There is probably a punning reference back to Mordant, dead in sensual pleasure, his cheeks rosy red against the white alabaster breast of Amavia. The contrast which Spenser makes between these and the isle of Delos, no longer wandering since it became the scene of a happier birth, that of Apollo and Diana [XII. 13], reinforces the connection with the earlier episode. They waste no time on Phaedria, and pass on from prostitutes to prodigality and ruin. The Quicksand of Unthriftyhed and the Whirlepoole of Decay, another sequence of cause and effect in the guise of a pair of opposites, are still within the aegis of the boatman, and the Palmer is content to point the moral in passing, in a sort of interior monologue on the part of Guyon, aimed at the reader.

As in the cave of Mammon, however, the very presence of evil and the need to avoid it, even though it does not tempt, is a strain which weakens rational control; and as Alma's hold becomes less complete, Phantastes begins to escape from his proper chamber and fill the mind with visions of 'Infernal Hags, *Centaurs*, feendes, *Hippodames*' [II. ix. 50]. The fantastic host of sea-monsters which bursts upon Guyon can only do so because he is tired, and as usual in Spenser's catalogues, the individual details define themselves by reference to the general symbolism of the poem. The 'Spring-headed *Hydraes*', the 'dreadfull Fish, that hath deserv'd the name/Of Death', the 'horrible Sea-satyre', for example, all hint at their origins in man's fallen nature. The important thing about them all is that they are not real, although irrational people might believe in them: they are the stuff of contemporary travellers' tales, and would be rated as such by the rational person, as the Palmer in fact rates them. Their appearance to Guyon at this point of the journey is a clue to the real power of Acrasia by whom they are conjured up. It is her special capacity through the weakness of the flesh to blind the eye of reason and to blur the distinction between fact and fantasy. This, more than the actual physical temptation she offers, is what makes her dangerous, and Guyon has to resist her insidious challenges for the rest of the journey until the Bower is destroyed. She represents a challenge especially relevant to Guyon who, as the knight of reason, has to maintain the proper relationship between the inhabitants of the three chambers of the mind, and prevent Phantastes from perverting his fellows. At this stage, the Palmer banishes these fantasies by smiting the sea, like Christ calming the waters, as Guyon asserts the mastery of reason.

In his tired state, Guyon tends to swing over from fear to sentimentality, as he hears the weeping maiden and desires to 'ease her sorrow sad', and when he recognises the nature of this impulse and resists it, his weariness assails him, reinforced by a dangerous touch of self-pity. The Sirens' song is a most poignant expression of Guyon's longing for rest, coupled with the momentary feeling that he deserves it for heroic labours already accomplished:

> O thou faire sonne of gentle Faery,
> That art in mighty armes most magnifide
> Above all knights, that ever battell tride,
> O turne thy rudder hither-ward a while:
> Here may thy storme-bet vessell safely ride;
> This is the Port of rest from troublous toyle,
> The worlds sweet In, from paine and wearisome turmoyle.
>
> [II. xii. 32]

With the help of reason he drives himself even past this, but pays the penalty of driving himself too hard, in the great fog of doubts and fears with which the tired body takes revenge on the mind:

> When suddeinly a grosse fog over spred
> With his dull vapour all that desert has,
> And heavens chearefull face enveloped,
> That all things one, and one as nothing was,
> And this great Universe seemd one confused mas.
>
> [II. xii. 34]

The only answer to such a state of hopelessness is a blind and dogged habit of virtue and an overriding sense of moral purpose until the black mood wears off; and so the Palmer and the boatman keep grimly at their posts, the one rowing, the other 'stifly' steering, until they come out into the light again and see the land ahead.

The fact that they reach the land demonstrates that Guyon has mastered Belphoebe's lesson and has proved himself in terms of the discipline of Diana; but that is only half the achievement of a full temperance, and he still has to prove his virtue in relation to the Venus who awaits him in the Bower. There has been no love in Guyon's pilgrimage: unlike the other heroes of the Quest he has no mistress, just as Medina alone of the three sisters has no lover. The only major human organs absent from the House of Alma are the sexual ones, and their turn does not come until the Mons Veneris of the Garden of Adonis. The Palmer includes love along with the passions of wrath, jealousy and grief to be rooted out at birth [II. iv. 35]; though it is important to realise that in this he plays the traditional role of Reason who, from the *Romance of the Rose* onwards, identifies 'love' with the carnal passion 'For delectation, not engendering',[1] and opposes it to the virtuous procreation which should be the object of love. Temperance is not opposed to sex but to its perversion; and its concern is with the disciplines which ensure that the sexual passion will not be

---

1 *The Romance of the Rose*, pp. 97–8.

abused when the time to experience it arrives. Alma is still a virgin 'That had not yet felt *Cupidoes* wanton rage' [II. ix. 18], but Spenser points out that she is ripe for marriage and wooed by 'many a Lord of noble parentage'.

The repressive vigilance of Diana's moral code, however, holds down man's sensual nature forcing it to find an outlet by indirect means, and the Bower of Blisse is Spenser's allegory of the effects of this repression. Acrasia is not, of course, a woman, but the symbol of man's own sensual nature seeking full possession, which is why Spenser shows her as the active partner 'greedily depasturing delight', leaning over the sleeping man and using him for her pleasure, as the nobler Venus in the Garden of Adonis uses Adonis for a worthier purpose. Acrasia's interest is only in pleasure, not in the more ardent processes of procreation, and the Genius at her gate is explicitly not the Genius who aids Venus at her work in the other garden. If she could, she would debase man to the level of swinish sensuality exemplified in Gryll; but for a person of such tried and rational temperance as Guyon, the temptation of simple nudity would be no more effective than Belial's plan for the seduction of Christ—'Set women in his eye and in his walk'. Denied, therefore, she works through the devious means which have already been suggested in her deceptive riddle, and in the delusions with which Guyon is beset on his journey over the lake. As man is a rational creature, her challenge is directed against the mind whose objectivity she seeks to obscure with the colours of fantasy. The Bower embodies the powers of the emotions to colour our thinking and make us accept as rational what is merely desired. The boatman can row past whatever he recognises as a temptation, but he is helpless in the face of intemperance masquerading as a virtue. For this reason Guyon leaves his boatman behind when he reaches Acrasia's island [38]; in an arena where temperance itself has to be defined anew, only the Palmer can be of use.

The quality of Acrasia's art in the Bower is to make everything appear better than nature, better than it really is. Although the art at times seems to despise the inadequacy of nature, 'as halfe in scorne/Of niggard Nature' [II. xii. 50], yet the two cooperate to produce something which looks better than either

alone, even though the motive behind the joint effort is emula-
tion of each other, and the effect is gained by hiding the imperfect under the perfect:

> One would have thought, (so cunningly the rude,
>   And scorned parts were mingled with the fine,)
>   That nature had for wantonesse ensude
>   Art, and that Art at nature did repine;   [II. xii. 59]

The results, however, exceed the beauties of nature alone:

>   So striving each th'other to undermine,
>   Each did the others worke more beautifie;
>   [II. xii. 59]

Moreover the art is the traditional Horatian art which conceals
itself from the beholder:

>   And that, which all faire workes doth most aggrace,
>   The art, which all that wrought, appeared in no place.
>   [II. xii. 58]

and at first glance it is difficult to see what is wrong with the
place. Everything in the garden seems bigger and better than
life: the porter at the door is

>   A comely personage of stature tall,
>   And semblaunce pleasing, more than naturall,
>   [II. xii. 46]

and the two Alma Tadema girls rising from their little fountain
'seem' to Guyon's inflamed senses the image of the morning
star, or of Venus herself 'newly borne/Of th'Oceans fruitfull
froth', with 'Christalline humour' dropping from their golden
hair. Above all, the Bower itself is more beautiful, more perfect
than anything in nature: it is an unfallen Garden of Eden, a
fragment of the Golden Age where winter never comes, and
spring and harvest reign together without change:

>   Thereto the Heavens alwayes Joviall,
>   Lookt on them lovely, still in stedfast state,
>   Ne suffred storme nor frost on them to fall,
>   Their tender buds or leaves to violate,

> Nor scorching heat, nor cold intemperate
> T'afflict the creatures, which therein did dwell,
> But the milde aire with season moderate
> Gently attempred, and disposed so well,
> That still it breathed forth sweet spirit and holesome
>   smell.   [II. xii. 51]

The word 'Joviall' pulls one up with a start, for Jove's reign was of the Silver Age with its cycle of seasonal change, and the unfading temperateness of the Bower belongs to Saturn and his Age of Gold. And this is what is wrong with it: the Bower is unnatural because seemingly unfallen, a fact to which Spenser draws attention in the next stanza:

> More sweet and holesome, then the pleasaunt hill
> Of *Rhodope*, on which the Nimphe, that bore
> A gyaunt babe, her selfe for griefe did kill;
> Or the Thessalian *Tempe*, where of yore
> Faire *Daphne Phoebus* hart with love did gore;
> Or *Ida*, where the Gods lov'd to repaire,
> When ever they their heavenly bowres forlore;
> Or sweet *Parnasse*, the haunt of Muses faire;
> Or *Eden* selfe, if ought with Eden mote compaire.
>   [II. xii. 52]

The comparisons are all to places of great beauty, but beauty to be marred by the intrusion of the Fall or its effects, manifested, for the most part, in terms of sexual temptation. The reference to the nymph who bore the giant babe is obscure, but it certainly reminds us of Amavia: Tempe recalls the fate of Daphne for denying her father's wish for grandchildren and refusing Apollo's love (*Met.* I). Her virginity is the opposite excess to that of Amavia, the nymph as opposed to Bacchus. Ida provided the occasion from which the Fall of Troy ultimately sprang; and Parnassus, the haunt of the Muses, may be cited because it was also the scene of the tragic contest between Apollo and Marsyas of which the Muses were the judges. Spenser quotes one instance after the other, until he reaches the most beautiful and the most tragic of them all, the Garden of Eden.

The Bower in its more than earthly beauty would make us forget all this, and Acrasia embodies the strength of our sensual

nature to charm and lull us into forgetfulness of our fallen
state and to inhibit our attempts to repair it. The point is made
in the first description of the Bower in canto VI, although the
full significance does not become apparent until the end of the
book:

> No tree, whose braunches did not brauely spring;
>   No braunch, whereon a fine bird did not sit:
>   No bird, but did her shrill notes sweetly sing;
>   No song but did containe a louely dit:
>   Trees, braunches, birds, and songs were framed fit,
>   For to allure fraile mind to carelesse ease.
>   Carelesse the man soone woxe, and his weake wit
>   Was ouercome of thing, that did him please;
> So pleased, did his wrathfull purpose faire appease.
>
> [II. vi. 13]

The unnatural perfection of its forest, presented in such highly
formalised rhetoric, gives us the first taste of the art of the
Bower, the effect of which is to make man 'carelesse' when he
should be full of care. The very title of the Bower of Blisse is an
indication of its counterfeit nature: true bliss is to be found in
heavenly, not in earthly bowers,[1] and Timias, waking from
his swoon in the next book, thinks at the sight of Belphoebe
that he is in heaven, and thanks God for his grace in sending
'thine Angell from her bowre of blis/To comfort me in my
distressed plight' [III. v. 35]. Acrasia is the figure of blind Cupid
making us see the world through rose-coloured spectacles, and
inspiring sonnet lovers with their hyperboles about their less
than perfect mistresses. Her bower is the embodiment of all the
erotic fantasies which the mind conjures up when in the grip
of the repressed passions, all the visions of the Rose which
young men tossing on their beds have dreamed up in love's
despair. Although Guyon has to face it as a result of his own
virtuous self-repression, the state of mind which the Bower
expresses is not essentially different from the traditional
'loveris maladye' engendered in the 'celle fantastik', that
deliberate over-heating of the imagination which Professor

---

[1] See, for example, Chaucer's translation of Boethius, *De Consolatione*,
book III, prosa 2, ed. F. N. Robinson, p. 399.

Robertson has diagnosed as the vice of the so-called 'Courtly Lovers'.[1] Acrasia is the mother of all forms of cerebral eroticism, including that of Cymochles, the voyeur who watches the naked girls through half-closed eyes. We see no actual love-making in the Bower, only the provocation of desire beforehand and the pleasing languors afterwards, which is why Acrasia is a force of sterility. Her temptation is not to make love but to take up a corrupt and intemperate attitude towards love itself, and the sexual activity to which she ultimately gives rise will be the unnatural and perverted kind which belongs to Busyrane.

Acrasia is the symbol of human sensuality which would not only blind the eye to the primary purpose of sex but, in creating a world of attractive fantasies, would make us content with our fallen state and plunge her victims into eternal sloth. For the sleeping Verdant, the quest itself has ceased to exist, and the Bower is a veritable bower of sloth, where all the inhabitants are perpetually resting, slumbering or sitting down. Genius at the gate is sitting, his garments 'Not fit for speedy pace, or manly exercize' [46], and within the porch the comely dame, 'Excesse, did rest' [55], while the very grapes bend down to the lips to save the effort of reaching. Guyon cannot destroy Acrasia but he can destroy her bower, and in doing so he exorcises from the mind all the fantasies bred by longing or repression or memory which would prevent the Christian from seeing the world as it really is. Evil has to be recognised before it can be destroyed, and Guyon's task is to clear human vision for all the heroes who follow. The net which he throws over Acrasia is that with which the toiling blacksmith, Vulcan, ensnared Mars and Venus in the midst of their amorous excesses; and the chains of adamant in which he binds her are those of the second Adam, although Spenser's description is a typically ambiguous one—'For nothing else might keepe her safe and sound' [II. xii. 82]. She is far from dead and lives on, safe and sound, in the strength of the old Adam.

Spenser is not the puritan denouncing sexual passion which he is still sometimes taken to be: if he were, indeed, there would be no quest for Britomart to achieve. He is making the traditional rational defence against whatever would pervert sex from its

[1] Pp. 98 ff.

proper function, and the Garden of Adonis cannot arise until the Bower of Blisse is in ruins. Although no lover himself, Guyon is yet vitally necessary to the conduct of love in *The Faerie Queene*, for the accomplishment of his quest defines the misleading delusions and sterile pleasures which stand in the way of virtuous love and Britomart has need of his clear sight in the House of Busyrane. In avenging the bloody-handed child and establishing Amavia's innocence, Guyon vindicates the fallen human flesh and puts Verdant in the place of Mordant, and his quest leads logically, therefore, on to that of Britomart as it has itself followed inevitably after that of Red Cross.

[7]

The Bower of Blisse is a place of intrusive art, where the birds and the trees are described with such formal rhetoric that they suggest the mechanical beauties of the garden which Jack Wilton saw in Rome rather than those of Nature herself.[1] This is because the Bower is a bastard creation of the human mind and contrasted, therefore, with the true fertile creation of Nature herself. It might seem surprising that Spenser, the Arch-Poet, should yet make art a symbol of evil in the Bower of Blisse; and one wonders where he stood in relation to the great debate over art and nature in the period, whether he believed in hard or soft primitivism, and whether he saw art as the destroyer or the healer.[2] The word carried very many meanings, but in whatever sense it was used, Spenser certainly saw it, like everything else in life, as Janus-faced, capable of good or evil and presenting the eternal choice. The supreme artist is God and his art is entirely good; Cambina's chariot of Concord is covered with designs 'Such as the maker selfe could best by art devize' [IV. iii. 38]. In so far as human art cooperates with that of God, it is good, and where it opposes, bad: it can cause the Fall or repair it.

The kind of art with which Spenser is most concerned is, of

[1] Thomas Nashe, *The Unfortunate Traveller*, in *Selected Writings of Nashe*, ed. Wells (London 1964), Stratford-upon-Avon Library vol. I, pp. 246–7.
[2] E. W. Tayler, *Nature and Art in Renaissance Literature* (Columbia, 1964), chap. I.

course, that of poetry; and we have seen how deeply he felt the responsibility it carried, and what enormous powers for good or evil he attributed to it: in Sidney's words, 'With a sword thou mayest kill thy father, and with a sword thou mayest defend thy prince and country'. *The Faerie Queene* embodies a good deal of literary criticism and comment on modes of traditional and contemporary literature which Spenser clearly felt to be pernicious and, in one way or another, to hinder the Christian in his quest. The episode of Busyrane is, as we shall see, one such passage, and Calidore's pastoral holiday another. The art of Acrasia's bower, too, has a literary application: it is a sort of sophist rhetoric which would make the false seem the true; and the over-formal and obtrusive figures which characterise its description draw attention to this fact. Bad art of this kind is Spenser's symbol for the sophistry which Acrasia practises; but Spenser goes further than this, I think, and attacks through it some tendencies in the poetry of his time of which he was deeply suspicious.

The most curious fact about the Bower of Blisse is its close approximation to the golden world of poetry as Sidney describes it so feelingly in the *Apologie*:

Onely the Poet, disdayning to be tied to any such subjection, lifted up with the vigor of his owne invention, dooth growe in effect another nature, in making things either better then Nature bringeth forth, or, quite a newe, formes such as never were in Nature, as the *Heroes, Demi-gods, Cyclops, Chimeras, Furies*, and such like; so as hee goeth hand in hand with Nature, not inclosed within the narrow warrant of her guifts but freely ranging within the Zodiack of his own wit. Nature never set forth the earth in so rich tapestry as divers Poets have done, neither with plesant rivers, fruitful trees, sweet smelling flowers, nor whatsoever els may make the too much loved earth more lovely. Her world is brasen, the Poets only deliver a golden. (p. 156)

It is to be expected that the demi-gods and Chimeras should occur both in Sidney's description and in Guyon's voyage over the Idle lake, for both writers are thinking of the same source in Homer; but the Golden world with its fruitful trees and rich flowers comes very near to the Bower. Even the grapes are there with which Excesse greets her visitors: 'Nay, he dooth, as if your journy should lye through a fayre Vineyard, at the first give you a cluster of Grapes, that, full of that taste, you may long to passe further.' (p. 172) The evil Genius at the gate has the power to make us fall 'Through guilefull semblaunts, which he makes us see.' [II. xii. 48], which comes very close to both Sidney's and Aristotle's definition of poetry as fiction. The whole Bower of Blisse is a poetic fiction in concrete form.

Sidney seems to have had no misgivings about the power of poetry to improve upon nature and, indeed, his whole defence is based upon the capacity of the poet to create out of his 'erected wit' images of perfect virtue which will inflame the reader with the desire to emulate them. He is thinking primarily of heroic poetry, especially the *Aeneid* and the *Odyssey*, and their pictures of heroic virtue aroused in him a passionate and generous response which he felt to be wholly conducive to virtue: 'Far as the image of each action styrreth and instructeth the mind, so the loftie image of such Worthies most inflameth the mind with desire to be worthy, and informes with counsel how to be worthy' (p. 179). Sidney admits the power of poetry to give an intensified image of evil as well as of good, and to paint it with a blacker, more repellent face of woe than it ever has in real life; but even here he stresses the delight which such imitations provide, echoing Aristotle's insistence that: '. . .those things which in themselves are horrible, as cruell battailes unnaturall Monsters, are made in poeticall imitation delightfull' (p. 173) and praising Tragedy above all for its 'sweet violence'. For Sidney, the noblest poetry is classic epic, and its power to move men lies in its capacity to 'feign' an almost prelapsarian virtue.

Spenser's method of persuading men to virtue is a different one. He was clearly more aware of the potency of the 'infected will' than Sidney, more sceptical about man's ability to be reformed by the mere sight of virtue. His own way is, as we have seen, to analyse the processes of vice and induce his reader both to participate imaginatively in the sensations of falling before temptation, and to recognise rationally the steps leading to that fall: the virtues of Arthur are necessary to the poem as a means of defining both virtue and vice, but they do not draw the reader to good as the errors of the separate heroes repel him from evil.

In the last analysis, Spenser is more traditionally Christian than Sidney, whose admiration for the classical epic perhaps caused him to hold up the self-sufficient, unfallen virtue of the pagan heroes for our total approval, just as Chapman venerated the wisdom of Homer with more ardour than would be possible for a plain Christian. There is more than a touch of Pico's Neo-Platonism, as expressed in his *Oration on the Dignity of Man*, in Sidney's enthusiastic veneration for the creative powers of the poet:

Neyther let it be deemed too sawcie a comparison to ballance the highest poynt of mans wit with the efficacie of Nature; but rather give right honor to the heavenly Maker of that maker, who, having made man to his owne likenes, set him beyond and over all the workes of that second nature, which in nothing hee showeth so much as in Poetrie, when with the force of a divine breath he bringeth things forth far surpassing her doeings, . . .   (p. 157)

Spenser, himself, I think, could never have talked with such adulation of human nature, even in the case of the poet; and it is interesting to notice that Sidney himself recognises in the ideal creations of poetry a danger to our awareness of the Fall: as he continues in the passage quoted above: '. . . with no small argument to the incredulous of that first accursed fall of *Adam*: sith our erected wit maketh us know what perfection is, and yet our infected will keepeth us from reaching unto it' (p. 157). I would suggest that Spenser was more conscious than Sidney of the 'argument to the incredulous of that first accursed fall of Adam' implicit in the classic epic; and that his Bower of Blisse is an allegory of these dangers inherent in some of the 'Golden' poetry of his period just as the pastoral interlude of book vi is critical of the pastoral idyll. Such an intention would be in keeping with one object of book ii, which is to challenge the classic ideal of a self-sufficient temperance and put in its place the humbler Christian virtue based on the need for Grace. Instead of making man aware of the Fall, poetry, as Sidney conceived of it, could make him complacent in the thought of a potential human greatness standing in no need of Grace. What for Sidney was the source of all virtue may have offered, for Spenser, a particularly subtle temptation to sloth.

7

Chastity

The first three books of *The Faerie Queene* reproduce in their
sequence the order of Red Cross's progress through the House of
Holiness, beginning with Fidelia and passing by way of Penance
and Speranza to Charitas. As Guyon's achievement makes holy
the quest of Britomart, which is to marry and bear a child, so the
emphasis in book III moves from the problem of sin to that of
death and the human answer to it; and the relationship of book
III to IV differs from that of I to II with the change of theme.
Whereas the first two books follow parallel courses because they
deal with different aspects of the same thing, namely, right-
reason in its relationship to faith and to virtuous action respectively; the relationship between books III and IV is one of
continuity, with the same characters bridging the six-years' gap
in publication, even though, as we shall see, some of them change
their roles in the process and are, so to speak, reborn. The
continuity is carefully maintained, however, because it has a
symbolism appropriate to the theme: the two books deal with
love and procreation, the continuity of the race and of the
British line; and, as always in the poem, form and content fit
each other.

In book III we move into wider fields than Guyon can encom-
pass: the ebon spear of Britomart unhorses him because it has
behind it the whole force of Nature; it is the emblem of the love
of God by which the universe was created and is maintained, and
its power springs, therefore, from a higher and more mysterious
reason than even Guyon can attain to. The heroic line is carried
on with a heroine whose mission is to fit herself for the husband
through whom she may fulfil her destiny in producing 'Most
famous fruits of matrimoniall bowre' [III. iii. 3] in contrast to
those of the Bower of Blisse. In view of Spenser's practices in the

field of number symbolism,[1] one wonders whether it is merely accidental that this important statement about Britomart's historical role should occur in a stanza with such triple symbolism in its numbering. Unlike Artegall, Britomart is not, of course, a character out of Tudor history books; her name combines Mars with Britain and her marriage to Artegall symbolises the espousals of Britain and the Tudor line. The Tudor peace and the harmony between Briton and Saxon with the restoration of the ancient British dynasty to the throne is referred to when she sets out on her quest wearing Angela's armour, and again in Paridel's account of the royal line of Brute which 'far abroad his mighty branches threw,/Into the utmost Angle of the world he knew' [III. ix. 47]. The outermost rind of allegory in book III is historical, as Spenser indicates when he invokes Clio [III. iii. 4], and involves Britomart in the genealogy of Briton kings. In addition to her role in British history she is also linked with the wider dynasty of the Elfin heroes. Britomartis was one of Minerva's pseudonyms, and Alastair Fowler has shown how closely Spenser identifies her with the goldenhaired, helmeted daughter of Jove:[2]

> Like as *Minerva*, being late returnd
>   From slaughter of the Giaunts conquered;   [III. ix. 22]

It must be remembered, too, that Hercules killed Busiris, whose name and nature suggests Busyrane, so that in a variety of ways, she is linked with the story of Jove, his children, and their war with the Titans.

As always in *The Faerie Queene*, however, the heroic is built upon the foundation of normal human psychology: in learning to be a heroine, Britomart must first learn to be a woman, and her progress towards this goal provides the theme of book III. She is woman growing into the knowledge of her own sexual nature, and in preparing to be the mother of a line of kings she has first to discover the true, fruitful purpose of sex. Book III is the book of sex, treating it with astonishing and modern frankness and, like the *Romance of the Rose*, exploring its implications in relation to human mortality. For this reason, the

1 Fowler, *Spenser and the Numbers of Time, passim.*
2 Pp. 124 ff.

decorum of the book in all its ramifications is governed by love: the divinities who dominate it in person, or in the tapestries of Malecasta or Busyrane, are Venus or Cupid, and much of the action takes place in conjunction with the natural element of Venus, the sea. There are frequent love laments of a traditional kind, such as that of Britomart straight out of Petrarch— 'Huge sea of sorrow, and tempestuous griefe' [III. iv. 8], or that of Arthur in the guise of the sleepless lover in the same canto [III. iv. 55], or Scudamore's lament over Amoret [III. xi. 9]. The casual similes throughout the book often bear on the same point:

> The loving mother, that nine moneths did beare,
> In the deare closet of her painefull side,
> Her tender babe, it seeing safe appeare,
> Doth not so much rejoyce, as she rejoyced theare.
>
> [III. ii. 11]

Even the landscapes themselves have an erotic suggestiveness which occurs too frequently to be accidental: there are the little cloven, wooded valleys where Timias is attacked by the forester with his long boar-spear [III. v. 17], or where the witch has her cottage [III. vii. 4]; and above all there is the Garden of Adonis on its wooded hill, that explicit symbol of the Mons Veneris.

The fertility myth embodied in this great sequence of the Garden is both the mathematical and the allegorical centre of the poem, the source of all the raw material which it is Spenser's aim to fashion according to the pattern of virtue. There Venus aided by the true Genius of generation performs her divine task, not as the woman receiving the man but as Great Nature using Adonis for her procreative purpose. Spenser does not identify her work with any specific theory of creation, whether in terms of forms or of seeds, for to do so would be to limit the application of the poem. Nor is he postulating any philosophical theory of reincarnation—it is allegory, not philosophy which we are reading, and the flowers which decay and revive again are merely an allegory of the miracle by which form mysteriously survives, however often its individual manifestations may die. Spenser's theme is the great cycle of death and rebirth by which Adonis remains 'eterne in mutabilitie' although 'subject to mortalitie' [III. vi. 47]: the infinite capacity of Chaos to take on new being, and the perpetual supply of forms from the Garden ensures that as the old ones are beaten by time's flaggy wings or mown down by his scythe, there will always be new ones to take their place and maintain that eternity by succession which replaces the immortality of Eden. The sequence is a great Elegy in which the flowers, fading and being born again, pay due tribute to the powers of winter but offer also the promise of the new spring. It is natural in this context, therefore, that Spenser's myth should include a reference to an altogether different kind of immortality, that which elegiac poetry can give:

> Sad *Amaranthus*, made a flowre but late,
> Sad *Amaranthus*, in whose purple gore
> Me seemes I see *Amintas* wretched fate,
> To whom sweet Poets verse hath given endlesse date.
>
> [III. vi. 45]

We find the same juxtaposition of these two types of immortality in Shakespeare's sonnets:

> But wherefore do not you a mightier way
> Make war upon this bloody tyrant, Time?
> And fortify yourself in your decay
> With means more blessed than my barren rhyme?
> Now stand you on the top of happy hours
> With many maiden gardens yet unset, . . .   (XVI)

and the flower is the inevitable metaphor for any treatment of the theme.

There has been much discussion about the location of the Garden of Adonis, whether it is at the celestial or the terrestrial level of creation, whether in or out of the dimension of time.[1] In one verse the flowers and the garden itself belong unmistakably to the world of mortality:

> Great enimy to it, and to all the rest,
> That in the *Gardin* of *Adonis* springs,
> Is wicked *Time*, who with his scythe addrest,

---

[1] For example, Josephine W. Bennett, 'Spenser's Garden of Adonis Revisited', *JEGP* 41 (1942), 53–78. Also Alastair Fowler, *Spenser and the Numbers of Time*, pp. 136 ff.

Does mow the flowring herbes and goodly things,
And all their glory to the ground downe flings,
Where they doe wither, and are fowly mard:

[III. vi. 39]

but a few verses later, the garden is described as something
beyond the reach of mortality and time, an unfallen Eden
without winter or change of season:

There is continuall spring, and harvest there
Continuall, both meeting at one time:
For both the boughes doe laughing blossomes beare,
And with fresh colours decke the wanton Prime,

[III. vi. 42]

The garden itself is idyllic, and yet devouring time appears to
enter into it and destroy its flowers even there: Spenser is very
ambiguous about where the destruction takes place, whether
within or without the garden. It seems clear to me that he is
describing the terrestrial level of creation, just as he is dealing
with the specifically terrestrial problem of mortality. His subject
is the sexual act and its consequences, and the bower itself is the
womb, Venus's 'joyous Paradize/Where most she wonnes, when
she on earth does dwel' [III. vi. 29]. It is at once timeless yet
subject to time, because it involves the mental state which
accompanies the physical act. That the Bower and its story
allegorizes the act of love-making is apparent both from the
sexual imagery in which it is described,

And eke attonce the heavy trees they clime,
Which seeme to labour under their fruits lode:

[III. vi. 42]

and from Spenser's own confession that he has been there and
enjoyed it:

But well I wote by tryall, that this same
All other pleasant places doth excell, [III. vi. 29]

It is something outside of time and mortality, however, in that
the lovers' experience of sexual fulfilment contains its own form
of eternity. Spenser is describing the experience which Donne

expresses in *The Sunne Rising*, for example, where, in each other's arms, the lovers seem to escape from the 'houres, dayes, moneths, which are the rags of time'; or that of the happy world of the *Good-Morrow*, 'Without sharpe North, without declining West'. Love defeats time on the psychological level by the pattern of timeless moments it engenders, just as on the physical level it produces its own eternity by succession, and the former is justified by the latter. The Garden is a place of happy regeneration, where the Fall is undone, where Adonis rises again and Psyche, once more united with Cupid, bears her child, Pleasure; but the idyll is only sanctified because the spring leads to harvest. The same idyllic pleasure forms the chief temptation of the Bower of Blisse.

Here Amoret has her upbringing and takes on her specific quality of womanhood, what Chaucer would have called 'kinde'. She is the embodiment of the procreative sexual instinct in woman, and in rescuing her, Britomart is rescuing something within herself in danger of being perverted, and demonstrating the obligation of all women to meet the same challenge. Book III marks the first half of her quest: in setting out on the journey which will reach its first resting point with the rescue of Amoret, Britomart is growing up, awakening both physically and mentally to puberty, and liberating the new-born instinct within her from the fantasies and hobgoblins with which tradition, literature and her own feminine nature have surrounded it. As Guyon destroys one set of fantasies emanating from the tempting pleasures of the Bower, so Britomart has to destroy the web of fears which Busyrane has woven around sexual love to inhibit its proper acceptance and use.

[2]

Britomart's companion on the way, Glauce, is as complex a figure of symbolism as her predecessors, Una and the Palmer. She is the nurse and suggests, therefore, both the youthfulness of her charge and the succession of generations with which the quest is concerned, a point further underlined by the contrast between her own age and Britomart's youth. Her name, too, points in the same direction, linking her with 'wanton Glauce' who is among the Nereides in the great procession of fertility at the wedding of Thames and Medway [IV. xi. 48]. At this stage of her development, Britomart is unawaked and innocent of sex, aware that there is such a thing to which one day she will come, but not as yet having any real inkling of its nature:

> So thought this mayd (as maydens use to done)
> Whom fortune for her husband would allot,
> Not that she lusted after any one;
> For she was pure from blame of sinfull blot,
> Yet wist her life at last must lincke in that same knot.
>
> [III. ii. 23]

Her first adventure, with Malecasta, presents her with the whole range of sexual temptations. Malecasta is an Acrasia, and her castle a Bower of Blisse, with its Lydian harmony and sweet birds 'Ay caroling of love and jollity' [III. i. 40]: she is described in all the images of intemperance, feeding the little spark of wantonness with coals, 'giving the bridle' to the unruly horse of the passions, and inevitably, when she steals to Britomart's bed, putting on the symbolic mantle of the scarlet woman. Yet to Britomart, it all means nothing: the six knights of courtship scarcely affect her,

> But to faire *Britomart* they all but shadowes beene.
>
> [III. i. 45]

and in her exchange with them, she parrots the traditional phrases of Courtly Love, obviously not understanding their implications or recognising that the 'maistry' which she so innocently condemns is normally equated with marriage:

> For knight to leave his Ladie were great shame,
> That faithfull is, and better were to die.
> All losse is lesse, and lesse the infamie,
> Then losse of love to him, that loves but one;
> Ne may love be compeld by maisterie;
> For soone as maisterie comes, sweet love anone
> Taketh his nimble wings, and soone away is gone.
>
> [III. i. 25]

The fact that the mistress, 'the truest one on ground', whom the knight refuses to forswear is called *'th'Errant Damzell'* completely passes her by [III. i. 24]. As yet, Britomart has no more womanhood than a boy, and strikes 'manly terror' into the hearts of her enemies: she is the 'vermeill Rose' safely guarded by its thorns; and in her innocence she romanticises Malecasta's passion, imagining that it springs from the same idealism as her own:

> Full easie was for her to have beliefe,
> Who by self-feeling of her feeble sexe, . . .
> Could judge what paines do loving harts perplexe.
>
> [III. i. 54]

Her own feelings are at the romantic, school-girl stage, and the image which she sees in the mirror is the reflection of her own idealism, an image of the perfect hero who

> restlesse walketh all the world around,
> Ay doing things, that to his fame redound,
> Defending Ladies cause, and Orphans right, . . .
>
> [III. ii. 14]

As she herself complains, the image she sees is no man 'But th'only shade and semblant of a knight' [III. ii. 38], and it is 'the semblaunt pleasing most your minde', as Glauce gently points out. This is very far from the passion of Malecasta, or of Myrrha, or Biblis or Pasiphae, but it is as strong: Britomart is firmly set upon the path of love, and all the unnatural charms with which the nurse tries to cure her cannot drive out what Spenser sees as a divine instinct. Although Glauce bids her 'spit upon my face,/Spit thrice upon me', as Christ was spat upon [III. ii. 50], and turns her 'contrarie to the Sunne/ . . . for she the right did shunne' [51], yet none of these can make her swerve from her quest. She still carries on fashioning an ideal husband out of her imagination:

> And in her feigning fancie did pourtray
> Him such, as fittest she for love could find,

Wise, warlike, personable, curteous, and kind.

[III. iv. 5]

She suffers, of course, but the very hackneyed love lament which Spenser puts into her mouth, imitated from Petrarch by every love poet from Wyatt onwards, is Spenser's indication that the wound which Gardante gave her in Malecasta's bower was a very slight one. It is, as yet, sonnet suffering and a long way from the trials which Florimel undergoes in her own little boat. Gardante was only the first of the six steps of courtship and there is far to go before Noctante is reached—in fact Britomart never reaches him within the poem. Nevertheless, her history in these early cantos provides a clue to the nature of the temptations which she will have to overcome at the end of the book. Her initial conception of love is very much a thing of the mind, influenced by the popular mythology concerning the nature of love, by memories of courtly love situations and the poetic agonisings of Petrarchan lovers. It is of these and similar factors that Busyrane will try to take advantage, and Britomart will have to exorcise them in order to fulfil her destiny.

By canto IV, Archimago has already 'her singled from the crew/Of courteous knights, the Prince, and Faery Gent' [45] as a possible future victim; but Spenser does not take up the subject again until canto XI, by which time Britomart has grown up a good deal more and is ready to feel the active pricking of Cupid's darts. This is the significance of Scudamore, Cupid's man with a Cupid on his shield, whom Britomart finds apparently asleep but who quickly awakes and declares the pains he feels for the loss of Amoret. Scudamore at this stage of the story, before he undergoes a metamorphosis, as we shall see, in book IV, personifies the stirring of physical desire in man or woman, and marks in Britomart the fact that the sexual nature is now awake, and that she is now old enough to feel Cupid's darts. His lament for Amoret shut away and tortured by Busyrane is Britomart's own dawning realisation of the physical instinct which is imprisoned within herself and in need of release. In the brief exchange between the two, Britomart passes from a state of detached pity to an active identification with his sufferings, a progress which Spenser describes with some irony. When she first hears his sobs, we are told 'That pitty did the Virgins hart of patience rob' [III. xi. 8]; and in no time she has offered her help, and Scudamore has appropriated her to his own purposes and made his sufferings hers:

> What huge heroicke magnanimity
> Dwels in thy bounteous brest? what couldst thou more,
> If she were thine, and thou as now am I? [III. xi. 19]

Amoret is held in 'thraldome and continuall feare' by Busyrane who tortures her because she remains steadfast in her love to Scudamore. Busyrane's castle defines the source and nature of these fears, and in entering the castle and destroying the power of Busyrane, Britomart is facing and mastering the fears which surround her own newly born physical instinct. It is these which, by inhibiting the proper and desired fulfilment of the sexual instinct, turn it into a source of torment, and Britomart has to dispel them before she is ready to seek a husband. Her journey through the castle is a journey within her own mind and the discovery of some of the strange inhabitants there, and it is one which she undertakes in a fearful yet coldly rational frame of mind, not in passion. She leaves Scudamore behind because his very nature keeps him out of such a voyage of discovery: he cannot pass the fearful barrier of flames since he himself is the cause of them and their intensity is the exact complement of his own desire—there were no flames or fears until Cupid lit the fire. Britomart takes a long look at the contents of the castle, as Spenser continually remarks: 'The warlike Mayde beholding earnestly...' [III. xi. 53]; 'And as she lookt about, she did behold,/...whereto though she did bend/ Her earnest mind, yet wist not what it might intend' [III. xi. 54]. Spenser mentions the 'busie eye' with which she inspects the Masque of Cupid; yet he does not suggest the sort of cerebration which Guyon exercises in the person of his Palmer as he meets the temptations of Acrasia. Instead, Britomart goes through by a sort of rational instinct, an absolute certainty of purpose in the face of which all that Busyrane can do simply melts away, even though she does not necessarily understand the reason why. Spenser is describing that feminine intuition which recognises its real enemies by unerring instinct, in contrast to the masculine rationalism of Guyon who needs to formulate the reason for what he does.

Britomart's enemy is the mediaeval 'Drede', at whose first impact, she feels herself in the wrong role, not that of Minerva slaying the giants, but of a rebellious Titan challenging omnipotent Jove:

> What monstrous enmity provoke we heare,
> Foolhardy as th'Earth's children, the which made
> Battell against the Gods? so we a God invade. [III. xi. 22]

Her rational courage asserts itself, however; and in going through the flames, her sword drawn, her shield before her, she assumes once more her proper Jovial role, armed with the divine thunderbolts, 'That through she passed; as a thunder bolt/Perceth the yielding ayre,...' [III. xi. 25]. Drede is a natural human phenomenon—the virginal trepidations and fears in the face of a new and profoundly disturbing instinct; but the interior of the castle shows that Buysrane's art has improved on nature and enriched it with all kinds of fantasy. His castle embodies the whole corpus of myth which surrounds sexual love, distorting it and making it terrifying for the initiate. The arras of Cupid's triumphs and the Masque which follows depict all the sins and sufferings of love; the agonising of sonnet lovers, the apprehensions and the pangs of conscience afflicting Courtly Lovers, the great Ovidean tragedies of love and the bestiality to which Cupid has reduced gods and heroes alike. This is the image of love which Busyrane forces upon Amoret so that her normal desires are turned into torment; and the image is a very literary one. These fears are the fruits of the *Metamorphoses*, on the one hand, and of traditional Courtly Love romances and sonnet attitudes, on the other; and Spenser is drawing attention to the responsibilities of literature in this most important field of human life, and to the immeasurable harm which the neglect of its responsibility is capable of doing. Busyrane tortures Amoret in order to make her forswear her essential nature and become his own; but in this case, the captive Amoret is a part of Britomart herself, and so stays staunchly true to Scudamore as Britomart herself sticks unflaggingly to her own amorous quest. In

reproducing what is in fact an inner struggle and anatomising it
so fully for his reader, Spenser is driving out fire with fire,
producing love poetry to destroy the distorted images which the
traditional literature of love enshrines.

The 'goodly arras' of Cupid's triumphs shows Cupid as the
victor of the gods and the gods reduced to beasts in his service:

> Now like a Ram, faire *Helle* to pervart,
> Now like a Bull, *Europa* to withdraw: [III. xi. 30]

he appears as a triumphant Mutability, or a successful Titan
challenging the gods 'to make his empire great', and wreaking
havoc on kings and on 'fearefull Ladies tender hart'. It is a
picture calculated to fill a young girl with misgivings; but if we
look at it more carefully, we see that it is frightening only
because Busyrane means it to seem so, and not to look any
further is to fall into his trap. The first thing we are told, for
example, is that there is gold 'lurking privily' underneath the
silk.

> As faining to be hid from envious eye;
> Yet here, and there, and every where unwares
> It shewd it selfe, and shone unwillingly;
> Like a discoloured Snake, whose hidden snares
> Through the greene gras his long bright burnisht backe
>   declares.   [III. xi. 28]

The chamber is a sort of Mammon's cave trying to conceal its
true identity, and the snake, which suddenly assumes such enormous proportions in the long-drawn-out last line, is clearly
waiting for Eve. In other words, Spenser is warning the reader
at the beginning of the episode that the arras itself conceals a
temptation and should not be taken simply at its face value. The
descriptions of Cupid's triumphs, and the evidence they seem to
offer of the debasement of the gods by love, could in fact point
to a quite different conclusion from that which Cupid would
draw: Jove in the role of a bull takes on a magnificence which
caused Europa's fearful heart 'lively' to tremble when she saw
'The huge seas under her t'obay her servaunts law' [III. xi. 30];
and coming to Danae, he metamorphoses himself into something
altogether more glorious than Mammon, 'Whenas the God to

golden hew him selfe transfard' [31]. The divine love-affairs themselves breed not only Helen but Hercules

> But faire *Alcmena* better match did make,
> Joying his love in likenesse more entire;
> Three nights in one, they say, that for her sake
> He then did put, her pleasures lenger to partake.

[III. xi. 33]

The reference to the Trinity catches the eye, and the whole sequence has an ambivalence which reminds us that the so-called tragedies of love are not all 'mournfull', and that there is more than one way of interpreting Cupid's sneer that '*Jove* to earth is gone' [35]. The full significance of this is not apparent until the *Mutability Cantos*, when we recognise that Jove's amours have their necessary function in establishing the order of Mutability. In the meantime, the arras offers a warning that the conventional mythology of love should not be accepted uncritically; and Britomart, though still a little dazzled by the golden image of Cupid which she gazes at 'The whiles the passing brightnes her fraile sences dazed' [49], yet presses instinctively forward.

She is not deterred by the mottoes on the doors, 'Be bold, be bold, be not too bold', because she is, after all, the 'bold Britoness'. They are, of course, put there by Busyrane as a further part of his distorted image of love, and could be the motto for any sonnet lover who may be bold enough to steal a kiss but is never bold enough to press on to a fuller consummation: it is a formula designed to keep the lover in perpetual servitude but never fulfilled. For those, however, who are determined to cross the forbidden threshold and be too bold, the Masque of Cupid awaits within as a further deterrent. This follows the stock pattern of the Courtly Love tradition, beginning with Ease and Fancy, and working through to Shame, Reproach and Repentance as the inevitable offspring. Britomart, though shaken by the initial storm of wind, thunder and lightning which heralds the approach to the Masque, remains steadfast as the uncanny pageant passes by, its formal allegory and explicit remoteness from life, 'as on the ready flore/Of some Theatre', suggesting her detachment from it all. She views it as a spectator, conscious now of its unreality; and Spenser's use of the masque form serves this purpose, I think, to suggest that all is unreal and artificial, lacking even the verisimilitude of drama. Everything in the castle is fantasy, as Spenser has already indicated by the fact that there are no people within:

> But more she mervaild that no footings trace,
> Nor wight appear'd, but wastefull emptinesse,
> And solemne silence over all that place: [III. xi. 53]

This is not to say that such fantasies cannot hurt; Amoret's sufferings are real enough to tear the heart out of her breast, and yet it is her own conception of the nature of love which torments her; she is like Tess of the D'Urbervilles, tortured by traditional guilts and fears, even though there is no cause in reason or in nature for them. The terrifying image of Cupid on his 'lion ravenous' is in the last analysis only a fantasy 'in wavering womans wit', and because Britomart recognises this, the whole pageant vanishes, not to be seen again. Britomart knows it for what it is and is ready to go beyond it, to the source from which it all springs, in Busyrane himself.

In the heart of the castle is Busyrane, the Enchaunter 'figuring straunge characters of his art' with Amoret's 'living blood', while she is bound with iron bands to the brazen pillar [III. xii. 30]. Busyrane is one with Archimago and Acrasia who are enchanters like himself: he is our own fallen nature working against virtue and life, seeking to blind the eye of reason and to drag the Silver Age down to the level of bronze and iron. Where Acrasia would make us forget the true function of sex by drowning us in its pleasures, Busyrane would make us flee it altogether or pervert it through the fears with which he surrounds it. His strength lies in the lusts of the flesh which came with the Fall, and in the shame at their nakedness which overcame Adam and Eve; and out of this combination come all the unnatural fantasies which the poets and mythmakers have woven around physical love, and which Spenser sees both as the symbol of the condition itself and as the means by which that condition is aggravated. His fantasies may be banished as Britomart banishes them, but he himself cannot be destroyed, any more than Acrasia; and, indeed, as we shall see, it is necessary to preserve him because some form of taboo based on fear is necessary to preserve the sexual instinct in a state of health. He can, however, be controlled, and Britomart controls him partly by the right-reason which Guyon learned to use in the Bower of Blisse, partly by the instinct of womanhood which Amoret gained from her upbringing in the Garden of Adonis. Britomart, therefore, can Christianise Busyrane, forcing him to forswear his 'balefull books' and to unsay his 'sad verse' and his 'bloody lines'. Although Britomart is challenging the basic fears, Spenser always reminds us of their projection in literature and always approaches them primarily as the poet whose job is to do better.

We are given an extraordinarily vivid impression of the overwhelming sense of relief as the burden of fear dissolves and the feeling of acceptance steals in:

> The cruell steele, which thrild her dying hart,
> > Fell softly forth, as of his owne accord,
> > And the wyde wound, which lately did dispart
> > Her bleeding brest, and riven bowels gor'd,
> > Was closed up, as it had not bene bor'd,
> > And every part to safety full sound,
> > As she were never hurt, was soone restor'd:
> > Tho when she felt her selfe to be unbound,
> > And perfect hole, prostrate she fell unto the ground.
>
> [III. xii. 38]

It is not by any cataclysmic revelation or violent emotional upheaval that Britomart has come to the knowledge and frank acceptance of her own physical nature; the word 'softly' suggests that it is as inevitable for her as growing up—which, in fact, is what it is. It is not, perhaps, the accepted ideal of virtuous womanhood which Spenser is advocating—it is a conception calculated to bring a blush to the cheek of a young Victorian person and a sonnet mistress alike; but it is a conception of virtue geared directly to the challenge of the Fall. Britomart is straight out of the *Romance of the Rose*, and on the side of Nature against Death. She has a lot to learn which the *Romance* does not attempt to deal with, for sin as well as death has to be overcome;

and book IV is largely concerned with the new possibilities of sin which arise once the sexual instinct has asserted itself. In book III, however, she completes the first stage of her quest, which is to become a virtuous woman in Spenser's specific definition of the term; and the conclusion of the 1590 version of the poem shows her contemplating the hermaphroditic sexual embrace of Amoret and Scudamore, and wishing that her physical bliss were then and not in the future. In this, she has allied herself with the Garden of Adonis and dissociated herself from the false and tragic myth of Venus and Adonis in Malecasta's tapestries. She does not do this without a wrench, and one of the most true and charming moments of the whole sequence comes at the end when, as she leaves the castle, she realises that all the beautiful tapestries have vanished, and she is filled with momentary regret:

> Returning backe, those goodly roomes, which erst
> She saw so rich and royally arayd,
> Now vanish utterly, and cleane subverst
> She found, and all their glory quite decayd,
> That sight of such a chaunge her much dismayd.
>
> [III. xii. 42]

It is not easy to give up the great and beautiful fabric of myth and romance, however morally desirable it may be to do so.

[3]

If we accept Britomart's growth to sexual maturity as the central theme of Book III, we shall find that the rest of the book falls into place around it. Florimel, in particular, has always presented a problem, though one that arises largely through an indiscriminate emphasis on the continuity of books III and IV and the assumption that she plays an identical role through both. I shall argue in connection with book IV that there is change as well as continuity between the two books, and that characters are metamorphosed in a way which forms an essential part of Spenser's symbolism. In any case, we should remember that six years elapsed between the publication of the two books, and that Spenser's readers came to book III without any assumptions concerning what was to follow. As it stands in the 1590 version, it is complete in itself, and to read it this way eliminates some of the problems which arise if we consider Florimel throughout her whole career.

Florimel obviously embodies a variety of meanings, all of them running parallel to each other in full compatibility. It has often been noticed that her story owes much to the myth of Proserpine: as Ovid recounts it in *Metamorphoses*, book v, Proserpine, the daughter of Ceres, Goddess of plenty, wished to remain a virgin, and Venus, worried by the increasing number who sought to escape from her power, bade Cupid strike Pluto with his arrow and inflame him with the love of the maiden. As a result of this, Pluto carried off Proserpine to the underworld, plunging into the caverns of the sea with his chariot and leaving her girdle floating on the waters, while her mother set out to seek her through the world. The extent to which Spenser drew upon this myth for his story is obvious, although he added a good deal of his own embroidery.

On one level of interpretation, she seems to be a symbol of ideal beauty, the gleam which all must follow and which makes Arthur wish, when the symbolic night of the world robs him of his vision, that

> that Lady faire mote bee
> His Faery Queene, for whom he did complaine:
> Or that his Faery Queene were such, as shee:
>
> [III. iv. 54]

In this sense, she is one with the platonic forms from which material beauty is derived, and she is linked, therefore, with the forms in the Garden of Adonis. Her name, Florimel, puts her among the flowers which grow there until, joined to first matter, they go out into life and are mown down by time's scythe, to return to the garden once more. Book III and, indeed, the subsequent books of *The Faerie Queene*, are full of imagery of flowers withering with time, and Florimel is their emblem. The third book shows her completing the first tragic half of the cycle, the form losing its beauty in the embrace of ever-changing chaos, the spring flower perishing in the frosty embraces of winter, Proserpine carried by Pluto into the darkness of the underworld—all combine in the single myth of spring and winter.

Florimel's story in book III is a tragic one, but Spenser makes it a very specific kind of tragedy and one of relevance to the central theme. The world into which she so dramatically bursts in the first canto is that of the forest, full, like the Bower of Blisse, of the wild beasts of the passions—'Beares, Lions, and Buls, which romed them around' [III. i. 14]; and the point at which Spenser continually hammers throughout the book is that she is driven into flight by her obsessive virgin fears. At first she has every justification for fear as she flies from the lustful foresters, though even at the beginning of her saga there is a touch of irony in the comparison of her hair as it streams behind, to a comet at whose appearance the soothsayers foretell 'death and dolefull drerihed' [III. i. 16]. There is less excuse for her flight later, however, when she flees from every man, including Arthur himself; and a note of half apologetic criticism creeps into Spenser's description:

> With no lesse haste, and eke with no lesse dreed,
> That fearefull Ladie fled from him, that ment
> To her no evill thought, nor evill deed;
> Yet former feare of being fowly shent,
> Carried her forward with her first intent:
> And though oft looking backward, well she vewd,
> Her selfe freed from that foster insolent,
> And that it was a knight, which now her sewd,
> Yet she no lesse the knight feard, then that villein rude.
>
> [III. iv. 50]

By canto VII Spenser is talking of her 'vaine feare' [1], and by VIII he laments that her unhappy journey in the boat is 'causelesse of her owne accord' [1]; and the placing of these comments in the first verse of their respective cantos underlines his insistence that these virgin fears are excessive.

In Florimel Spenser is creating an antithetical figure to Britomart, one who, like the nymph of the waters in book II, turns her back eternally on Faunus and the wood-folk. She is what Busyrane would have made of Amoret if his tortures had succeeded, and that is why Britomart so firmly turns away from the initial chase after Florimel and never meets her throughout the book: her way is not to be that of virginity or virgin fears. Florimel runs a parallel and opposite course to that of Britomart, always in flight from the fears which it is Britomart's mission to face and overcome; and her story, for all her beauty and pathos, is a ruthless and astonishingly modern account of such virginity viewed as an aberration in a book dedicated to the praise of sexual love.

Florimel is a sad, almost heroic, figure because she so valiantly resists whatever seems to assail her; but her tenacious opposition to love—and we shall see later that her love of Marinell is no exception to this—breeds passions which Spenser analyses with great insight and considerable compassion. Her first real adventure comes in canto VII when she reaches the witch's cottage in a sequence which echoes Una's unhappy encounter with Corceca. One of the qualities of Florimel's story, indeed, is its similarity to the unhappier part of Una's: both come to similar cottages and both are rescued by Satyrane; but there is the significant difference that Florimel is in flight whereas Una is in pursuit, and Florimel carries no suggestion of the 'fruitfull virgin' which forms a real part of Una's symbolism as the Bride of Christ. The witch to whom Florimel comes has chosen to live alone, 'So choosing solitarie to abide,/Far from all neighbours' [III. vii. 6], and Spenser stresses the fact that her unsociability has made her sluttish, 'in loathly weedes,/And wilfull want, all carelesse of her needes'. Moreover, her solitariness has bred the slothfulness, the indifference to praise and fame, and the unexpressed, unfulfilled lusts which characterise her uncouth son. This sequence is, I think, Spenser's allegory of the dangers which beset the unnatural virgin life, and in finding herself there, Florimel is threatened by these effects of the path she has chosen.

She resists them virtuously and escapes from the witch and her son, but she cannot escape from the monster whom the witch creates, 'That feeds on womens flesh, as others feede on gras' [III. vii. 22]. The passage must refer to Isaiah, 40:6—'All flesh is grass, and all the goodliness thereof is as the flower of the field': it is a passage dealing with the brevity and mortality of the things of time as opposed to those of eternity, and one very relevant to the theme of book III and its fading flowers. There may also be a link with the hyenas mentioned earlier in Isaiah, 13:22, who will dwell among the ruins of Babylon. The witch's beast who pursues Florimel is surely Spenser's symbol for the action of time, the withering of beauty which none can escape, 'a malady most incident to maids': his task is to devour 'her beauties scornefull grace' [III. vii. 23], and having deflowered her white palfrey he sullies her virgin girdle. This is not the physical rape of Florimel, however, as it has often been interpreted, but the destruction of beauty, so that the virgin girdle is no longer a thing of such value: it is devouring time that has ravished her as it ravages the flowers from the Garden of Adonis:

> When forty winters shall besiege thy brow,
> And dig deep trenches in thy beauty's field,
> Thy youth's proud livery, so gaz'd on now,
> Will be a tatter'd weed, of small worth held:
>> [Shakespeare, Sonnet 2]

But time devours everyone, Britomart and Florimel alike, and one must ask, therefore, why the beast is created by the witch of solitariness. Spenser's answer would be that time ravishes the virgin in a specific and painful way, and that in coming from the witch's stable, the spotted beast represents the specific effects of time upon ageing virginity. He is covered with 'thousand spots of colours queint elect' [III. vii. 22], and the word 'queint' suggests an obvious sexual pun in the context of the story, a pun, moreover, which has been made more succinctly a little earlier when Spenser describes Florimel as 'nothing quaint' [III. vii. 10]. It is the pains and penalties of her own long-preserved virginity which are causing Florimel to wither so rapidly; and the point is reinforced by the episode in the *Metamorphoses* from which Spenser got a hint for his idea of the spotted beast. When Ceres went in search of her daughter Proserpine, she came to a little cottage for food and was insulted by a cheeky boy whom, for punishment, she turned into a spotted lizard [book v]. Like Ovid, Spenser sets up the antithesis between fruitfulness and the spotted beast, though he develops it in far greater detail.

The nature of these pains and penalties to which Florimel's way of life leads will be discussed shortly, but first we should consider the False Florimel whom the witch creates to console her broken-hearted son for the loss of the real one. The elements of which False Florimel is composed give us a clue to her nature; the purest snow 'from all men conceald' [III. viii. 6], tempered with 'fine Mercury,/And virgin wex, that never yet was seald', the 'perfect vermily' and the hair made of golden wires, suggest not only the materials of which the frigid but adored sonnet mistresses are composed, but the more literal art with which Mrs Otter or Lady Centaur repair the ravages of time in Jonson's plays. It is the art of make-up that Spenser is describing, and the mercury is used in the composition of a skin-wash. False Florimel embodies, among other things, the attempts of withered beauty to preserve its charms; and the picture is an unpleasant one, coming painfully near the bone in the way it brings to mind the image of the ageing Virgin Queen Elizabeth— although, of course, the subject is almost an obsession with the Jacobeans.

It is to Florimel's credit that she turns her back on the appeal of such art and never meets the False Florimel until, in book IV, her presence causes the other to vanish. Florimel's defence is in Satyrane who, we are told,

> rather joyd to be, then seemen sich:
> For both to be and seeme to him was labour lich.
>
> [III. vii. 29]

which is the antithesis of all false appearances through cosmetics or any other means. In grappling with the beast and binding it with 'The golden ribband, which that virgin wore/About her sclender wast' he expresses Florimel's heroic mode of coming to terms with her situation: she refuses to conceal her ravaged beauty with art, and comforts herself against all that the beast has done by the thought of her virginity. Satyrane, in book I, is an image of the will trained to conquer the beasts of the passions, and similarly at the tournament in book IV, he proves himself the chief knight of the court of Maidenhead, wearing its emblem on his shield in direct contrast to Scudamore's device of Cupid. We are told that he is one who in 'courtly services tooke no delight' [III. vii. 29], and Florimel, therefore, has inevitable recourse to him in times of crisis.

His victory over the spotted monster, however, is described in curiously equivocal terms which suggest that he is trying to control something fundamentally uncontrollable:

> As he that strives to stop a suddein flood,
>> And in strong banckes his violence containe,
>> Forceth it swell above his wonted mood,
>> And largely overflow the fruitfull plaine,
>> That all the countrey seemes to be a Maine,
>> And the rich furrowes flote, all quite fordonne:
>> The wofull husbandman doth lowd complaine,
>> To see his whole yeares labour lost so soone,
> For which to God he made so many an idle boone.

> So him he held, and did through might amate:. . .
>
> [III. vii. 34–5]

Satyrane's control of the beast is compared to that of the farmer whose attempt to bank in the flood simply causes it to pour over with all the more violence, destroying the very fruitfulness of which it should be the source, and even the verse itself gets out of control in support of the conception. In both the 1590 and 1596 editions the rhyme scheme is broken and the word 'enclose' is there in place of 'containe' in the second line of verse 34. 'Contain' is a modern emendation which obscures what seems to me to be a very broad hint from Spenser that all is not well. For time brings with it more than the loss of beauty; it also brings a host of passions which, like the farmer's flood, denied their normal outlet, now begin to break out in less legitimate directions and shake Florimel with what would nowadays be called the passions of ingrown virginity. The arrival at this point of Argante, a daughter of the rebellious Titans incestuously begot by Typhoeus on his mother earth [III. vii. 47], marks the beginning of this stage and indicates Spenser's profound horror at it. Argante is not merely the symbol of incest, though that is among her many aptitudes; she is like the Crone in the *Romance of the Rose*, the symbol of the naked, unrefined, uncontrolled sexual appetite, voracious for any man, but when denied, slipping over into all forms of female perversion. The fact that she has just captured and made the Squire of Dames her own implies a most subtle and virginal form of such perversion. The 'gentle lady' whom the squire serves refuses him her favours, but insists that he shall seduce as many women as he can and bring the evidence of his conquests to her [III. vii. 55]. She is a sort of voyeur, clinging tenaciously to her own virginity, but satisfying her unappeased appetites vicariously and at the same time, punishing her servant for his incontinence. This is the aspect of Argante to which Spenser draws specific attention; and the fact that the giantess so quickly overcomes Satyrane indicates that Florimel herself is assailed and shaken by the forces of perverted instinct to which her virginity has made her vulnerable.

All are rescued by the mysterious Sir Palladine [III. vii. 52], whose name suggests the Pallas Athene/Minerva with whom, as we have seen, Britomart is linked in her role of giant-killer. Spenser does not make it clear whether Florimel is saved by the grace of God, or by the remnant of true womanhood still remaining within her, or by both: it is certain, however, that the sexual values for which Britomart stands are the answer to what Argante represents, and because Florimel has not embraced these values, her trials are not yet over. The last is the worst; still fleeing as Daphne fled 'to save her maidenhead', she is at last driven to the symbolic sea which she has never before entered, and at once the old man asleep in his boat awakes and tries to rape her. The passage is full of gross sexual innuendos concerning the cock-boat to which Professor Hamilton has rightly drawn attention,[1] and the fact that all are spoken by Florimel herself indicates their significance. The old man is the embodiment of the repressed sexual passions in the aged virgin herself, flaring up for the last time and too strong to be controlled any longer, however hard Florimel still tries to resist them; and they vent themselves, therefore, in ways which Spenser mercifully leaves undefined, though he hints at auto-eroticism. It is an unpleasant, painful picture, but intended to be

[1] *The Structure of Allegory in The Faerie Queene*, p. 151.

so; and it is inevitable in terms of the mythology of the poem that Aeolus, who does his best to hinder so many noble voyages, makes no effort to hinder this one but keeps his winds 'From stirring up their stormy enmitie' [III. viii. 21].

Proteus saves her from the final assault and, lifting her with his rugged hands:

> with his frory lips full softly kist,
> Whiles the cold ysickles from his rough beard,
> Dropped adowne upon her yvorie brest: [III. viii. 35]

This is surely the kiss of death; the flower is at last beaten down by time and Florimel has gone into the darkness, a virgin to the end. The final episode in Proteus's Bower would seem to be Spenser's summing up of what Florimel stands for in relation to the theme of the whole book. Proteus is a figure of far-reaching symbolism in the poem; the marriage of Thames and Medway takes place in his hall, and his capacity for change identifies him with the ever-changing chaos to which the flowers in the Garden of Adonis are united in eternal succession:

> That substance is eterne, and bideth so,
> Ne when the life decayes, and forme does fade,
> Doth it consume, and into nothing go,
> But chaunged is, and often altred to and fro. [III. vi. 37]

He begins his changes 'when the life decays', that is, when Florimel dies, and he wooes her in a great variety of shapes, all of which she refuses:

> Sometimes he boasted, that a God he hight:
> But she a mortall creature loved best:
> Then he would make himselfe a mortall wight;
> But then she said she lov'd none, but a Faerie knight.
>
> Then like a Faerie knight himselfe he drest;
> For every shape on him he could endew:
> Then like a king he was to her exprest,
> And offred kingdomes unto her in vew,
> To be his Leman and his Ladie trew: . . .
>
> [III. viii. 39–40]

Clearly Florimel is running true to form and no guise will serve her turn. In this, Spenser establishes her as the archetype of virginity which opposes itself to all the creative processes of nature and refuses to let the great wheel turn. Though subject to mutability, Florimel turns her back on the physical regeneration which mutability makes possible; and though the virginity she preserves may traditionally rate more highly than the sexual way, Spenser points out the penalty which has to be paid for such high aims in this world. The fame which she achieves for her valiant fruitlessness is not, therefore, that which comes to Britomart for her human heroism, but that of heaven; and Spenser prophesies that her reward will not be in this world but in the next:

> Most vertuous virgin, glory be thy meed,
> And crowne of heavenly praise with Saints above,
> Where most sweet hymmes of this thy famous deed
> Are still emongst them song, that far my rymes exceed.
>
> [III. viii. 42]

Her place is not in a book devoted to fertility, and his 'feeble muse' is inadequate to the task of celebration—'Fit song of Angels caroled to bee' [43]. Cantos VII and VIII contain a very frank and dispassionate analysis of a way of life with which Spenser had little sympathy: he is a Renaissance man looking at a mediaeval ideal and finding it outworn. Florimel's story might be subtitled 'The triumph of Busyrane'.

But this interpretation raises the further problem of Marinell for whose love, after all, Florimel flees all other embraces. A closer look at Marinell will resolve the apparent contradiction. There is an obvious layer of political allegory in the episode when Britomart meets him by the 'rich strond' and wounds him so deeply; it is the Briton maid defeating Philip of Spain, not in terms of the Armada but on the Spanish Main where so many Spanish treasure ships were being plundered. This surface allusion, however, reinforces other and deeper layers of meaning which are more relevant to the special significance of Florimel. Marinell is of the sea, as his name and parentage make plain; he is the son of a sea-nymph and DuMarin, and he should participate, therefore, in the sea's abundant fertility. Instead, he guards the rich strand against which his mother and her sea-nymphs have to take care not to bruise their fins 'and surbate sore/Their tender feet upon the stony ground' [III. iv. 34]. Like the sterile Philip of Spain, he turns the sea into a sort of Mammon's cave; he is a Volpone of the sea, preferring the false increase of its jewels to the true increase of love, and in this he resembles Malbecco who puts his riches before his wife. It is the same 'profitless' usury which Shakespeare is contrasting with the true in sonnets IV and VI, and Florimel very properly loves him because he is the complement of herself.

The whole sequence dealing with Florimel and Marinell is a coherent but difficult one, and perhaps it had to be difficult, for Spenser was treading on dangerous ground. With a virgin queen on the throne whose ageing beauty was only too similar to that of both Florimels, he had to be wary, and this perhaps accounts both for the complexity of the allegory and also for some aspects of the Belphoebe–Timias story. In the letter to Raleigh and in the proem to book III, Belphoebe is explicitly related to Elizabeth, while the adventures of Timias contain unmistakable references to Raleigh. Spenser pays his patron the compliment of making him alone follow the lustful foresters when Arthur and Guyon chase after Florimel, and the fight and subsequent cure through tobacco [III. v. 32], would seem to refer to Raleigh's chequered progress into the Queen's favour. Such explicit identification of characters is rare in *The Faerie Queene*, yet in this case it is underlined and amplified in book IV. One wonders whether Spenser perhaps included this as a sort of insurance policy against the Queen's identification of herself with either of the two Florimels, or even her possible resentment of a general criticism of virginity. At least, with such an admirer as Timias, she need never find herself in the plight of Florimel in her cock-boat. It is unnecessary, however, to take so low an estimate of Spenser's motives, for he clearly distinguishes between the virginity which is simply a fear of womanhood, and that nobler kind which is chosen as a means of freeing the individual for great and fruitful effort in another field. This is the sort of activity which belongs to Belphoebe, who is the pattern of active virtue and the controlled will. Spenser treats the Queen's virginity as he treats the fact that she is the ruler in a world where man has a higher place in the natural hierarchy; both are unnatural but both divinely appointed, and justified by the fruitful blessings which they bring to the nation. The fruitful virgin is, as we have seen, a basic concept of *The Faerie Queene* both in religious and secular terms; but Spenser seems to have no sympathy whatever with the mediaeval ideal of virginity which has its source in the attempt to escape from the world.

One more sequence remains to be discussed, that of Paridel and Hellenore which, for all its underlying reference to Paris and Helen, is treated in book III in a happily comic vein. It affords a comic interlude between the genuine tragedy of Florimel and the strange, even frightening adventures of Britomart in the castle of Busyrane, and ensures that the balance is tilted on the side of comedy, which is proper in terms of the conception of love which Spenser is putting forward. Paridel's remark, when he hears of Florimel's death and sees her stained girdle, contains a quality of irony which helps to keep the episode in proportion. He protests that he will not give up the search for Florimel as long as any hope remains:

> Yet will I not forsake my forward way,
> Till triall doe more certaine truth bewray [III. viii. 50]

He will, in other words, carry on the chase as long as there is a virgin left alive. Malbecco is treated in the same way, as the comic cornuto who 'low louted on the lay' before the comic bragging soldier with his traditional fustian,

> But minds of mortall men are muchell mard,
> And mov'd amisse with massie mucks unmeet regard.
> [III. x. 31]

There are innumerable jokes and sexual puns about young women mated with men 'Unfit faire Ladies service to supply', and deprived, therefore, of 'kindly joy', or stealing off in 'misconceiving night'.

It is the treatment, however, rather than the theme itself which is comic, as Spenser makes clear when he describes the Ovidean language of love which the guilty pair practise as 'A sacrament prophane in mistery of wine' [III. ix. 30]. The

genealogy which Paridel gives for himself and Hellenore sets
the Trojan myth firmly in the centre of the poem, and relates
both himself and Britomart to the heroic and anti-heroic lines
between whom the whole struggle of *The Faerie Queene* takes
place. In terms of book III, Hellenore is of especial significance,
for she represents one reason why Busyrane must not be killed,
even if it were possible to kill him. Hellenore is a woman without any sexual fears or inhibitions at all, and Spenser suggests
through her, I think, that even Busyrane, properly used, may
have his value, just as the fear of the Blatant Beast in book VI
helps some people to be virtuous. At this stage, Spenser treats
Hellenore with a certain amount of tolerance as he describes the
satyr ringing his matin bell so oft, because in the special context
of book III, her incontinence is no worse a fault than that of
Florimel. Myrrha, if not more admirable, is perhaps more
natural than Daphne. As is so often the case in *The Faerie
Queene* Spenser raises lightly at the end of one book what is
going to provide the main theme of the next. Book IV is concerned with the moral exercise of the sexual passion which book
III has brought to birth, and the passions of lust and jealousy
belong more properly there.

Spenser's book of Chastity issues a challenge to the whole
tradition of love literature and to the time-honoured conception
of Cupid. Chaucer's Troilus does not blame Cresseid for his
pains nor Astrophil, Stella for his frustration—the particular
woman hardly enters into it: it is Love seen as an external force
which seizes hold of people and involves them even against
their will. But Spenser's image of love in Britomart is of something which rises from within and which it is in her power to
release for herself, to choose and direct. He turns an impersonal
force into a human instinct and moves from the world of myth
to that of psychology. In so doing, he throws the onus of choice
and action more firmly onto the individual will and is able to
incorporate love more completely within the discipline of virtue
than in any previous literature.

8

Friendship

[1]

The relationship between books III and IV is a complex one and their order of composition is not clear; but however they were written, the gap in publication faced Spenser with a special literary problem. He had to bring book III to a real conclusion so as not to leave his readers suspended in the middle of an episode, and he had later to reopen it and pick up the threads again in order to allow the sort of continuity he needed. The answer is the changed ending of III in the 1596 edition, and the very great pains which Spenser took to dovetail the fourth book into the third so that the reader remembers the significance of what has already happened. We are reminded of Florimel's 'unworthie paine', of Amoret's 'hart-binding chaine', and of the sufferings she underwent as a 'virgine wife' for love of Scudamore. The only change in detail, the separation of Scudamore from Amoret, makes it possible for the story to be continued and for Scudamore to be revived as a character in book IV, whereas in the normal pattern of *The Faerie Queene*, his task would be finished at the end of book III. This is of the utmost importance to the total structure and meaning of the two books.

It has been argued that book III contains a religious and philosophical statement about the right true end of human love worked out in psychological terms, and that it traces Britomart up to the moment of her emancipation from some of the traditional attitudes towards sex. Book IV takes up the theme at this point and explores the new range of moral problems, temptations and solutions which accompany the awakened sexual instinct. At the same time it considers these, more than book III, as an aspect of that divine creativity by which God brought the whole universe into being: of all the books of the poem, that of Friendship is the most metaphysical.

Virginal fears, like the temptations of faith and temperance, are private and personal, to be encountered and overcome within the individual mind. Love as a sexual relationship, in contrast, involves another person and has social consequences, so that the virtues of the second three books are social ones, and the allegory gradually moves from within the mind to involve outer realities. The change is never total and the psychological allegory is always there in a greater or less degree, but there is an increasing tendency through book IV for the figures to develop into characters in their own right or to become allegories of external forces. We shall see one form of this in the changing role of Scudamore from a quality to a person; another, in the altered significance of Florimel's girdle: in book III it is clearly the virgin zone, but by the tournament of IV. v, it has become the girdle of chastity, the Cestus which Venus wore when she chose to live 'in wively sort' [IV. v. 3]. The proem to book IV heralds the new emphasis: it deals with the fame which comes not merely to those who love but to 'them that love, and do not live amisse', and it is addressed to Elizabeth, the Queen of Love in her social role of 'Prince of peace' [iv].

The beginning of book IV takes up the story where book III ended, with Britomart and Amoret together and, like much in the two books, the opening sequence makes its point on both literal and allegorical levels. As a literal narrative of two girls, it gives a sympathetic and amusing picture of the new self-consciousness of adolescent sex. Amoret is exaggeratedly aware of her virginity and of the masculine threat to it—'His will she feard'—and acutely conscious of physical proximity:

> For *Amoret* right fearefull was and faint,
> Lest she with blame her honor should attaint,
> That everie word did tremble as she spake,
> And everie looke was coy and wondrous quaint,
> And everie limbe that touched her did quake:
>
> [IV. i. 5]

This is realism and yet it is a good deal more, as the curious last line indicates, for we should expect it to be Amoret's limb which quaked, whereas it is, in fact, Britomart's. Spenser is fusing the two girls into one, insisting that Amoret is still a part of Britomart's own nature as she was in book III. Only in this light does the later episode make sense, where Britomart goes to sleep in the shade and Amoret, wandering off into the forest, is at once seized by Lust; and the same is true of the uncharacteristic behaviour of Britomart described in canto I. 7—the 'fine abusion of the Briton mayd', as Spenser calls it:

> For other whiles to her she purpos made
> Of love, and otherwhiles of lustfulnesse,
> That much she feard his mind would grow to some
> excesse   [IV. i. 7]

We should hardly expect such wanton teasing by Britomart on the literal level, even to hide her 'fained sex', but as an allegory of Britomart herself toying with her newly felt instincts, it is more in character. The same method of interpretation works with the succeeding episode of the young knight who jousts with Britomart for possession of Amoret. Britomart's answer is to keep Amoret for herself, but to admit the virtuous admiration of herself by the knight [IV. i. 15]. In other words, she allows male admiration but firmly keeps her virginity; there is to be no sex without marriage:

> But either he should neither of them have, or both.
> [IV. i. 10]

The result of this first direct sexual challenge to Britomart is to force her to define her sexual position more clearly to herself, and once this is done the uneasy uncertainties of the opening sequence are left behind. This is why Amoret is 'freed from feare', and, getting into Britomart's bed as she has not done before, 'found right safe assurance theare' [IV. i. 15]. The two can now openly admit their sexual longings to each other, safe in their determination to remain chaste.

[2]

Britomart is now ready to begin the second stage of her quest and face the sexual temptations of lust and jealousy to which her own awakened nature exposes her. At this point, therefore,

Spenser introduces the first group of the villains of book IV, Paridell, Blandamour, Duessa and, source and product of them all, Ate, the archetype of evil in the last three books of the poem. She is the occasion of one of the great set pieces of the poem, defining by negatives Spenser's conception of love, both human and divine. She is the source of all dissension, both public and private, among men [19], and her dwelling is 'Hard by the gates of hell' [20], to complement her activities which are directed against the saving mercy of heaven [30]. Her underground den is surrounded by thorns and 'wicked weedes' which like intemperance grow 'at first of little seedes' [25], and all occasions of historical and mythological discord stem from her, including the golden apple and the feast of the Lapithes, where so many Centaurs 'under great *Alcides* furie fell' [23]. Her name places her firmly within the mythological framework of the poem, for it was Ate who attempted to delay the birth of Hercules. Moving from the moral to the metaphysical level, Spenser makes her an 'unnatural' character in all the full Elizabethan sense of the word. Her squinting eyes and unmatching feet and ears are contrary to the harmony of nature, and in keeping with this her sole aim is to destroy the great chain of concord and reduce everything once more to chaos:

> For all this worlds faire workmanship she tride,
> Unto his last confusion to bring,
> And that great golden chaine quite to divide,
> With which it blessed Concord hath together tide.
>
> [IV. i. 30]

The love to which Ate is opposed is that primal love by which God created the universe, as Spenser describes the process in the *Fowre Hymnes*, when form was imposed upon the jarring atoms of first matter and harmony upon the warring elements:

> The earth, the ayre, the water, and the fyre,
> Then gan to raunge them selves in huge array,
> And with contrary forces to conspyre
> Each against other, by all meanes they may,
> Threatning their owne confusion and decay:
> Ayre hated earth, and water hated fyre,

Till Love relented their rebellious yre.

[*An Hymne in Honour of Love*, lines 77–84]

Chaos came first and love after which is why, in the Garden of
Venus, Concord has both hate and love by the hand, but love is
the younger and the stronger.

If book III of *The Faerie Queene* is that of creation, book IV
celebrates the concord which creation itself implies and by
which it is maintained; and the metaphysical dimension is
nearly always present in the description of moral and heroic
behaviour. The heroes of book IV are the peace-makers who, at
whatever level on which they operate, are ultimately imposing
the harmony of form upon chaos. Alastair Fowler has analysed
the symbolism of the four elements which runs throughout the
book,[1] and every instance in which a group of four jarring
knights is forcibly pacified by Arthur or Britomart forms a
paradigm of Divine love. The most elaborate instance is the
fight of Britomart and Scudamore against Druon, Claribell,
Blandamour and Paridell in canto IX. Claribell and Blandamour
attack Britomart [30], because both exemplify excesses of love
opposed to her full virtue [21]. In contrast, Druon, who delights
in single life, and Paridell, who feels no love at all for the women
he seduces, are opposed to love itself, and so their attack is
directed against Cupid's man. Left to themselves, the four like
Ate would make chaos come again; and it is natural that their en-
deavours should be associated with the malevolent blasts of Aeolus:

> As when *Dan Æolus* in great displeasure,
> For losse of his deare love by *Neptune* hent,
> Sends forth the winds out of his hidden threasure,
> Upon the sea to wreake his fell intent;
> They breaking forth with rude unruliment,
> From all foure parts of heaven doe rage full sore,
> And tosse the deepes, and teare the firmament,
> And all the world confound with wide uprore,
> As if in stead thereof they *Chaos* would restore.

[IV. ix. 23]

Because love is such a necessary thing both to the human

---

[1] *Spenser and the Numbers of Time*, chap. IV.

microcosm and to the whole of creation, Spenser makes it his main object in book IV to identify its chief enemies, especially those forces of self-destruction which live in the heart of love itself. The most important section of the book is the great episode of Cambel and Triamond, whose original title in the edition of 1596, which has Telamond for Triamond, suggests that the sequence is designed to embrace the whole world.[1] That the episode represents the triumph of concord over discord is obvious, but it should be noticed, too, that it represents the battle between two conceptions of love, both noble and both traditional, the love which is physical and that which is spiritual. It is a statement of Spenser's own conception of the relationship between Eros and Agape. The symbolism of Agape's name prepares us for the nature of her three sons who, born of the union of a mortal and a fay, have the same mixed constitution, half physical, half spiritual, as the soul itself, and bring to mind the triple soul of man, as Professor Roche has pointed out.[2] This love of soul for soul is the truest, the most intense and unshakeable love relationship possible to mankind:

> For as the soule doth rule the earthly masse,
> And all the service of the bodie frame,
> So love of soule doth love of bodie passe,
> No lesse than perfect gold surmounts the meanest brasse
>
> [IV. ix. 2]

but it suffers from the inescapable limitation that it has no answer to mortality, as Spenser makes clear both by his account of Agape's visit to the Fates, and his description of the pairs of heroic friends in the Garden of Venus whose loves are immortal but whose lives are subject to time: 'Whose lives although decay'd, yet loves decayed never' [IV. x. 27]. The love and the exchange of souls between the three brothers can strengthen each other, but not create the eternity by succession which belongs to the Garden of Adonis.

Cambel, in contrast, has Canacee's magic ring with all the traditional sexual symbolism attached to it. He has 'hope of happie speed,/Conceived by a ring' whose special virtue was 'to

1 Thomas P. Roche Jr, *The Kindly Flame* (Princeton, 1964), p. 16.
2 Pp. 15 ff.

staunch al wounds, that *mortally* did bleed' [IV. ii. 39]; and his power in the battle is to die and rise again, like some 'newborne wight' [IV. iii. 23], or

> Like as a Snake, whom wearie winters teene,
> Hath worne to nought, now feeling sommers might,
> Casts off his ragged skin and freshly doth him dight.
>
> [IV. iii. 23]

or, more explicitly,

> Like as a withered tree through husbands toyle
> Is often seene full freshly to have florisht,
> And fruitfull apples to have borne awhile,
> As fresh as when it first was planted in the soyle.
>
> [IV. iii. 29]

The snake and the apples belong to the Fall and mortality, but the 'husbands toyle' emphasises the continuity of the new spring and sexual procreation. The battle between Cambel and the three brothers is yet another variation on the ancient opposition between flesh and spirit, Venus and Diana, and its long-drawn-out agony suggests above all the weariness and sterility of life thus unnaturally divided against itself:

> Long while they then continued in that wize,
> As if but then the battell had begonne:
> Strokes, wounds, wards, weapons, all they did despise,
> Ne either car'd to ward, or perill shonne,
> Desirous both to have the battell donne;
> Ne either cared life to save or spill,
> Ne which of them did winne, ne which were wonne.
> So wearie both of fighting had their fill,
> That life it selfe seemd loathsome, and long safetie ill.
>
> [IV. iii. 36]

Spenser's answer is a love which includes and transcends both sides, as God's own love involves both the contemplation of his infinite beauty and its propagation through the universe. Cambina's Hermetic rod is that with which Mercury points upwards to the divine mysteries in Botticelli's *Primavera*,[1] but

---

1 Edgar Wind, chap. VII.

its results are to turn blows to kisses and hatred into marriage;
and in combining in herself the two Platonic Venuses, Cambina
heals the breach between body and soul. It is this full relationship on all levels to which Spenser gives the name of Friendship,
the same friendship for which Venus pleaded with Diana in book III.

Because of Cambina's central relevance, Spenser makes her
stand out from the rest of the episode which is itself a sort of
inset within the book. Her arrival is a stage entry, like that of
Truth in her chariot when she comes to the barriers and stops
the fighting in Jonson's *Masque of Hymen*:

> All suddenly they heard a troublous noyes,
> That seemd some perilous tumult to desine,
> Confusd with womens cries, and shouts of boyes,
> Such as the troubled Theaters oftimes annoyes.
>
> [IV. iii. 37]

It is with logical irony that Spenser makes the entry of the
queen of peace the cause of confusion and disquiet among the
crowd, for her power is beyond human understanding and
derives from the art of God himself, 'Such as the maker selfe
could best by art devize'. Only the old heroes are fit to drink of
her Nepenthe, and by it they become worthy to join the
immortals [IV. iii. 44].

[3]

Although the legend of Cambel and Triamond itself is limited to
two cantos, and the characters play only a small part outside of
these, the theme of friendship is treated in a variety of ways
throughout the book. The opposition between physical and
spiritual is implicit in the great tournament of canto IV for
Florimel's girdle, itself a rather ambiguous object involving
both, for it begins as a symbol of virginity and ends as one of
married chastity. On this occasion, the knights of Maidenhood
whose champion is naturally Satyrane, are opposed to the lover
knights, Cambel, Triamond and Scudamore. The prize is
carried off by Britomart who unites in herself the virtues of both
sides: as a virgin warrior set upon a quest of marriage, she is a
Diana who will turn into a Venus.

The relationship of Timias and Belphoebe rings a further change upon the theme. As we have seen, the sequence is more explicitly involved with contemporary history than anything in the earlier books, and must be read against the background of court politics and the long and losing battle which Raleigh fought to retain the Queen's favour.[1] It is not, however, a simple transcript of history but a selection of those aspects of history which are relevant to the themes of books III and IV. Because the two books are concerned with physical and spiritual love, the relationship between Timias and Belphoebe is considered from this angle, and Spenser concentrates attention upon the clash between the sexual values in love with which Raleigh identified himself and the royal cult of virginity. From the first moment he sets out, Timias is a figure like Sidney's Astrophil, continually seeking to master lust but always being conquered by it. In trying to save Florimel, he is wounded by the lustful forester, and in his chivalric attempt to rescue Amoret, he is hindered by her body behind which Lust shelters. From time to time, Spenser utters what sound like personal warnings to his patron against future hazards:

> Now God thee keepe, thou gentlest Squire alive,
> Else shall thy loving Lord thee see no more,
>
> [III. v. 26]

There is the suggestion of some kind of topical reference in the description of Belphoebe's nymphs who come running up to the rescue:

> And every one to runne the swiftest stryv'd;
> But two of them the rest far overpast, . . .   [III. v. 38]

and his embracing of Amoret, which so arouses Belphoebe's anger, is the predictable culmination of his whole history. There would seem to be a reference to Raleigh's marriage here, though Amoret is not to be equated with Elizabeth Throckmorton; she is not a person but a quality, the inclination towards married love to which the Queen objected so strongly in her favourites.

Walter Oakeshott, *The Queen and the Poet* (London, 1960).

In book III, Spenser's attitude towards Timias is one of tolerant criticism. In a book praising physical love, Timias's feelings are right and natural, yet, mistaking Belphoebe's true nature, he aims too high. She is not a mistress, but Diana's maid, the imperial voice of fame beyond the reach of ordinary human reactions; and Timias seeks to reduce her to the role of the normal obdurate Petrarchan mistress. Whatever criticism the sequence contains is aimed at Timias, and is perhaps Spenser's comment on Raleigh's willingness to participate in the courtly cult of erotic idolatry which surrounded the Queen. By book IV, however, Spenser's attitude has changed. In being angered at his embrace of Amoret, Belphoebe steps down from her lofty platform of fame and becomes a Diana meddling in the affairs of Venus instead of performing her proper job. Spenser would seem to be levelling an oblique criticism at the Queen for allowing personal affections to obstruct her public duties, and diverting Timias from his true quest, which was a more active and imperial one in Spenser's eyes. There is the suggestion of this in the reconciliation between Belphoebe and Timias, for the 'happie life with grace and good accord' [IV. viii. 18] which Timias achieves on his return to favour makes him forget his service to Arthur and become 'mindlesse of his owne deare Lord/The noble Prince' [IV. viii. 18]. Even the means by which he comes back into Belphoebe's graces carry a suggestion of irony: the ruby heart which the dove bears to her could contain a reference to the return of the great Carrack in 1592, when Raleigh was let out of the Tower in order to stop the looting and preserve the Queen's share of the booty. I would suggest that in book IV, Spenser is pleading with the Queen to be a Belphoebe indeed and, in rising above the level of personal involvement, to set Raleigh once more upon the road to fame in service to the state.

As the central character of books III and IV, Britomart herself has inevitably to face and resolve the dichotomy between the two aspects of love. She has spent her time in book IV battling with the variety of perversions which arise when the physical and the spiritual are divided; and her own complete heroism consists in her ability to deal with the conflict when it arises within herself, and to reconcile the demands of the flesh which she had learned to accept by the end of book III with the higher demands of her spiritual nature. This is the theme of canto VII. As Britomart goes through the forest, she relaxes after the tournament, and alighting to rest her weary limbs, she falls asleep—'There heavie sleepe the eye-lids did surprise/Of *Britomart* after long tedious toyle' [IV. vii. 3]. Meanwhile Amoret, 'of nought affeard', wanders away through the wood and is seized by the monster Lust: 'Feebly she shriekt', we are told, but too feebly to wake Britomart; and once in Lust's arms she no longer thinks of crying for help:

> For she deare Ladie all the way was dead,
> Whilest he in armes her bore;...   [IV. vii. 9]

the grief and tears only come when he puts her down and she wakes again. The sequence does not imply that Britomart falls unguardedly into a love affair, for Amoret escapes from Lust's cave before her turn comes to be devoured, and in full horrified recognition of the evil he embodies. The ethics of Spenser's period would not allow him to plunge his heroine into sin in a manner comparable to the fall of a hero. He makes the point, therefore, that Britomart is still not fully aware of the strength of her own instincts, and that once aroused they are almost impossible to control: she has, in fact, to learn the wisdom of what the Palmer said in book II about occasion, and the fire springing from the little spark. At this stage she can no longer escape from the grasp of Lust by her own unaided efforts, even though she is awake to its true nature; and Spenser gives a slightly sardonic picture of Amoret's attempts to run away 'Ne feeles the thorns and thickets pricke her tender toes' [IV. vii. 21] —and of the blind panic she experiences 'like a ghastly Gelt'. Her own body stands in the way of her rescue and prevents Timias from destroying the monster.

Only the Grace of God can save her in these circumstances, as it came to the aid of Red Cross and Guyon when they were too weak to save themselves:

> Ne living aide for her on earth appeares,
> But if the heavens helpe to redresse her wrong,
> Moved with pity of her plenteous teares.   [IV. vii. 23]

Help comes in the form of Belphoebe who embodies, at this point of the poem, the noblest moral instincts of Britomart's own nature. She is a figure of the virginity which Britomart struggles to retain, a Venus Urania whose idealism destroys lust; above all, a Diana in the woods 'hunting then the Libbards and the Beares/...To banish sloth, that oft doth noble mindes annoy' [IV. vii. 23]. She is the instinct towards Fame, and by her Britomart is enabled to summon up all her inner strength, her idealised conception of physical love, her sense of her heroic mission, to bring her physical nature into proper subjection. From this moment she can go on in the strength of her own tried and tested virtue, just as Amoret is healed by Arthur's 'pretious liquour' [IV. viii. 20] and can travel in his company 'safe as in a Sanctuary', because he has learned

> The course of loose affection to forstall,
> And lawlesse lust to rule with reasons lore;
>
> [IV. ix. 19]

The rescue of Amoret by Belphoebe is Britomart's reconciliation of the conflict between Diana and Venus within herself, and she is at last ready to meet her lover in the flesh instead of seeking a disembodied ideal. Her relationship with him will now be one in which virtue and pleasure are reconciled. She has still, however, a further step to take. Her path in book IV has been one of abstinence, and she has drawn on the strength of Diana to bridle her desires; but in the security of this strength she must now revert to her proper and ultimate role, which is that of Venus. Her battle with Artegall marks this change, for she loses the fight but wins a victory of a different kind. The blow which sheers off her helmet reveals her femininity and, in being conquered, Britomart learns the proper way for her sex to conquer. From this point, she can play the woman's role and cease to go against the 'course of kind' [IV. vi. 30], a fact which delights both Scudamore and Glauce. She is forced to put off her own sex and play the man again in book V, but only because Artegall has played the woman with Radegund, and she has to redress the balance in a battle which Spenser presents as essentially unnatural.

[4]

Although Britomart never abuses the powers which her beauty
gives her, they are powers which are capable of abuse, as we
see in the effect of Radegund upon Artegall in the next book;
and Spenser therefore rounds off the sequence with a warning
of this danger to both the sexes. The subject is treated earlier,
in the Bower of Blisse, of course, in the power with which
Acrasia dominates her lovers; but book II deals with it as something rising from within: Acrasia is not a woman but Guyon's
own sensuous nature challenging the strict rational control
which he would exercise over it, in contrast to book IV, where it
is seen as a force affecting us from outside. The story of Poeana
is an allegory of the dangerous power of woman's looks as
defined in the contemporary theories of the physiology of sex.
She is the daughter of Corflambo of the flaming eyes whose
contagious fires set Amyas aflame in canto VIII, when he met
Aemylia in the grove. As Corflambo is clearly Spenser's symbol
for the animal spirits which dart from the lover's eyes—in this
case Aemylia's—and inflame the other party with desire,
Poeana must, therefore, personify the power which this ability
to arouse desire confers upon a woman. She is a more formidable
figure than we might think, the embodiment of the active
effects of sex-appeal, and even Arthur has to tread warily in her
presence. When he first sees her, the might of woman's eyes is
almost enough to disarm him—'The Prince halfe rapt, began
on her to dote' [IV. ix. 6], and he is only able to conquer her
because he has already destroyed the occasion and source of her
power, Corflambo himself. The two are the dominant figures in
the physiology of desire, and his victory over them is his demonstration in book IV of the perfection of his virtue.

The difference between Acrasia and Poeana is symptomatic of
the change from internal to external, from private to social,
which takes place in book IV. Britomart's meeting with Artegall
at the very centre of the book forms the watershed; and from
then on Spenser is increasingly concerned with the relationship
of the sexes to each other, and goes on to explore the sort of
female power which is compatible with a traditional hierarchy
in which the male is the dominant figure. The proper hierarchy

of the sexes is treated more fully in the book of Justice, but the problem is raised in the complex story of Amyas and Aemylia, Placidas and Poeana, which sums up so much of book IV and leads on into the next one. The basic story is yet another variant on the theme of Cambel and Triamond: the masculine love of Amyas and Placidas is weighed against the sexual appeal of Poeana and proves the stronger, although Spenser makes the point, as he did with Cambina, that neither love is enough on its own. The marriage of the four lovers produces a harmony which transcends either and creates in human terms the pattern of the four elements. It depends, however, on the natural hierarchy of the sexes, and Arthur is careful to destroy the unnatural 'maisterie' which Poeana has exercised, by making her subject to Placidas and putting him in charge of all her lands:

> From that day forth in peace and joyous blis,
> They liv'd together long without debate,
> Ne private jarre, ne spite of enemis
> Could shake the safe assuraunce of their state.

[IV. ix. 16]

It is in the light of this that we should consider the development of Scudamore through book IV, and his emergence by canto X as a heroic character in his own right. In book III, as we have seen, he is no more than the personification of an inner trait, a figure of the pangs and frustrations of the awakening sexual instinct; and in this role, he falls into the wildly irrational jealousy at the obviously fictional account of Amoret's infidelity [IV. i. 49] which is to be expected of such love. As Cupid's man, he is neutral, capable of expressing either sex, and having served to reveal the nature of Britomart in book III, he moves over to the same role in relation to Artegall. Before he knows Britomart, Artegall feels only a general interest in the opposite sex—it is the loss of Amoret which angers him at the tournament—and he welcomes Scudamore as soon as he sees him. The union of Artegall and Britomart gives Scudamore as great a pleasure as the loss of his own Amoret grieves him, because he is still, in part, the personification of a human instinct in Artegall, as he was formerly of Britomart. By canto X, however, there is a change in his role: when he tells his tale of the capture of Amoret, he comes to the front of the stage and takes on the form of the traditional male lover in *The Romance of the Rose*. His quest for Amoret and his capture of her from the Temple of Venus is the male equivalent of Britomart's rescue of Amoret from Busyrane's castle. Like Amoret who 'never joyed day' since Scudamore 'her bought/In perilous fight' [IV. i. 2], Scudamore himself 'never joyed howre' since she first wounded his heart [IV. x. 1]. His progress to the Garden of Venus is one of growing up, like that of Britomart; the bridge he has to cross with its 'curious Corbes and pendants' at one end, and its gated castle at the other, contains obvious symbolism of both sexes; and as Britomart has to overcome Drede, so Scudamore has to pass by the equally traditional figure of Daunger before he can reach the rose itself.

It is a different rose from that of the *Romance*, not just the sexual conquest, but the achievement of the perfected virtue of sexual love in the lap of Concord, attended by all the graces; and Spenser turns this ideal conquest of Venus's maid by Cupid's man, therefore, into an heroic exploit:

> No lesse did *Daunger* threaten me with dread,
>   When as he saw me, maugre all his powre,
>   That glorious spoyle of beautie with me lead,
>   Then *Cerberus*, when *Orpheus* did recoure
>   His Leman from the Stygian Princes boure.
>
> [IV. x. 58]

The reference to Cerberus, so consistently coupled with Hercules throughout the poem, makes the comparison to Orpheus the more striking: Scudamore's heroism is not that of a Hercules and, as we already know from the whole story of books III and IV, he is destined to lose the Eurydice he has won. Lovers are all of the line of Mordant and Amavia and have mortal tragedy mixed with their triumphs. Yet the capture of Amoret by Scudamore, which should logically be told at the end of book III, and from which so much of the unhappiness of book IV derives, is kept until the end and then raised to a heroic prominence which makes us forget what has gone before. Spenser is redressing the balance of the sexes, bringing forward the active male principle to match and finally dominate the female, as the proper relationship of the sexes is reasserted. Love is full of suffering for both sexes:

> For every dram of hony therein found,
> A pound of gall doth over it redound. [IV. X. 1]

Britomart will find this as much as Scudamore, and yet the outcome justifies it all. The meeting of Scudamore and Amoret, like that of Artegall and Britomart, makes possible the fruitful concord of generation, and Scudamore's conquest of Amoret is followed logically, therefore, by the great pageant of fertility at the marriage of Thames and Medway in the next canto. Spenser's method of telling his tale in reverse rather than in chronological order throws the emphasis onto the essential cause and effect within the sexual relationship and, at the same time, presents the whole process as a perpetual cycle rather than as a particular instance with a beginning, a middle, and an end. In this context, Florimel can rise from her dark prison and Marinell return to his proper element, the sea, with the same inevitability as Proserpine makes her return with each new spring.

Although books III and IV are both concerned with love, it is obvious that their unity is not a simple one, and that book IV builds upon but progresses beyond the statement of book III. The wedding of the Thames and the Medway is founded in the Garden of Adonis, but it incorporates the further conceptions of order and concord which have been explored through book IV. This development in theme involves, as we have seen, a development in method, the main quality of which is a loosening of the strict logic of allegory and a general changing of roles by the various characters. Cambell and Triamond have a specific symbolism in canto III which they shed later: Poeana dwindles from being the allegoric daughter of Corflambo into a mere wife: Florimel, having originally chosen the heavenly way, comes back into circulation on earth, and her girdle changes from that of virgin to wife. In reading the two books, and more particularly in reading book IV, one is aware of stories and characters melting into each other in a manner which resembles that of Ovid's *Metamorphoses* more than anything else; and the fact that Ovid's poem is largely concerned with love would justify Spenser's choice of it as his model on the grounds of literary decorum alone. In a deeper sense than this, however, books III and IV are based on the principle of metamorphosis, for mutability and creation are ultimately different names for the same thing. The perpetual regeneration and infinite plenitude of nature arise from the insatiable desire of first matter to partake of divine beauty, so that it takes on form after form in the endless circle of generation and corruption. In the words of Leone concerning First Matter:

According to Plato, it desires and loves the forms of all created things with a love like woman's for man. And as this love, appetite, desire are not to be appeased by the actual presence of any one form, it is ever enamoured of another that is absent and, abandoning the one, seizes on the other; so that as it cannot be actualized in all forms at once, it assumes them all successively one after the other. Its many parts do indeed embrace all forms simultaneously, but since each part desires to enjoy the love of all forms, they must needs be transmuted into one another in continual succession. For a single form is inadequate to sate its appetite and love, which greatly exceeds all satisfaction, so that no one form can fulfil this insatiable appetite. Thus first matter causes both the continual production of those forms which it lacks, and the continual destruction of those which it possesses. Hence some call it harlot, because of the variety and inconstancy of its loves; for no sooner does it love one than it desires to leave it for another. Yet it is this adulterous love which beautifies the lower world with such and so wondrous variety of fair-formed things. So that the creative love of this first matter, and its desire for ever new mates, and the delight it takes in ever new copulations, is the cause of the creation of all created things.[6]

That is why Spenser's Proteus is at once a disreputable but a most necessary figure in the scheme of creation; and the power of change which he embodies is woven, therefore, into the very structure of Book IV. The apparent looseness of the book does not represent a loss of control but a very subtle use of symbolic form, and the change of method with the change of theme when we come to book V is very marked. As usual, Spenser prepares the reader for what is to come, and leads out of the one book into the other. Themes especially relevant to justice have already been introduced in connection with friendship,

---

[1] Leone Ebreo, *The Philosophy of Love*, trans. F. Friedeberg-Seeley and Jean H. Barnes (London, 1937), pp. 84–5.

and book IV ends with Cymodoce's curiously legal plea for the liberation of Florimel which sets the key for the new book:

> To whom she answerd, Then it is by name
> *Proteus*, that hath ordayn'd my sonne to die;
> For that a waift, the which by fortune came
> Upon your seas, he claym'd as propertie:
> And yet nor his, nor his in equitie,
> But yours the waift by high prerogative.
> Therefore I humbly crave your Maiestie,
> It to replevie, and my sonne reprive...
>
> He graunted it: and straight his warrant made,
> Under the Sea-gods seale autenticall,... [IV. xii. 31–2]

It is a clear case of linkage, and Spenser's notice to the reader that all the virtues form a ring.

9

Justice

The legal language which appears at the end of book IV forms a part of the literary decorum of the book of Justice, and is there in names such as Grantorto, or in the legal puns by which, for example, Munera's wealth is described—'Through strong oppression of his powre extort' [V. ii. 5]. The same decorum enters even more obviously into the patterns and symbols of book V, whether in the many refences to the justice of Jove and Hercules, or in the image of the scales which appears in a variety of forms throughout. There are the literal scales of the communist giant, or the metaphorical ones in which the coffer of Amidas is balanced against the island of Bracidas, for example. The method of telling the story at times resembles that of a law-book with its illustrative examples concerning John Doe and Richard Roe: the episodes of Sanglier and of Amidas and Bracidas have something of this generic quality.

The conception of justice which Spenser advances has already been introduced in book IV and follows logically on it. Friend-ship breeds concord which in its turn demands justice to main-tain it, and Spenser defines the latter very simply as giving to each man his own:

> So was their discord by this doome appeased,
> And each one had his right...   [V. iv. 20]

This is the justice which Artegall dispenses at the tournament in celebration of Marinell's wedding. The false Florimel is as fair as the true in all men's eyes, so that even Marinell cannot tell which is which until Artegall himself sets them side by side; and in the same way Guyon gets his horse, Marinell his victory, and Braggadocio is stripped of his undeserved honours. Justice of this kind between individuals, or where relatively simple moral principles are involved, demands no more than the patience to ferret out the truth; and Artegall spends much of his time in the earlier cantos sifting the evidence in preference to letting battle decide the justice of a cause. But as the scope of his activities becomes wider and the causes more social, Spenser is forced to define his basic assumptions about the nature of justice, which is the purpose of the episode of the giant with the scales.

The sequence is concerned with mutability, and considers the problems set by the Fall from the particular point of view of justice. The giant, seeing everything around him in a state of change—the universal change which Spenser has already lamented in his proem to the book—seeks to restore all things 'In sort as they were formed aunciently;/And all things would reduce unto equality' [v. ii. 32]. The equality which he wishes to restore is that of the Golden Age, before Mutability moved things from their proper places, and when there were neither rich nor poor, kings nor subjects; and he plays in relation to justice, therefore, the same role as Acrasia in relation to love, refusing to accept the Fall as the irrevocable basis of his politic as she of her ethic. Inevitably, as the hero, Artegall challenges the false justice of this attempt to return to a prelapsarian state; for him mutability is inescapable:

> He maketh Kings to sit in soverainty;
> He maketh subjects to their powre obay;
> He pulleth downe, he setteth up on hy;
> He gives to this, from this he takes away.   [v. ii. 41]

It is not, however, random: God has replaced the equality of the Golden Age by an ordered hierarchy which, though it may appear to change all the time, yet keeps its basic proportions unaltered by what Miss Williams calls a sort of cosmic justice,[1] though cosmic equity would, I think, be a truer description. The sea eats away the land in one place, only to deposit it elsewhere, as happens in the case of Amidas and Bracidas; the flowers die and return to earth, only to rise again in the endless cycle of the Garden of Adonis [v. ii. 39–40]. Spenser's conception reflects the passionate desire of his period to retain the structure of the social hierarchy while allowing for the enormous changes which were going on in the membership of its various

[1] P. 180.

levels. The task of justice is to maintain the hierarchy against the forces of egalitarianism, on the one side, and the unbridled exploitation of private power on the other. It is a mean between a complete permissiveness and a rigid discipline, which allows for change within an ordered pattern.

Book V is the least popular of all parts of *The Faerie Queene*, and little has been written in its favour apart from the very spirited defence by Professor Dunseath.[1] One reason for this is the ambiguous nature of justice as Spenser envisages it. It is at once the most splendid and the most heartbreaking of virtues, the most 'heroic' to enact yet the least satisfactory in its results. On the heroic side, the knight of justice, unlike all previous heroes, is fighting real not metaphorical battles; and the very word 'chivalry' implies the kind of knightly horsemanship which is denied to Guyon, for example, but is essential to a knight fighting external foes. For this reason Spenser places justice first in his hierarchy of heroic virtues:

> Nought is more honorable to a knight,
>> Ne better doth beseeme brave chevalry,
> Then to defend the feeble in their right,
>> And wrong redresse in such as wend awry.
> Whilome those great Heroes got thereby
> Their greatest glory, for their rightfull deedes,
> And place deserved with the Gods on hy.   [v. ii. 1]

But because justice is a social virtue designed to maintain order in the society which love has brought into being, the materials upon which it must work are more recalcitrant than the inner passions which Red Cross or Guyon are so anxious to subdue. Like other virtues, of course, it begins at home with the need to establish the proper hierarchy of reason and passion within the hero himself; and like other virtues, too, it is only learned through personal failure. Artegall is not truly just until he has learned to accept the justice of his punishment at the hand of Radegund, and his humble behaviour at this stage is in marked contrast to his anger and pride after the tourney in which Britomart defeats him. But this is only preliminary to his real

---

[1] T. K. Dunseath, *Spenser's Allegory of Justice in Book V of The Faerie Queene* (Princeton, 1968).

task, which is to impose heroic values upon unheroic people and virtue upon those who unlike himself have no desire to be virtuous. The bitterness of so much of book v springs from the fact that the justice which the hero himself is capable of learning, though only by the most painful means, is even more difficult to apply to other people. As Spenser widens the scope of justice to embrace domestic and foreign affairs, the gap between the ideal and the real grows progressively greater. The poet must have realised how little the episodes of Belge and Gerioneo resembled the English exploits in the Low Countries; and when he describes the actual facts of contemporary politics, for example, such as the predicament of Henry of Navarre in terms of Bourbon's rescue of the ungrateful Flourdelis, he writes with a note of vigorous cynicism. The only episode in which the justice portrayed in Spenser's allegory coincides with the historical facts is the defeat of the Soldan, and here the victory belongs to God, not to man. It was the winds, not the fleet, which destroyed the Armada, as Spenser faithfully acknowledges when he makes Arthur drive the Soldan's horses into their destructive flight by uncovering his shield. Even here it is symptomatic of the tone of book v that Arthur, not Artegall, is the agent of God's grace. Almost all the victories of the book are gained by the ideal hero rather than the human knight, and to a greater extent than in any other part of the poem, Arthur plays the truly Herculean role, in his conquest of the Soldan's horses, of Gerioneo and of the Lernean monster who lives under the altar [v. xi. 32]. Artegall, in contrast, is perhaps the least effective of all the heroes and his most strictly Herculean exploit is to wear woman's clothes as Hercules did for Omphale.[1] He is almost too late to rescue Irena, and as soon as he has done it, his triumph is soured by the assault of Detraction and Envy. Professor Dunseath is surely wrong in calling Arthur's role in book v a 'muted' one.[2]

The Fall is depressingly present throughout, and justice can only be just by compromising with the evils which it is its job

---

[1] Dunseath traces the association of heroism with Hercules in book v, though he does not comment on the Herculean role of all the other heroes in the poem.

[2] P. 190.

to conquer. Arthur uses some of Malengin's own guile to outwit him; and Artegall, like Elyot's Governor who must be able to swim, is as good a swimmer in the troubled waters of the world as Pollente himself:

> For *Artegall* in swimming skilfull was,
> And durst the depth of any water sownd.
> So ought each Knight, that use of perill has,
> In swimming be expert through waters force to pas.
>
> [v. ii. 16]

In an age of iron, justice needs the help of the iron man and force must be used to bridle force. The Elizabethans after Macchiavelli were very conscious of the different standards necessary for public and private virtue, and recognised that the good man was not necessarily the good king; but Spenser seems not to have accepted any such dual scale of values. The cause of sin in society lies in the Original Sin of the individual, and the same discipline, therefore, is necessary for both. The lesson which Artegall has to learn is the ruthless if disciplined use of force, and his personal failure with Radegund springs from a misplaced impulse of mercy rising, it is true, from sensual weakness, but representing nevertheless a human and normally admirable reaction to such a situation.

Justice is a bleak virtue, the nearest of all to the unrelenting quality of Diana, and in so far as it is softened by Artegall's normal humanity, it becomes less effective. In heaven it is tempered by mercy which, as it is God's own peculiar quality, is the nobler virtue of the two:

> Sith in th'Almighties everlasting seat
> She first was bred, and borne of heavenly race;
> From thence pour'd down on men, by influence of grace.
>
> [v. x. 1]

There is, however, no place for mercy in the dangerous world of Elizabethan politics, and the irony of the Mercilla episode is that she is unable to exercise her own quality, although Spenser is clearly a little uneasy about the human need to deny the most divine of virtues and very loth to admit the fact. At the trial of Duessa, Mercilla 'would not let just vengeance on her light' [v. ix. 50], but instead, lets fall a tear, and it is not until the next canto that we are told that 'strong constraint' has enforced her to pass sentence [v. x. 4]. Spenser takes great pains to justify Mercilla's ultimate lack of mercy by enumerating all the charges which Religion and the Peoples' cry lay against Duessa and, with even more cogency, referring earlier in the book to the plots against the Queen. The episode of Dolon's attempt on Britomart's life, which Spenser associates with the denial of Christ himself [v. vi. 27],[1] prepares the way for the outcome of the trial, and provides the reason why Artegall is opposed to mercy from the start and Arthur is swayed to the same side against his kinder nature.

The reality of the Fall comes most starkly to the surface in Spenser's definition of justice as a virtue which has no room for mercy; and it is Astraea herself who left her iron man 'And willed him with *Artegall* to wend', when human wickedness drove her from the world. Talus is not, of course, synonymous with justice but represents the force which justice needs if it is to prevail—'For powre is the right hand of Justice truely hight' [v. iv. 1]. He is the force of the law in contrast to the arbitrary use of force out of private interest; and in this respect book v reflects the social conflict between the power of the law and the tradition of private justice which Professor Fredson Bowers has shown to be the inspiration of the contemporary revenge play.[2] Talus only uses his flail at the command of justice and cannot use it any other way; he will not, for example, rescue Artegall once the latter has fallen under the just doom of his promise to Radegund:

> Yet all that while he would not once assay,
> To reskew his owne Lord, but thought it just t'obay.
>
> [v. v. 19]

In the cause of justice, however, his violence knows no bounds, since justice is ineffective 'Unlesse it be perform'd with dreadlesse might' [v. iv. 1]; and Spenser emphasises the horror of his

---

1 It seems to me that Spenser is associating Peter's sin with the treachery of Dolon rather than with Britomart herself as Dunseath argues, p. 169. She does, after all, escape, and does not fall as Peter does.
Fredson Bowers, *Elizabethan Revenge Tragedy* (Oxford, 1967).

just vengeance and the ruthlessness with which his force is applied. The communist giant is shouldered off the higher ground onto the rocks below, so that 'His timbered bones all broken rudely rumbled' [v. ii. 50]; and Malengin suffers an even more violent fate:

> all his bones, as small as sandy grayle
> He broke, and did his bowels disentrayle;   [v. ix. 19]

Only by a correspondingly ruthless violence does Britomart complete the justice which Talus had first enforced so brutally against Radegund's regiment of women, but which Artegall then threw away by his weakness. This is an aspect of Spenser's conception of justice to which, I think, Professor Dunseath pays too little attention.

Where then does equity, Britomart's particular virtue in book v, enter into the picture? Mercy is a 'heavenly thing' whose application at the personal or the political level could destroy the social hierarchy. Justice, at the other extreme, is the enforcement of the law which, strictly applied, 'Oft spilles the principall, to save the part' [v. x. 2]. This, although in one sense a protection of the individual against the abstract and the general, in another, can entail the sacrifice of the spirit of justice to the rigid letter of the law: Amidas is legally entitled to both the land and the coffer, as Artegall in strict justice deserves his slavery or as Adam and all his sons deserved death. Equity, therefore, is that part of justice designed to preserve the spirit against the tyranny of the letter and to ensure that the detailed application does not violate the larger principles of justice. It is a virtue derived from justice as the moon derives its light from the sun, but it is equally heroic, as the heroism of Britomart equals that of Artegall. Its power is to use injustice to correct injustice and break the law to re-establish the law once broken. It is not connected with mercy, although it may in the end make mercy possible.[1]

Britomart is specifically identified with the principle of equity in canto VII, and its workings are exemplified in her battle with Radegund. Spenser makes it clear that in allowing

---

[1] For an illuminating analysis of justice, equity and mercy in relation to Shakespeare's *Measure for Measure*, see Ernest Schanzer, *The Problem Plays of Shakespeare* (Routledge Paperbacks), pp. 114–120.

himself to be enslaved by Radegund, Artegall commits an act
of injustice and an offence against the natural hierarchy of the
sexes. The point is made flippantly at the beginning when the
two combatants dress for battle: Artegall puts on the armour
suitable for the task which is properly his, 'as best was seeming
for a Knight', whereas Radegund, in contrast, arms herself 'as
best it likt her selfe to dight' [v. v. 1], which is in the most
unsuitable feminine frills:

> All in a Camis light of purple silke
>> Woven uppon with silver, subtly wrought,
>> And quilted uppon sattin, white as milke,
>> Trayled with ribbands diversly distraught...
>>> [v. v. 2]

When, however, the moon eclipses the sun and Radegund's
feminity triumphs in the masculine field, a Venus disarming
Mars, the tone changes, and Spenser plays up the profound
indecorum of the situation. The hero is degraded by his own
justice to the depths of unheroic activity; the fundamental
justice of the normal sexual hierarchy is violated, and the action
becomes symbolic of a world in discord.

Such an unnatural state can only be repaired by an equally
unnatural excess at the other extreme, and so Britomart has to
assume once more the part of the male warrior and balance
Artegall's feminine role by her own equally unfitting masculine
one. She becomes the figure of Hercules conquering the
Amazon queen while he descends to the level of Hercules at his
most unheroic. In the description of her fight, Spenser emphasises
the unnaturalness of what is happening and the new perversions
which follow from the old:

> Ne either sought the others strokes to shun,
> But through great fury both their skill forgot,
> And practicke use in armes: ne spared not
> Their dainty parts, which nature had created
> So faire and tender, without staine or spot,
> For other uses, then they them translated;
> Which they now hackt and hewd, as if such use they
>> hated,

So long they fought, that all the grassie flore
Was fild with bloud, which from their sides did flow,
And gushed through their armes, that all in gore
They trode, and on the ground their lives did strow,
Like fruitles seede, of which untimely death should
                    grow.   [v. vii. 29, 31]

Not only is all proper use of arms lost in this unnatural fury,
but Britomart is forced to endanger her own sexual nature and
deny her own procreative quest: the battle in defence of her
love is one of such monstrous violence that it threatens the
very nature of love itself. The long account which Spenser
gives in canto v of how both Radegund and Clarinda fall in
love with the captive Artegall is probably included to remind the
reader of the natural sexual pattern and make the horrors of
the battle all the more apparent.

There is no place for mercy in this situation which misplaced
mercy has itself created, and Britomart beheads Radegund
with as little compunction as Talus would have shown. It is
equity that one unnatural deed should correct another, and in
this it performs its proper function which is to support justice.
Once Radegund is removed, Britomart can restore the proper
hierarchy of the sexes and, stepping down from her own bad
eminence, reinstate Artegall in the place for which his mas-
culinity fits him if he uses it justly. Her profound and disciplined love enables her to resist the temptation to exploit her
superior power when to do so would be merely to perpetuate the
original injustice. Professor Dunseath has analysed the stages
by which Britomart becomes capable of this final, most important act of self-abnegation.[1] That her love is only human has
been hinted at by the fact that she was wounded both by
Gardante and Busyrane in book III, and her first reaction to the
news of Artegall's delinquency is the all-too-human one of
anger and jealousy which saps her faith in her divine mission
to marry him and distracts her from the pursuit of her quest. It
is not until she discovers him in Radegund's castle, humble
and enfeebled, that her own compassion and humility are
aroused; and Spenser invests her reactions with a sense of

[1] Pp. 166–82.

inevitability and justice by describing the meeting in terms which, as Professor Dunseath has pointed out, bring to mind the return of Odysseus to Penelope. The roles are, of course, interchanged, with Britomart playing the male and Artegall the female part, but both are now ready to take their proper places, Artegall through the wisdom he has learned, and Britomart through love. In first conquering and then humbling herself, Britomart follows the pattern which Spenser associates with Belphoebe in book II, when he compares her first to Diana and then to Penthesilea [II. iii. 31]: her final and greatest act of heroism and the culmination of her long training in love is to recognise the implications of her sex and to find its fulfilment in terms of justice. It is an episode which has dated more than most parts of *The Faerie Queene*, and one which nowadays we find it difficult to take seriously, although Spenser clearly conceived of it as the climax to the book and showed some courage in including it:

> During which space she there as Princesse rained,
> And changing all that forme of common weale,
> The liberty of women did repeale,
> Which they had long usurpt; and them restoring
> To mens subjection, did true Justice deale: [v. vii. 42]

It is a tactful formula which allows Spenser to acknowledge the presence of a woman on the throne while, at the same time, asserting the abnormality of this fact; and the word 'restore' indicates that he felt that women would be much better off in their proper role of Venus instead of that of Mars or Diana.

Britomart's battle with Radegund shows good coming out of evil and explains the rather riddling vision of the temple of Isis. No one has ever been very happy about the crocodile; yet its ugly fierceness which ends in love is the equivalent in theme and in tone of the unwomanly battle which restores the proper relationship of the sexes; and the vision is prophetic in all its details. The moon of equity takes its light from the sun of justice and preserves that light while the sun is hidden; and on another level, the priests of Isis anticipate the just sense of values which enables Britomart to lay down her arms once they have served their purpose. Spenser tells us that they

> mote not taste of fleshly food,
> Ne feed on ought, the which doth bloud containe,
> Ne drinke of wine, for wine they say is blood,
> Even the bloud of Gyants, which were slaine,
> By thundring Jove in the Phlegrean plaine.
>
> [v. vii. 10]

Like Britomart they forswear the rebellious pride which was the quality of Radegund and the rebellious giants alike.

Canto VII epitomises the whole theme of the book of Justice, in its image of the harsh discipline which the Fall has made necessary and its hint—though in a glass darkly—of the ultimate good to which that discipline may lead. In this it forms, together with the whole of the book, the most explicit instance in the poem of the symbolism of the Law and the Gospels. The world of book V is a 'stonie' one, and there are constant episodes which recall the Old Testament—the judgement of Solomon, for example, or Moses burning the golden calf—'And burning all to ashes, powr'd it downe the brooke' [v. ii. 27]. Yet even Talus himself, it is hinted, will lead on to a kinder, more fruitful time as the bitterness of the Law prepares for the Gospels. His flail, 'With which he thresht out falshood, and did truth unfould' [v. i. 12], separates the chaff from the fruitful grain; and Spenser develops the image when he describes the rout of Grantorto's supporters in a way which suggests new lives and new springs to come:

> But he them overthrew both man and horse,
> That they lay scattred over all the land,
> As thicke as doth the seede after the sowers hand.
>
> [v. xii. 7]

The same point is implied in the proem, at the heart of what might seem one of the bitterest passages of the poem, when he is describing the new men of stone who have taken the place of the flesh and blood of the Golden Age:

> And men themselves, the which at first were framed
> Of earthly mould, and form'd of flesh and bone,
> Are now transformed into hardest stone: [proem 2]

He compares them to the stones

Such as behind their backs (so backward bred)
Were throwne by *Pyrrha* and *Deucalione*:

It will be remembered that these same stones turned into men, and that the whole myth was generally equated with the story of Noah and interpreted as a prophecy of human redemption. The Law clears the ground and sets the seeds. We shall see something of the fruits in Spenser's treatment of courtesy.

10

Courtesy

[1]

'But where ye ended have, now I begin' [VI. i. 6], says Calidore when he meets Artegall at the beginning of book VI, echoing a similar meeting between Guyon and Red Cross; and books V and VI form a complementary pair, as I and II, or III and IV, although the relationship is a different one in each case. The Blatant Beast has already made his entrance at the end of book V as the embodiment of all the envy and detraction to which Artegall's forceful imposition of justice gives rise, and courtesy is designed to combat the range of evils which justice itself in part breeds but is powerless to quell. The beast springs up in book V as the result of a local and particular instance of giant-killing, but in book VI his range is more general. He approximates to the 'Evil tongues' of the *Romance of the Rose* or the sonnet cycles, attacking whatever is vulnerable whether innocent or guilty, whetting his tongue 'Gainst all, both good and bad, both most and least' [VI. vi. 12]. In mauling Serena after her indiscreet but innocent love-making with Calepine, he embodies all the ill-nature in society which seizes upon the least flaw in reputation. He is the biggest beast of all the forest kind, and his intermittent appearances through the book are modelled on those of the elusive Blatant Beast who is often heard but rarely seen in the Arthurian legends. In choosing him as his symbol, Spenser was presumably thinking of the slanderous word or whispered piece of gossip, so difficult to trace and even harder to counter. The unlovely human quality which the beast embodies appears throughout book VI in a variety of forms, but finds its most active expression in Turpine, the character upon whom Arthur demonstrates the nature of complete courtesy. Turpine represents the heartlessness and malice of the crowd towards anyone who has laid himself open to censure; and in the episode where Calepine defends himself by hiding behind Serena, Spenser

suggests in a brutally unforgettable image that in such situations the woman fares worse than the man. Turpine is a con-
glomeration of all the evil traits of human nature which are
too cowardly to become criminal and which, falling outside the
scope of Talus and the law, demand another answer than justice.

Spenser traces this aspect of human nature back to the guilt and
shame which came with the loss of primal innocence. The word
'shame' is repeated like a refrain through the book, and the
epithet 'shameful' is that by which its evils are most commonly
stigmatised. The opening adventure with Crudor and Briana
sets the tone: 'A shamefull use as ever I did heare,/Sayd
Calidore' [VI. i. 14]; 'Not unto me the shame,/But to the shamefull doer it afford' [VI. i. 26]; 'Then doe your selfe, for dread of
shame, forgoe/This evill manner' [VI. i. 27]. Arthur's chastise-
ment of Turpine in canto VI is a long cadenza on the term:
'He for such basenesse shamefully him shent,... And eke all
knights hast shamed with this knightlesse part' [33]; 'Yet further
hast thou heaped shame to shame' [34]; 'foule cowardize,/Is
greatest shame' [35]; 'for shame is to adorne/With so brave
badges one so basely borne' [36]. In reply Turpine 'gan devize,
to be aveng'd anew/For all that shame' [VI. vii. 2].

Not only is 'shame' in all its variety of meanings the most
frequent term of censure, but the book abounds in episodes to
which the term is peculiarly applicable, little epiphanies of
shameful behaviour which carry almost the force of an emblem
—a knight hiding behind his lady to protect himself from attack,
a man on horseback attacking one on foot, or an armed knight
fighting with an unarmed one. In the account of Priscilla,
Spenser breaks through the shell of formal language with a
calculated indecorum which gives the reader a sudden shock:

> Yet not content, more to increase his shame,
> When so she lagged, as she needs mote so,
> He with his speare, that was to him great blame,
> Would thumpe her forward,...   [VI. ii. 10]

The description of Serena among the cannibals is a most ambi-
tious attempt to define the very quality of shame and, with
characteristic Spenserean rhetoric, make the reader experience
the feeling itself. Serena lies asleep in her naked purity, and

there is a grim, predictable humour in the way the savages whet their knives and strip their elbows bare. As they thank their god for the 'heavenly Grace' which has sent them such a prey, and prepare to make a sacrifice of her 'guiltlesse bloud' [vi. viii. 38], they become one with the crucifiers of Christ, and the passage takes on the sort of irony of George Herbert's 'Sacrifice' —'Was ever grief like mine?'. Having prepared the reader in this way, Spenser then launches out into the great description of Serena's beauties, which he enumerates part by part:

> Her yvorie necke, her alabaster brest,
>> Her paps, which like white silken pillowes were,
>> For love in soft delight thereon to rest;
>> Her tender sides, her bellie white and clere,
>> Which like an Altar did it selfe uprere,
>> To offer sacrifice divine thereon;
>> Her goodly thighes, whose glorie did appeare
>> Like a triumphall Arch, and thereupon
> The spoiles of Princes hang'd, which were in battel won.
>
> [vi. viii. 42]

The force of this traditional icon derives largely from its context, and from the contrast it enforces between the unfallen beauty of Serena and the only too fallen impulses of the savages, the latter so intrusive that the catalogue of her beauties begins to make us uncomfortable. The reader feels a mounting sense of embarrassment at things exposed to public view which should remain private, at deep taboos violated. Spenser has, in fact, evoked that deep inborn fear of being exposed naked which he believes to be the heritage of the Fall, the sense of shame which came to Adam and Eve and made them seek to cover their nakedness. It is inevitable that when Serena is rescued she feels this shame at her nakedness, even though it is night and her rescuer is her lover:

> So inward shame of her uncomely case
>> She did conceive, through care of womanhood,
>> That though the night did cover her disgrace,
>> Yet she in so unwomanly a mood,
>> Would not bewray the state in which she stood.
>
> [vi. viii. 51]

We get as near in this passage to the very quality of the Fall
as it is possible to do, and it is with this that book VI is principally
concerned. It is something which sullies innocence and stains it
with its own feeling of shame, and lying in the heart of man it
penetrates into every corner of human activity. Book VI is full
of instances of innocence broken into and destroyed: unlike the
Garden of Adonis where love is secure and without shame:

> Franckly each paramour his leman knowes,
> Each bird his mate, ne any does envie
> Their goodly meriment, and gay felicitie.   [III. vi. 41]

the lovers of book VI are always interrupted, however innocent
and legitimate their embraces. Aladine and Priscilla are
'Joying together in unblam's delight' [VI. ii. 43], when they are
attacked without reason or provocation: Calidore himself breaks
in upon Calepine when 'In covert shade him selfe did safely
rest,/To solace with his Lady in delight' [VI. iii. 20]; Serena,
wandering in the wood 'Without suspect of ill or daungers
hidden dred' [VI. iii. 23] is swept off by the Blatant Beast, just
as later on, when asleep, 'Fearelesse of ought, that mote her
peace molest' [VI. viii. 34] she is seized by the savages. Moreover
Spenser makes it clear that one can and should expect nothing
better, and that Serena is wrong to assume an innocence which
the fallen world will no longer allow. His description of her
innocent wandering in the wood 'as liking led/Her wavering
lust after her wandring sight,/...thus loosely wandring here
and there' [VI. iii. 23–4] is a very loaded one. The destruction of
the pastoral idyll by the brigands, though on a larger scale, is
only the final instance of the pattern which runs throughout. Although we are apt to think of book VI as the most idyllic of them
all, the world it presents is a fallen one, and an important function of the idyll is to remind us that Ardens and Edens are no
more to be found. Book VI is, in some ways, a mirror image of
book V; the latter showing the vain attempts of the hero to
enforce his ideal vision upon a world unwilling to receive it, the
former presenting an ideal vision which the world continually
shatters.

Shame, the least tangible and the most pervasive symptom of
Original Sin, besmirches the ideals within the mind, and the

answer to it must be found, therefore, within the mind itself, in a deeper idealism and a surer sense of values. 'But vertues seat is deepe within the mynd', writes Spenser in the proem to book VI, and he opposes to the stain of the Fall the profoundest human vision of truth, namely, the inspired vision of the poet. This is the theme of the proem, which rejoices in leaving the battle-fields of justice for the more delightful pastures of poetry, in a passage very reminiscent of Sidney's *Apologie*:

> The waies, through which my weary steps I guyde,
>   In this delightfull land of Faery,
>   Are so exceeding spacious and wyde,
>   And sprinckled with such sweet variety,
>   Of all that pleasant is to eare or eye,
>   That I nigh ravisht with rare thoughts delight
> My tedious travell doe forget thereby;   [proem. 1]

The source of this delightful vision is 'the sacred imps, that on *Parnasso* dwell', and the 'goodly fury' which they infuse is attainable only by the poet, 'Ne none can find, but who was taught them by the Muse'. Spenser's symbol of the poet's vision is the dance of the Graces to which Colin, the poet, pipes; and he gives the name of courtesy to the values which they embody.

The Graces carried a wide range of symbolic meanings for the Renaissance, as Professor Wind has shown.[1] Spenser describes them in their characteristic position:

> That two of them still froward seem'd to bee,
> But one still towards shew'd her selfe afore;
> That good should from us goe, then come in greater
>   store.   [VI. x. 24]

Their circular dance was the traditional symbol of generosity,[2] a quality very relevant to the theme of book VI; but it lent itself also to the Platonists as an image of the circle of love in its many applications—the divine love emanating downwards to chaos and kindling in it the love of form from which all creation proceeds; the human love which, inspired by beauty, inflames

[1] *Pagan Mysteries*, chaps. II and III.
[2] Wind, chap. II, pp. 28 ff.

the lover with the desire to embrace and propagate the eternal forms. For Spenser the Graces lent themselves, in addition, to a specifically Christian interpretation as a symbol of Grace— God's love of man through Christ raising him up, Man's love of God drawing down Grace upon himself. This double movement of receiving and giving makes up the full circle, and Spenser continually mentions the Graces in association with the circle or the ring. The hundred naked maidens are 'raunged in a ring,/And daunced round' [VI. x. 12], and the Graces themselves form a garland around Colin's mistress so that she stands like a jewel

> Amidst a ring most richly well enchaced,
> That with her goodly presence all the rest much graced.
>
> [VI. x. 12]

In the same way, their counterparts on earth, Pastorella and her maidens, form a ring with Pastorella at the centre,

> and round about
> Environ'd with a girland, goodly graced,
> Of lovely lasses, . . .   [VI. ix. 8]

The constant punning on the word 'graced', always in association with the image of the ring, suggests that Spenser was well acquainted with the symbolism commonly associated with the three. Gloriana herself forms part of the pattern, surrounded by all the virtues 'which round about you ring' [proem. 7]; and Spenser sees himself as the poet participating in the dance of the Graces, thereby gaining the inspiration and motive for his poem:

> Then pardon me, most dreaded Soveraine,
> That from your selfe I doe this virtue bring,
> And to your selfe doe it returne againe: [proem. 7]

Whereas in book V, Gloriana is linked with Astraea, in book VI she has the more gracious role of Venus, sum of all the Graces,[1] dispensing her benevolence to those of mankind who seek it.

The vision of the Graces is one of perfect courtesy, the equivalent of the perfect justice which Astraea took with her to heaven

---

[1] Wind, chap. III, pp. 36 ff.

as being too noble for the world. The Graces' hill is a symbolic landscape, bordered with 'all trees of honour' in whose tops, in its proper place,

> the soring hauke did towre,
> Sitting like King of fowles in majesty and powre.
>
> [VI. x. 6]

while at the foot a gentle stream

> His silver waves did softly tumble downe,
> Unmard with ragged mosse or filthy mud,
> Ne mote wylde beastes, ne mote the ruder clowne
> Thereto approch, ne filth mote therein drowne:
>
> [VI. x. 7]

It is a place from which all evil is banished and where all happiness is ever-present: on the Grace's hill, even the Petrarchan mistress is at last kind:

> Pype jolly shepheard, pype thou now apace
> Unto thy love, that made thee low to lout;
> Thy love is present there with thee in place,
> Thy love is there advaunst to be another Grace.
>
> [VI. x. 16]

For this reason it is as remote from the real world as the pure justice of Astraea, and can only exist in the poet's mind. The damsel at the centre of the ring, who crowns the whole assembly like a precious gem, is compared to

> the Crowne, which *Ariadne* wore
> Upon her yvory forehead that same day,
> That *Theseus* her unto his bridale bore,
> When the bold *Centaures* made that bloudy fray
> With the fierce *Lapithes*, which did them dismay;
> Being now placed in the firmament,
> Through the bright heaven doth her beames display,
>
> [VI. x. 13]

but Spenser insists that the comparison is to Ariadne's crown in heaven: on earth things are very different, and Hercules himself was involved in the unheroic affair of the Lapithes and Centaurs.

Pure courtesy exists only as an ideal, and the knights of courtesy in the real world are too involved with their own and other people's sins to have time to dance with the Graces. Even Calidore, the best of them, is too earthly to enter into their presence: he hides in the wood and does not know who they are —he has to ask the poet 'what mote these dainty Damzels be' [VI. x. 19]. His clumsy intrusion into their revels, which sends them all flying, is the archetypal example of prelapsarian innocence broken into by the facts of the Fall.

Like Astraea, the Graces have been driven from the world by human blindness, but in place of Talus they have left behind Colin, the poet, to transmit their values and lift mankind up to civilisation again. This, as we have seen, is Spenser's myth for the task of the heroic poet and for his own duty in the generic role of Colin Clout. He chooses the pastoral pseudonym because the name has, so to speak, a foot in the world of the ideal and the real. Colin belongs to the world of Greek pastoral, in which the shepherd speaks with the voice of poetry piping in an age of gold; but Clout comes firmly down to earth with Skelton's very practical application of poetry to the purposes of satire. The name is a two-edged one, involving the two great traditions of the pastoral, the idyllic vision and the practical reform designed to make the vision prevail; and Colin Clout is the bridge between the two, epitomising Spenser's conception of the dual function of poetry.

Book VI is his attempt to convert into practical human ethics as much of the innocence of courtesy as human nature has the capacity to achieve. Pastorella, as she sits on her 'little hillocke', piped to by shepherd swains, is a simulacrum of the Graces; and human courtesy, like divine, has its origin in love. It stems, in Spenser's analysis, from the remnant of innocence still left in Adam's sons, exemplified in the natural altruism of the Salvage Man, or in the instinct which makes the knight keep his word to the sleeping Arthur when he could so easily have betrayed him to Turpine [VI. vii. 25]. It counters the effects of the Fall by turning the forces of shame against themselves and marshalling them in the cause of honour, in the same way as justice turns force against force in the cause of law. Honour is shame put to benevolent uses; and the Salvage Man, therefore, who has not yet reached the stage of human civilisation or corruption, has neither shame nor honour: he is invulnerable to both Turpine and Disdain, but on the negative side he lacks Arthur's skill to relieve the pains of Serena's wound.

At the same time, courtesy builds upon justice, but a justice in respect of intangible rights which is established by consideration and deference instead of by force, and which is only possible because of the fact of love:

> What vertue is so fitting for a knight,
>> Or for a Ladie, whom a knight should love,
>> As Curtesie, to beare themselves aright
>> To all of each degree, as doth behove?
>> For whether they be placed high above,
>> Or low beneath, yet ought they well to know
>> Their good, that none them rightly may reprove
>> Of rudenesse, for not yeelding what they owe:
>>>>>>> [VI. ii. 1]

Spenser's syntax does not make it clear to whom 'their good' alludes, whether to the courteous knight himself or to those towards whom he shows courtesy. The implication is that there is no distinction between the two, and that the courteous man loves his neighbour as himself. Courtesy goes beyond justice, however, in giving men more than their just deserts and insisting on mercy whenever possible. Arthur spares and redeems his enemies instead of killing them provided that they forswear their evil ways, as they do for the most part in book VI; and Calidore rounds off his adventure with a lesson on Christian mercy:

> Who will not mercie unto others shew,
>> How can he mercy ever hope to have?
>> To pay each with his owne is right and dew.
>> Yet since ye mercie now doe need to crave,
>> I will it graunt, your hopelesse life to save;   [VI. i. 42]

The Christian overtones are very obvious, and it is only fitting that Crudor should be made to swear a Christian oath, 'By his owne sword, and by the crosse thereon' [VI. i. 43]. In contrast to justice which pulls down, courtesy lifts up: the heroes of book

VI always raise the fallen and restore them to their rightful place. On the most literal level Calidore does not hesitate to carry the wounded Alanus [VI. ii. 47–8], whereas Turpine refuses to carry Serena across the river. In a more metaphorical way, Calidore raises Tristram to knighthood, and Calepine lifts up the child from the animal level of Bruin the bear to the level of human civilisation represented by Sir Bruin; and the Christian symbolism of the act is pointed by the scriptural echoes of the whole episode. The child is 'gotten, not begotten', and through his timely appearance, the lands do not return again

> To that foule feend, who dayly doth attend
> To leape into the same after our lives end.   [VI. iv. 31]

We shall see the same pattern repeated in Calidore's rescue of Pastorella. Of all types of heroism in the poem, courtesy is the most steeped in the symbolism of redemption.

[2]

This is the very complex virtue which Calidore has to master and, as in the previous books of the poem, his education comes through the experience of failure. For the first eight cantos he is the perfect hero of courtesy, never deserting his quest for any consideration; and Spenser praises him for 'Sewing the *Blatant Beast*' and 'Reaping eternall glorie of his restlesse paines' [VI. ix. 2]. We are warned, however, in unusually strong terms, of the Fall to come—'the great dishonour and defame/Which should befall to *Calidores* immortal name' [VI. ix. 1]. The truancy of Calidore among the shepherds is one of the most puzzling and controversial episodes in *The Faerie Queene*, for Spenser appears to be censuring his hero for behaviour which is presented as worthy of praise. He explicitly criticises Calidore for forsaking his quest yet, at the same time, shows that the love of Pastorella inspires him to a finer, more human courtesy than he has been capable of before. The pastoral interlude is of the greatest beauty, the section of the poem which, as Miss Williams rightly insists, lingers finally in the memory as the quintessential image of human courtesy at its purest: whatever strictures Spenser may be passing upon it, there can be no doubt that it was an image to which he himself responded very deeply.

In this respect, Spenser was one with his period in which, as Professor Tayler and others have shown,[1] the vogue of the pastoral idyll was closely linked with nostalgia for the Golden Age. As a vision of innocence, the idyll appealed deeply to the world of the Reformation and Counter-Reformation obsessed to an unusual degree by a sense of Original Sin. At the same time, in providing the image of an age when changes of fortune and season had not yet begun, and men lived without toil off the fruits of the earth which a kindly Nature produced, it appealed equally to a century harassed by the speed of change and the many new forms of getting and spending which forced themselves upon human consciousness. The pastoral idyll is the natural response to the new and more complex organisation of city life and the smoky furnaces of the new age; and the true opposite of Meliboe's cottage is not the Court but the cave of Mammon.

Spenser clearly felt the nostalgia for simpler, more innocent ways of living but recognised the danger that such an ideal could easily become a form of escapism. His profound sense of the Fall made him mistrustful of any daydreaming after an innocence irrevocably lost, and forced him to distinguish very precisely between the ideal which spurs one to profitable effort and that which inhibits action or breeds complacency. The problem was possibly forced upon him in an acute form by the great burst of pastoral idyllicism in the poetry of the 1590s. His own previous exercise in the pastoral had been predominantly satiric, and he may have felt that the contemporary obsession with the idyllic mode distracted the mind from the evils of the world and perverted poetry from its high task of producing virtuous action. He would have been on the side of Raleigh's answer against Marlowe's romantic 'Come live with me and be my love'. That his criticism of Calidore among the shepherds is linked with his disapproval of these current trends in poetry is

[1] E. W. Tayler, *Nature and Art in Renaissance Literature, passim.*

shown, I think, by the especially literary nature of his picture of
the shepherd's life: the shepherds fleet away their time in the
traditional ways of pastoral cliché, 'playing on pipes and carol-
ling apace', varied with the occasional dancing or wrestling
match, and the only incursion into the world of action is the
fight with the tiger which has all the mannered unreality of
Greene's romances.

This is the world of nostalgic wishful-thinking into which
Calidore is drawn; the inspiring vision of the Graces is a harder
thing, and not to be reached until the evils in its way have been
destroyed. To escape into a fictional world of innocence as
Calidore tries to do is not essentially different from believing in
Acrasia's fantasies, and leads equally into sloth. It is significant
that apart from the pastoral characters, the only characters in
book VI who live the simple life, enjoying nature's bounty
without the sweat of Adam, are all less than men. The Salvage
Man lives off the natural fruits of the earth and retains his
primal innocence, but Spenser pictures him as a primitive
creature needing to be lifted up to full human stature by the
civilising influence of Arthur. He is like the simple, pre-human
species in Golding's *The Inheritors*, only innocent because not
yet human. At the other extreme are the brigands who form
a parody of natural man, doing no work and, like Volpone,
denying the need for toil:

> ne did give
> Them selves to any trade, as for to drive
> The painfull plough, or cattell for to breed, . . .
> [VI. viii. 35]

Ironically Spenser makes these parodies of innocence the agency
by which the true innocence of both Serena and the pastoral
scene is destroyed.

Spenser's criticism of Calidore is that he takes refuge in an
ideal world when he should be reforming the real one. He first
comes to the land of the shepherds in search of the Blatant
Beast, but is assured by the inhabitants of this innocent and
happy place 'that no such beast they saw,/Nor any wicked
feend, that mote offend' [VI. ix. 6]. This alone should have
been enough to warn off anyone whose sole quest was to find

and capture it; but Calidore, like Guyon in Phaedria's boat, takes a rest and, seeing Pastorella,

> Ne any will had thence to move away,
> Although his quest were farre afore him gon;
>
> [VI ix. 12]

His love of Pastorella is an ennobling passion and he outshines the unlucky Corydon at every turn, but it is virtue in an inferior cause. He takes his armour off so that he may woo her as a shepherd, and Spenser makes his comment through a characteristic image:

> And doffing his bright armes, himselfe addrest
> In shepheards weed, and in his hand he tooke,
> In stead of steelehead speare, a shepheards hooke,
> That who had seene him then, would have bethought
> On *Phrygian Paris* by *Plexippus* brooke,
> When he the love of fayre *Oenone* sought,
> What time the golden apple was unto him brought.
>
> [VI. ix. 36]

The reference is to Paris in his days of innocence; but the fall of Troy is to come. Pastorella, too, is at fault in preferring the shepherd to the knight, and Spenser describes ironically how she fails to appreciate the noble courtesies which the hero shows on his arrival:

> But she that never had acquainted beene
> With such queint usage, fit for Queenes and Kings,
> Ne ever had such knightly service seene, . . .
>
> [VI. ix. 35]

The reason for her ignorance is the fact that she has been 'bred under base shepheards wings' and, having fallen from her own natural high estate, will be unable to love true courtesy until she is raised again to the royal place which Calidore recognised as her due when he first saw her.

Calidore's fault is not that of loving, but of stooping to the shepherd's level in his love, and a hero descending to the level of the pastoral is an offence against literary decorum which Spenser turns into the symbol of a moral frailty. Meliboe

himself draws attention to Calidore's lack of wisdom in leaving
the station in life which the heavens have alloted to him:
happiness is found not in trying to change one's fortune but in
making the best use of what is given, 'Sith each unto himselfe
his life may fortunize' [VI. ix. 30]. Love, however, blinds
Calidore's eye as effectively as Acrasia blinded Verdant, and
Spenser describes his reactions in language reminiscent of that
of the Bower of Blisse:

> Whylest thus he talkt, the knight with greedy eare
>   Hong still upon his melting mouth attent;
>   Whose sensefull words empierst his hart so neare,
>   That he was trapt with double ravishment,
>   Both of his speach that wrought him great content,
>   And also of the object of his vew,
>   On which his hungry eye was alwayes bent;
>   That twixt his pleasing tongue, and her faire hew,
> He lost himselfe, and like one halfe entraunced grew.
>
>   [VI. ix. 26]

The description in these 'sensefull words' evokes all the organs
of sense except those of touch, since Calidore's love is a virtuous
one, but this omission does not alter the fact that his love is of
a sufficiently sensual kind to cloud his judgement. 'Entrapt of
love' in this way, he mistakes the shepherds' idyll for true coin:
he agrees with Meliboe's conventional strictures on the 'vaine-
nesse' of the court, even though the courtesy which he serves
takes its name from the noblest court of all; and he flies from
'this worlds gay showes' to what he believes to be

> this safe retyre
> Of life, which here in lowlinesse ye lead,
> Fearelesse of foes, or fortunes wrackful yre, . . .
>
>   [VI. ix. 27]

The brigands shatter his illusions, but until that time, the
'gentle knight' is content to stay 'Amongst that rusticke rout
in all his deedes' and to forsake the heroic for the pastoral. The
Graces flee his presence because they are beyond the compre-

hension of 'the ruder clowne' and Calidore has placed himself in
that category. He has made his choice between soft if innocent
pleasure and hard virtue, and he has no comprehension of the
golden mean between the two which is true courtesy.

Yet even as he condemns Calidore, Spenser simultaneously
indicates the presence of other factors which, while they do not
excuse Calidore's fault, nevertheless ensure that the fault itself
serves the purposes of virtue. We have here again the dichotomy
which runs through the poem, between the human obligation to
seek virtue and the divine purpose which fulfils itself no matter
what we do. In giving up his heroic quest and becoming a
shepherd, Calidore becomes the means by which Pastorella is
raised to her proper station; and the necessity of destroying the
brigands forces him to discover the heroic pastoralism, the blend
of action and idealism, on which courtesy depends. In stooping
to the shepherd's condition, Calidore has unwittingly put on
the mantle of the good shepherd, and his debasement is in the
pattern of Christ taking on humanity as the means to human
redemption. Love has driven him to choose the path of ultimate
virtue, to become the shepherd hero.

The Christian symbolism of the apparent death and resurrec-
tion of Pastorella is emphasised very forcibly by the many
great streams of imagery in the sequence which turn her rescue
into a redemption and make courtesy the most Christ-like
of all the virtues. The cave in which she is imprisoned carries
all the cumulative force of the image which has built up
throughout the poem; and the little flicker of human light
which is the sole illumination is not enough to show things as
they are, but forces a dependence on the lower instead of the
higher senses:

> Ne lightned was with window, nor with lover,
> But with continuall candlelight, which delt
> A doubtfull sense of things, not so well seene, as felt.
>
> [VI. X. 42]

It is a place of Hell and damnation—'she thought her self in
hell,/Where with such damned fiends she should in darknesse
dwell' [VI. X. 43]; and when the battle in the cave breaks out,
and even the small spark of human light is quenched, it

becomes a place of chaos and old night in which all distinction of degree and of form is lost:

> But making way for death at large to walke:
> Who in the horror of the griesly night,
> In thousand dreadful shapes doth mongst them stalke,
> And makes huge havocke, whiles the candlelight
> Out quenched, leaves no skill nor difference of wight.
>
> [VI. xi. 16]

From both hell and chaos Calidore's subsequent activity brings regeneration. Pastorella, plunged into chaos, is the 'bloosme of comely courtesie' of the proem which, like the flowers in the Garden of Adonis, has been sent down into the world:

> Her wretched life, shut up in deadly shade,
> And waste her goodly beauty, which did fade
> Like to a flowre, that feeles no heate of sunne,
> Which may her feeble leaves with comfort glade.
>
> [VI. x. 44]

But the fate of the flower is not the end: she is restored to her parents and rejoined to her lover so that the circle of creation can continue through marriage. The 'little purple rose' on her breast which has been so long hidden is at last uncovered, and the flower starts its cycle over again.

As courtesy answers mutability in terms of the Garden of Adonis, so it answers sin in terms of divine mercy, lifting up the fallen, harrowing Hell,

> But Calidore with huge resistlesse might,
> The dores assayled, and the locks upbrast.   [VI. xi. 43]

above all, restoring the dead to life:

> So her uneath at last he did revive,
> That long had lyen dead, and made againe alive.
>
> [VI. xi. 50]

The redemptive quality of courtesy, which has been apparent in the action throughout, is defined most explicitly here in conjunction with the image of the good shepherd.

[3]

Courtesy is not, therefore, just another virtue, but one which involves all its predecessors and builds most explicitly upon them, uniting love and justice upon a foundation of Grace. Calidore is the spiritual son of Britomart and Artegall: he represents the happiest fusion of Christ and Hercules of all the heroes in the poem, and in his regenerative love, completes the ring of virtues which began in love in book I. Miss Williams has pointed out that everything turns out right in the end, in book VI;[1] even Mutability herself, translated into Lady Fortune to fit the decorum of this mediaeval setting, seems to be the instrument of a benign providence. Fortune's wheel, which plays a large and explicit part through the book both in lifting up and casting down, has a mysterious and benevolent purpose behind its apparently random revolutions. Fortune fails Timias in his fight with Disdain [VI. viii. 10], but helps Arthur [VI. viii. 15]; she betrays Pastorella [VI. x. 38–9], and heaps yet greater pain on her by making the Brigand captain fall in love with her, yet in the end this apparent bad fortune turns out to be good, 'as Fortune had ordayned' [VI. xi. 3]. She supports Calidore when he attacks the brigands and finally restores Pastorella who had been originally exposed in the open fields to 'fortunes spoile' [VI. xii. 16]. Evil leads into good and even the Blatant Beast has his uses, exposing what is truly shameful in the monasteries as well as wounding innocence.

The apparent optimism of book VI must, however, be treated with some reservation: its ending is that of the traditional fairy-tale, and of all the books of the poem, it is written most clearly in the mode of the popular romance. To mistake it for real life is to fall into Calidore's own error and succumb to the escapist charm of the pastoral idyll. Spenser is not postulating a Golden Age returned but using the appropriate poetic 'kind' as an allegory to express the poet's ideal vision of life. It is the product of the erected wit which can escape in imagination but not in action from the corrupted will, and Spenser is at pains to ensure that we recognise this fact. The radiance of the pastoral vision is always shadowed by the proximity of shame;

Pp. 208–9.

and the tensions between what man was and would be, and what he actually is, are more extreme here than in any other book of the poem. Spenser's pastoral embodies and anatomises the subtlest temptation in *The Faerie Queene*, the temptation to fall in love with innocence and thereby forget the fact of sin.

The ways of Providence in book VI are inscrutable and painful, and though ultimately kindly, they need to work through human suffering. This has been the pattern throughout the poem, but it is defined explicitly in the episode of Mirabella which, as is so often the case in *The Faerie Queene*, treats in a small way what is to receive full treatment in the following book. The trial of Mirabella in Cupid's Court anticipates the greater trial in the Court of Nature in the *Mutability Cantos*; her parable is couched in the idiom of Courtly Love, as befits the decorum of the book of courtesy, but its implications concern love in a wider, more Christian sense. Mirabella's abuse of love exceeds that of the usual courtly mistress in that she perverts not only the laws of Cupid but those of God himself:

> Whylest she, the Ladie of her libertie,
> Did boast her beautie had such soveraine might,
> That with the only twinckle of her eye,
> She could or save, or spill, whom she would hight.
> What could the Gods doe more, but doe it more aright?
>
> [VI. vii. 31]

For her pride, therefore, she is made to weep, 'of no man mercifide' [VI. vii. 32], and her punishment is by the Scorn and Disdain of which she herself has been guilty. Disdain is descended of the house

> Of those Old Gyants, which did warres darraine
> Against the heaven in order battailous,
> And sib to great Orgoglio which was slaine
> By *Arthur*, when as *Unas* Knight he did maintaine.
>
> [VI. vii. 41]

Yet Mirabella welcomes the punishment 'For penaunce of my proud and hard rebellious hart' [VI. viii. 19], and will not let Arthur kill him 'Least unto me betide a greater ill' [VI. viii. 30], for she recognises that the God of love himself has laid the punishment on her for her own good.

We are back for the last time with the underlying theme of the poem, that of the Law preparing for the Gospels. It is a progress symbolised by the development of the action within each book of the poem, but it is dominant in the relationship of the last two books to each other more explicitly than in any other sequence of the poem. Hitherto it has been there only in allusion, but now the theme rises to the surface in a great theological assertion about divine justice and redemptive love. The power of Talus to strike down is countered by that of Calidore to lift up, though the contrast is not an absolute one: courtesy needs the help of justice to survive in the world, as justice needs that of courtesy to remain human, and the difference is one of emphasis. The relationship between the two is defined in the common image by which both are described. Artegall, conquering Radegund on his first encounter with her, is compared to the kingly eagle justly pouncing upon the unworthy goshawk:

> Like to an Eagle in his kingly pride,
>   Soring through his wide Empire of the aire,
>   To weather his brode sailes, by chaunce hath spide
>   A Goshauke, . . .   [v. iv. 42]

In contrast, Arthur, when attacked by two knights at Turpine's instigation, is described in the image of the heron on whose sharp beak the attacking falcons impale themselves:

> As when a cast of Faulcons make their flight
>   At an Herneshaw, that lies aloft on wing,
>   The whyles they strike at him with heedlesse might,
>   The warie foule his bill doth backward wring;
>   On which the first, whose force her first doth bring,
>   Her selfe quite through the bodie doth engore, . . .
>   [vi. vii. 9]

Force is no part of ideal courtesy, but it is necessary in the world of men, and this is the lesson which Calidore has to learn. In doing so, he achieves his own virtue and converts Fortune into

Providence. *The Faerie Queene* gives throughout the impression of God's purposes being irrevocably fulfilled, and yet of man himself as the free agent. Spenser's answer to the paradox lies in Christ, both man and God incarnate, the heroic shepherd in whom divine justice and divine love are reconciled.

11

Mutability

[1]

Spenser never identifies himself totally with his characters, and
the vision of life which *The Faerie Queene* presents is a double
one, resulting from two simultaneous but different perspectives.
The predominant vision is that of the central characters, for
whom life appears to offer an inescapable moral imperative:
there is a quest to be attempted, a choice to be made between the
uncompromising opposites of good and evil, and only by scrupu-
lous and unflagging attention can salvation be achieved and the
will of God performed. The hero's responsibility, therefore, is to
model himself on Hercules in choosing the path of virtue and
slaying the giants and monsters of sin. Such is the earnest and
arduous conception of life upon which Red Cross, Guyon and
their successors base their actions. At the same time, however,
another, more kindly vision of life runs under the surface of the
poem, that of the omniscient poet who speaks with the voice of
God and who knows from the start what the characters themselves only grasp fleetingly by the time their adventures are
ended. From this point of view, the hero's success or failure in
his quest matters not at all and his errors are more fruitful
than his virtues—indeed, they turn out in the end to be the
very source of his virtues. In the world of the Fall, where evil is
ineradicable, God's Grace is correspondingly ubiquitous and
converts the Fall itself into ultimate good: the sins which the
hero as a human being inevitably commits carry their own
punishment and in this way their own correction; and the
figures with whom it is the hero's prime duty to do perpetual
battle—Orgoglio, Acrasia, Lust, Disdain—are God's agents in
his education. The appropriate myth for such a vision of life is
not that of Hercules's Choice, but that of the Old Law and the
New; and the proper ideal not the Herculean hero fighting and
conquering, but a hero redeemed through suffering who exem-

plifies the Christian paradox, 'Therefore that he may raise the
Lord casts down'.

It is the central paradox of *The Faerie Queene* that Cupid's
triumphs and Lucifera's sins are as necessary as the labours of
Diana and the sweat of Adam, and that the hero must struggle
with all his might to make the right choice even though his
way to salvation will be through error. Spenser's certainty
of God's benevolence, however, is not an invitation to ignore the
obligation of the quest: on the contrary, the perils of the quest
are the sole means by which that benevolence can be realised
and the divine purpose achieved. The only moral imperative for
Spenser is that we shall undertake the quest, and the attempt if
'but endeavoured with sincere intent', will bring us safely
home, regardless of incidental success or failure by the way. To
accept the quest and to persevere in it however ineffectively is
the only heroism.

This conception of human responsibility and divine purpose is
implied in the separate stories of the first six books but defined explicitly in the philosophical allegory of the *Mutability
Cantos*. Although Mutability does not appear in person until the
end of the poem, her presence has been manifest throughout.
She is there in books III and IV, in the Protean chaos whose
appetite for change is synonymous with death and birth alike;
and again in books V and VI, where the precession of the equi-
noxes and the apparently random revolution of Fortune's
wheel turn out, in the end, to be both equitable and providential.
It is she who, in the guise of time, outwears the 'warlike
numbers and Heroicke sound' of Chaucer's verses, but allows
Spenser to 'revive' them in his tale of Cambel and Canacee
[IV. ii. 33]. Mutability is present in a more pervasive sense than
this, however, and the whole poem is an extended pageant of
her witnesses. The strongest evidence supporting Alastair
Fowler's argument that the books of the poem correspond to the
days of the week lies in the fact that the hours, the months and
the seasons, but not the days, take part in Mutability's procession; the days have been embodied in the sequence of the books
themselves, and each book has already witnessed both to the
power of Mutability and to the validity of Nature's final judgement. Each book contains a story of heroic change, as the hero

moves from the initial possession of his virtue, through loss, to a
fuller understanding of its true quality. Nature's summing up of
the role of Mutability defines the progress of every hero through
the poem:

> I well consider all that ye have sayd,
> And find that all things stedfastnes doe hate
> And changed be: yet being rightly wayd
> They are not changed from their first estate;
> But by their change their being doe dilate:
> And turning to themselves at length againe,
> Doe worke their owne perfection so by fate:
>
> [VII. vii. 58]

The fact that all things 'worke their owne perfection so by fate'
implies the paradox of free human responsibility which yet
performs the will of God.

Mutability herself is Spenser's allegory of the fallen state: she
is identified with both cause and effect of the Fall, with the
rebellious pride from which it sprang, and the death which
came in its train. Unlike her sister Titans, Hecate and Bellona,
who for all the ambiguity of their natures are still content to
serve Jove's purposes [VII. vi. 3], Mutability acknowledges no
master and seeks to shoulder Jove himself from his right. She is
Earth's daughter and Chaos's grandchild [VII. vi. 26]; she is the
flesh with which Jove himself is too much in love to 'doe still
what he can' [VII. vi. 31]. In continuing the rebellion of the
Titans, she is one with all the giants and monsters whom the
Herculean heroes have sought to quell throughout the poem;
but she is in addition a Titaness of such beauty that Jove stays
his hand, as Artegall relented at the beauty of Radegund.
Mutability is a Venus–Titan rising from the sea of creation to
confront her maker, and uniting in herself both classical and
Christian myths of the Fall, the loss of Eden and the destruction
of the Golden Age:

> O pittious worke of MUTABILITIE!
> By which, we all are subject to that curse
> And death in stead of life have sucked from our Nurse.
>
> [VII. vi. 6]

The creation which Mutability assembles to support her
claim and hear Nature's judgement is inevitably the fallen
creation which owes her its allegiance: death is there as well as
life, and the only creatures banished from the gathering are
those outside the scheme of Mutability altogether, namely, the
'infernall powers' and the 'unruly feendes'. The meeting place
on Arlo Hill is a fallen Eden, once the haunt of Diana in the
old days of innocence, when her nymphs used to play and sport
with the 'woody Gods'—'For, with the Nymphes, the Satyres
love to play and sport' [VII. vi. 39]. But now, through the guilt
of foolish Faunus, the nymphs and the wood-folk have quarrel-
led, and Cynthia, like Astraea, has departed, leaving the place
to wolves and robbers [VII. vi. 55]. It is the familiar world in
which Diana is opposed to Venus, and in which the Satyrs, their
innocence destroyed by the sin of Faunus, breed their own opposite in the person of Satyrane. Even the 'joyance' of all the
creatures there in Nature's presence is described with a note of
sinister irony:

> Was never so great joyance since the day,
>   That all the gods whylome assembled were,
>   On *Haemus* hill in their divine array,
>   To celebrate the solemne bridall cheare,
>   Twixt *Peleus*, and dame *Thetis* pointed there;
>   [VII. vii. 12]

This was the occasion, it will be remembered, when the apple
of discord was thrown down.

Yet Spenser's comment upon it all is a happy one promising, if
not a Golden Age renewed, at least a Silver Age justified; and
Nature raises her eyes from the contemplation of the symbolic
ground with 'chearefull view' [VII. vii. 57]. The sin of Faunus,
although an image of the Fall, is treated as a happy event which
leads to ultimate good. The wood-god's crime is to forsake the
instinctive and innocent carnality of the satyr who rang his
matin bell so oft with Hellenore, for the self-conscious sexuality
of Cymochles in the Bower: it is Adam's fall from innocence to
knowledge. Yet he is forgiven after a little punishment and his
accomplice, Molanna, is first stoned and then married to her
lover, Fanchin, in a comedy version of the human progress from

the Old Law to the New. The grounds for this optimism have already been demonstrated in the first six books, and the procession of Mutability's witnesses sums up the complex moral of the whole poem in a great and concentrated emblem.

Like all the great processions in *The Faerie Queene* Mutability's pageant is full of paradox. It resembles the chronicle of Briton Kings or the procession of the rivers in suggesting the inter-penetration of good and evil, but it goes further than these in implying that as far as the maintenance of Nature's order is concerned, good and evil are identical. It is a procession in which the virtues and the vices are inextricably mixed, and yet the order of nature rests upon their joint shoulders. Sherman Hawkins has shown how Spenser embodied the twelve months in terms of the traditional calendar of the farmer's year, so that they walk past Nature's throne in the guise of twelve good labouring-men performing the cycle of yearly tasks.[1] The basic order of the elements and the seasons is already there; but by cooperating with this the human labourers establish and maintain the details of the pattern, and without their labours, the regular cycle of the human year would not exist. Instead of the purposeful round of sowing, cultivation and harvest there would be only the chaos of weeds which surrounds Ate's dwelling, and which provides Spenser and his whole period with a symbol of disorder. Human labour mends the old quarrel between Art and Nature through an art which seconds Nature's purposes and converts the potential of the four seasons into the fulfilment of the farmer's year. It also reconciles Diana and Venus, bridging the gulf between the austerities of the one and the fruitful pleasures of the other, as the sweat of the labouring men leads on to the increase of bounteous Ceres. In this respect, the pageant of the months summarises the ethical code of the quest, insisting on the need to avoid sloth, defining virtue as a union of Bacchus and the nymph, and asserting the vital responsibility of human virtue in the establishment of God's order. It epitomises the assumptions about human duty which impel every knight to follow the path of heroism.

[1] Sherman Hawkins, 'Mutabilitie and the Cycle of the Months', in *Form and Convention in the Poetry of Edmund Spenser*, ed. William Nelson (New York and London, 1963).

Yet the poem has taught us that this is only half the story: the quest may demand unremitting virtue from those who attempt it, but its achievement will come by way of human failure and sin, and this fact, too, is indicated by Mutability's procession. The order of Nature does not proceed from the exclusion of evil but incorporates it and subdues it to its own purposes, and Mutability does not have to change her character to serve the cause of ultimate virtue. The twelve honest labouring men prove to be a curiously ambiguous collection when looked at closely, suggestive of sin and death as much as life and virtue. They are all busy about their creative tasks, yet the deadly sins are of their company and the framework of the zodiac in which they are set is itself a reminder in stellar form of the illegal passions and lustful amours of Jove. March rides upon Jove's ram—'The same which over *Hellespontus* swam'; April goes upon his Bull—'. . .the same which led/*Europa*. . .'; May rides on the shoulders of the Twins, with the inevitable reference to Leda and the swan. June is 'All in greene leaves', like Lechery 'In a greene gowne' as in Lucifera's pageant: July 'boyling like to fire' is a figure of Wrath upon the Nemean lion, 'raging yet with ire'. August leads by the hand Astraea herself, the righteous and fruitful virgin, but Spenser reminds us that she was driven from the unrighteous world 'after Wrong was lov'd and Justice solde'. September is at once a harvester and a thief, 'laden with the spoyle/Of harvests riches, which he made his boot'. October is Drunkenness, his head all 'totty of the must', while November is Gluttony, 'grosse and fat,/As fed with lard'. December is the most interesting of all, reminding us on the one hand of the feasting and gladness appropriate to the birth of Christ, but on the other, of the mixed associations of Capricorn, and most specifically, perhaps, of tragedy, august and bearded in front but bald behind like the 'shaggy-bearded' Goat from which its name was traditionally derived. The Crucifixion as well as the Incarnation is implicit in Spenser's description, and this may be the reason why January and February alone are described without any tincture of sin, the birth of Christ having removed the burden. They testify, therefore, to the painful labours of the sons of Adam out of which the new spring and regeneration will come.

The Zodiac witnesses simultaneously to Jove's lusts and to his law, and this ambivalence is typical of the whole poem. *The Faerie Queene* resembles one of those Victorian pictures which presents different images when looked at from different angles, because it embodies the double vision of life as it appears to man and as it is understood by God. To man good and evil are in eternal opposition, to God, in ultimate harmony; and Spenser's method is to juxtapose the two faces of truth throughout the poem, and by the gradual pressure of reiteration, make the reader aware of the one behind the other. Reading the poem is a disconcerting experience in that it forces the reader to question and ultimately deny the relatively simple assumptions about good and evil which he is encouraged to hold at the start. Spenser's poetic rhetoric transforms a moral precept into the experience of moral exploration and discovery, so that when we finish we are forced to go back to the beginning again and re-evaluate in the light of the hints which were always there but which only assume significance later. If we turn back to the ominous opening of the poem, we can see, in the light of subsequent knowledge, the suggestions of rebirth and regeneration implicit in the first, very forbidding description of Jove:

> And angry *Jove* an hideous storme of raine
> Did poure into his Leman lap so fast,
> That every wight to shrowd it did constrain,
> And this faire couple eke to shroud themselves were fain.
> [I. i. 6]

On the surface, there is the promise of sin and mortality in the sinister ambiguities of the word 'shrowd'; but by the end of the poem, we know that Jove's anger is directed against the rebellious Titans; and that his lust, which dooms Red Cross and all mankind to the forest and to the shroud, is not only the source of death but of the life-giving fertility which is its answer. Even the forest with which the poem begins and ends changes its aspect in the interim: it is great Nature's forest in each case, as Spenser makes clear by taking his catalogue of trees in book I from *The Parliament of Fowls*, and by his reference in the *Mutability Cantos* to the description in the *Foules parley* which

Dan Geffrey took from Alanus [VII. vii. 9]. There is this difference, however, that whereas the forest of book I is a place of attractive and interesting variety which draws us into error, that of book VII shows the other end of the chain when, having experienced error and mutability, we discover at the heart of darkness the knowledge of Nature's benevolent purposes. The details of Spenser's descriptive method provide an allegory of the change in perspective. In book I, the description of the forest is that of the artist 'imitating' the work of another artist, but in book VII he refers beyond the creation of the artist, Chaucer, to that of Nature as expressed at the fountain-head of all such descriptions, the *Plaint of kindes*. The human art of book I is transcended by a higher art based on that of Nature herself.

The very myths of the poem take on the quality of a pun. Daphne and Myrrha are used, as we have seen, to embody opposite perversions of love, the excesses of sterile virginity and of unnatural lust; yet both are already there in more innocent form in the forest of book I, 'The Laurell, meed of mightie Conquerours', and 'The Mirrhe sweete bleeding in the bitter wound' [I. i. 9]. Seen in proper perspective, they take their places in the camps of Diana and Venus, and remind us of the hero's garland and the gifts of the fruitful manger. The coupling together of apparently conflicting images which we have seen to be a feature of the poem stems from this double vision. The description of Phantastes' chamber, for example, points in two directions:

> And all the chamber filled was with flyes,
>> Which buzzed all about, and made such sound,
>> That they encombred all mens eares and eyes,
>> Like many swarmes of Bees assembled round,
>> After their hives with honny do abound:...

> [II. ix. 51]

The satanic flies are countered by the innocent and beneficient honey-bees because, rightly apprehended, the two are ultimately the same; and the Bower itself, which is the creation of Phantastes, has the same ambivalence. At the sight of land, the Palmer hails 'The sacred soile, where all our perils grow' [II. xii. 37]; and the word 'sacred' carries its normal meaning of 'holy', as well as the pejorative senses of 'cursed' and 'detestable' to which the *Variorum* tries to limit it. Mutability herself, with her two faces of pride and of beauty, is the epitome of the whole. *The Faerie Queene* consists of an infinite series of puns, a sustained exercise in ambiguity woven around the Christian paradox which is its foundation and which could be its motto:

> Sin is behovely, but
> All shall be well, and
> All manner of things shall be well.

It is Acrasia's riddle extended to more than epic length.

[2]

The fact that the *Mutability Cantos* bring to the surface so much of the underlying mythology and meaning of the poem and make the only explicit comment on the theme of the whole would suggest that they should be considered as an epilogue rather than as fragments of an unfinished book. Professor Northrop Frye, for example, has argued that the poem is complete and that Colin, breaking his pipe when the Graces are put to flight, is symbolic of Spenser forswearing his art like Prospero when his work is done.[1] The description of Mutability breaking into the palace of Cynthia and almost plucking her from her throne, while the lower world trembles in fear that Chaos is come again, could refer to the country's fears concerning the death of the ageing Queen, which were particularly acute in 1597, the year of the Queen's grand climacteric. There is no clear evidence that the cantos were written earlier, and none that they were designed as part of a larger unit. The label under which the publisher launched them into the world—'Two Cantos/of Mutabilitie/Which, both for Forme and Matter, appeare/to be parcell of some following Booke of the Faerie Queene,/under the Legend/of/*Constancie*'—is too diffident in its claims to be taken as evidence of Spenser's intention.

It can be argued from sonnet LXXX of the *Amoretti* that by 1595 Spenser had curtailed his original grandiose scheme of two poems each consisting of twelve books to two of six, dealing

---

[1] Northrop Frye, *Fables of Identity* (Harbinger Books, 1963), p. 70.

with private and political virtue respectively:

> After so long a race as I have run
>> Through Faery land, which those six books compile,
>> give leave to rest me being halfe fordonne,
>> and gather to my selfe new breath awhile.
> Then as a steed refreshed after toyle,
>> out of my prison I will breake anew:
>> and stoutly will that second worke assoyle,
>> with strong endevour and attention dew.

The reference to 'that second worke', and the fact that courtesy joins hands with holiness to form an unbroken ring of virtues, suggest that Spenser saw book VI as the end of its sequence at the time of writing the sonnet. Presumably he intended to proceed with a second six books dealing with public virtues on lines parallel to what he had already done, and if this were so, one wonders what his seventh virtue would have been. One would expect book VII to echo book I in political terms, for Spenser shows himself extremely conscious of recurring pattern in *The Faerie Queene*, and the second three books follow the sequence of the first three. Books I and IV deal with God's love for his creation; II and V with human discipline, and III and VI with human love. If Spenser had kept to this pattern, Nature's judgement could conceivably have formed the centre-piece for the first book of the new series: Book VI ends with the Blatant Beast ranging the world again, and the poet suffering as a result, under 'a mighty Peres displeasure' [VI. xii. 41]. Nature's pronouncement of order within change might have formed the basis of a defence of hierarchy and provided a definition of the duties of both poet and peer.

Whatever Spenser's original motive in composing the cantos, however, the fact that they pick up and tie together so many threads from the rest of the poem suggests to me that Spenser changed his mind a second time about the structure of the poem, some time after writing Sonnet LXXX. Perhaps he felt that even the smaller project of twelve books was too much for him, or perhaps he recognised that his book of Justice had already encroached upon the field of political virtue. Whatever the reason, I believe that he abandoned a structure based, like that of his

Shepheardes Calendar, on the twelve months of the year for one built upon the seven days of the week, a structure of far greater allegorical relevance to the theme of the poem for they are, as Alastair Fowler has pointed out, the seven days of the creation.[1] In completing the week, Mutability herself brings the sequence to its proper conclusion, or at least, to its temporal conclusion, for the two stanzas of canto VIII remain, and their concern with eternity supports Sherman Hawkin's argument that they belong to the spiritual eighth day.[2] Spenser makes the transition from the world of time to the pillars of eternity 'When no more *Change* shall be', and in doing so, brings the whole poem into that perspective which the vision of Contemplation afforded in book I. Time and Mutability have been the subject, and now the dimension of eternity is introduced as the Heavenly Hymns follow the Earthly ones, or as secular mediaeval works such as *Troilus and Criseyde* conclude with a glimpse of Heaven. It is not a recantation but a reminder of other values and dimensions which are relevant yet do not invalidate by their perfection the struggles proper to the life lived in Time. The wholly traditional nature of Spenser's final juxtaposition of time and eternity is the clearest proof that we have here the true ending of the poem.

One can imagine other endings, with all the knights converging on the Court of Maidenhood and Arthur at last achieving his Gloriana, but this would be untrue to the spirit of the poem. The untidy life of the world which is Spenser's subject finds accurate expression in the unfinished action; and the constancy which he celebrates is not that of Heaven or even of Arthur's unflagging virtue, but only a constancy in change. Spenser is more like Yeats than Eliot, and his essentially unmystical type of mind has little place for transcendental vision. He prefers the struggles of life to the artifice of eternity, the mirror-scaled serpent, multiplicity, to the One. *The Faerie Queene* demonstrates to a supreme degree the point of the rhetorical question with which the Heart counters the arguments of the Soul in Yeats' poem—'What theme had Homer but original sin?'.

[1] Pp. 233.
[2] *Form and Convention*, p. 99 and n.

239

INDEX